Subjects of Desire

SUBJECTS OF DESIRE

Hegelian Reflections in
Twentieth-Century France

Judith Butler

Columbia University Press

New York

The Andrew W. Mellon Foundation, through a special grant,
has assisted the Press in publishing this volume.

Library of Congress Cataloging-in-Publication Data

Butler, Judith P.
Subjects of desire.

Bibliography: p. 253
Includes index.
1. Hegel, Georg Wilhelm Friedrich, 1770–1831—
Influence.   2. Desire (Philosophy)   3. Philosophy,
French—20th century.   I. Title.
B2948.B86   1987   128'.3   86-33458
ISBN 0-231-06450-0   —   ISBN 0-231-06451-9 (pbk.)

Columbia University Press
New York   Guildford, Surrey
Copyright © 1987 Columbia University Press
Preface to the Paperback Edition copyright © 1999
Judith P. Butler

Printed in the United States of America

Book design by Ken Venezio

p 10 9 8 7 6

Contents

Preface to the Paperback Edition

Subjects of Desire is my 1984 dissertation, revised in 1985–86. I wrote on the concept of desire, concentrating on Hegel's *Phenomenology of Spirit* and some of the central appropriations of that theme in twentieth-century French philosophy. Prior to my graduate studies, I was a Fulbright Scholar studying Hegel and German Idealism at the Heidelberg Universität, attending the seminars and lectures of Dieter Henrich and Hans-Georg Gadamer. As a graduate student in the Department of Philosophy at Yale University in the early 1980s, I trained in the tradition of continental philosophy, studying Marx and Hegel, phenomenology, Heidegger, Kierkegaard, Merleau-Ponty, and the Frankfurt School. I wrote the dissertation under Maurice Natanson, a phenomenologist who generously supported my scholarship, but let me know that French philosophy met its reasonable limit in the work of Sartre and selected writings of Merleau-Ponty. Studying at Yale in the late '70s and early '80s, I certainly knew about poststructuralist thought, but tended to place it outside the sphere of the continental philosophical tradition I meant to study. I occasionally attended a seminar by Derrida, and more often audited Paul de Man's lectures, but for the most part worked in the traditions of phenomenology, hermeneutics, and the Frankfurt School while seeking to acquire a background in German Idealism. It was in the context of a women's studies faculty seminar that I encountered the work of Michel Foucault. And it was not until I left Yale and became a visiting faculty member and then a postdoctoral fellow at Wesleyan University from 1983–86 that I became open to French theory in a way that I mainly resisted while at Yale. At the Center for the Humanities, I was exposed to critical theory in the French vein, and it was in the initial stages of that exposure that I revised the dissertation as *Subjects of Desire: Hegelian Reflections in Twentieth-Century France*, published by Columbia University Press in 1987. The final chapters on Deleuze, Lacan, and Foucault were not part of the dissertation proper, and they represent first forays into material that I have since come to understand deserve a more complex consideration.

I published the book too early, pressured by the job market, and I republish it now too late to make revisions. Any revised version of this work would be a new work altogether, one that I am not prepared to embark upon at this time. In 1985–86, I was not quite prepared to make the theoretical moves that I begin in the final chapters and that I subsequently made in the writing of *Gender Trouble*, published in late 1989. Although at the time of this writing I am not yet ancient, the book reads to me—to the extent that I can read it—as my juvenilia, which means that I ask the reader to approach it with abundant forgiveness in reserve.

The text is neither a comprehensive account of French Hegelianism nor a work in intellectual history.[1] It is a critical inquiry into a relation repeatedly figured between desire and recognition. If it were to have been a comprehensive treatment, it most certainly would have included a chapter on the work of Georges Bataille.[2] *Subjects of Desire* would have also considered the influence of Hegel's *Logic* in greater detail, especially on the work of Jean Hyppolite in which the *Logic* provides validation for the essential truths revealed in subjective experience in the *Phenomenology*.[3] To the extent that *Subjects of Desire* focuses on the *Phenomenology*, it could have included as well a consideration of Hegel's chapter, "Freedom of Self-Consciousness: Stoicism, Scepticism, and the Unhappy Consciousness." This key chapter's appropriation by Jean Wahl might reasonably be said to be the first major work on Hegel in twentieth-century France, indeed, it is the chapter through which the twentieth-century French reception of Hegel began. Wahl's short text, *Le Malheur de la conscience dans la philosophie de Hegel* (Monfort, 1929), established an appropriative reading of Hegel, bringing the internally divided consciousness to bear on both religious and existential themes, and emphasizing the *negativity* of consciousness that plays such a prominent role in the subsequent readings provided by Kojève and Hyppolite.

In 1995, I published an essay, "Stubborn Attachment, Bodily Subjection: Rereading Hegel on the Unhappy Consciousness," which constitutes a continued reflection on the Hegelian subject.[4] There I sought to show that Hegel offers a sequel to the Lordship and Bondage chapter that is rarely considered by those who prize the apparently emancipatory conclusion of the former chapter. Hegel offers a configuration of the subject in which subjection becomes a psychic reality, one in which oppression itself is articulated and entrenched through psychic means. My suggestion is that Hegel begins to explain the inversions of power that take place as it acquires the status of psychic reality, an explanation that allies him with insights usually credited to Nietzsche and Freud.

This text relies on available English translations of Hyppolite, Kojève, and Sartre, and works with selected essays in French with the consequence that the bulk of Kojève's untranslated writings (including the full version of his *Introduction à la lecture de Hegel*) remain largely unconsidered. His lectures, offered from 1933–39 at the École des Hautes Études, include extensive discussions of Hegel's relation to Kant, the place of poetic language, tragedy, and religion in the *Phenomenology*, and an extended discussion of the figure of Christ and the meaning of Christianity that did not survive into the abridged English translation.[5]

Kojève remains a difficult author to understand, claimed on the one hand by the Straussian tradition of Allan Bloom, Stanley Rosen, and Francis Fukuyama and heralded on the other hand as a Marxist by Pierre Macheray and others.[6] Even as Kojève insisted that Hegel's text is open to a set of historical appropriations unanticipated in Hegel's time, so his own reading of Hegel has become open to widely conflicting readings. And this predicament may well be the result of the kind of "reading" that Kojève himself put into place, one that sought less to be faithful to the letter of Hegel's text than to produce new interpretations that reflect the changed historical circumstance of reading itself. Hegel's text, as it moves through time, thus continually re-poses the question of its own readability, most clearly because the end of history that he foretells is not the end of time and not the end of the temporality of reading.[7] Thus Hegel's text, perhaps despite itself, opens up the question of the relation between time and readability. The future is, for Kojève, no longer constrained by teleology, and the future that Hegel anticipates is in some ways precisely the one that Kojève mourns as lost idealism. Kojève's "reading" brings into relief the temporality of Hegel's text, showing that the temporality into which it has survived demands a different kind of reading, one that does not move progressively with the same confidence. This predicament of temporality post-Hegel has lead some of the Straussians to conclude that history itself must resolve into "perennial" themes, and it has also led Althusserians to conclude that a structuralist analysis of society relieved of the conceits of diachrony is the preferable conclusion. But another perspective can be derived from Kojève, one that insists that temporality is irreducible to historicity, and that neither is reducible to teleology. The temporality of the concept is neither static nor teleological, but requires a doubly inverted reading that knows no closure, which will no doubt offend the avatars of common sense, but without which no approach to Hegel is possible.

The speculative sentence that Hegel outlines in the *Logic* underscores this problem of temporality as a predicament of reading. We cannot expect that language will transparently show the truth of what it says, but neither can we expect that this truth will be found outside of language. The truth is not the same as the narrative that the *Phenomenology* provides, and yet it is made manifest only through its exposition. The sentence moves in such a way that the familiar is rendered unfamiliar, and this pertains to the familiar grammar of the sentence itself. This becomes especially true when we consider the grammatical place of "negation," a term that not only undergoes semantically important shifts in meaning, but that also "acts" in essential ways in the unfolding of essential truths.

These functions of "negation" elicit the usual jokes on Hegel by contemporary analysts who insist that Hegel either be made plain or be rejected once and for all. Hegel has other plans in mind when he claims, for instance, in the *Phenomenology* that the speculative proposition destroys the general nature of the proposition (Miller 38). But the question is not what logical sense can be made of negation in Hegel, but how the very use of negation in Hegel calls into question our understanding of logical relations.

In the *Phenomenology*, negation emerges in a number of ways, and not merely in the service of an assimilating or domesticating conceptual

[x]

operation that subdues the alterities it confronts. In the section, "The Truth of Self-Certainty," consciousness negates its objects by consuming them; in Lordship and Bondage, negation appears first as the effort of both figures to annihilate one another and then transmutes into relations of domination and servitude. What does it mean that negation "appears" through these various figures? And how are we to understand the transmutations that the appearance of negation undergoes?

My suggestion is that in the *Phenomenology*, figures emerge to describe a state that has not yet achieved a stable logical status; indeed, the figure marks the instability of logical relations. Conversely, though, every logical relation assumes a shape or an appearance that is figural. If we are to read Hegel, what will this reading do to a grammar that is preconceived to express logical relations (the conceit of Husserl's *Logical Investigations* and the early Wittgenstein alike)? One reads along in the *Phenomenology* with the assumption that a stable reality is being described only to come up against the obduracy of descriptive language itself. We think we know at any given textual moment what negation "is" and what it does, only to find out by following the course of its action, indeed, by reading it, that our former convictions were unfounded. It is the term, in other words, that constantly undermines our own knowingness. The language we thought was reporting on the reality of negation turns out to take part in the activity itself, to have its own negating function and, indeed, to be subject to negation itself. The language of the text thus exhibits its own rhetoricity, and we find that the question of logic and that of rhetoric are indissociable from each other. Similarly, no claims of cognition can be made apart from the practice of reading: the temporality of the concept is not finally separable from the temporality of reading.

One of the more recent French readers of Hegel, Gérard Lebrun, in his *La patience du Concept: Essai sur le discours hégélien*, makes a similar point as he disputes the possibility of a Hegelian dogmatism and shows that Hegelian discourse actively initiates the reader into a new mode of philosophical thought.[8] Just as for Kojève, the reading of Hegel must traverse a temporality that is past (an idea of the future that is past), so the reading of Hegel's grammar according to the demands of the speculative sentence can be read "forward" only to find that the presuppositions that animated the reading must themselves be read in turn, compelling a reversal that does not quite undo what has been done (and that, at the very level of grammar, enacts a notion of negation proper to reading itself).

Jean-Luc Nancy makes this point in a different way in his recently published *Hegel: L'inquiétude du négatif.*[9] For him, the subject is not recoiled into itself, but is defined fundamentally as an act by which the self overcomes itself in its passage toward and into the world. The subject disperses itself into its world, and this self-surpassing is precisely the operation of its negativity. Nancy's work releases Hegel from the trope of totality, insisting that the "disquiet" of the self is precisely its mode of becoming, its final nonsubstantiality in time, and its specific expression of freedom. Nancy's work is rhetorically significant as well because in the place of a systematic exegesis of Hegel's work it provides a discontinuous set of meditations on the *Phenomenology* through the key terms by which the question of freedom is approached. Those who expect Hegel's *Phenomenology* to illustrate a clear teleology will be productively confounded by such a text.[10]

In fact, the status of teleology seems significantly contentious in the reconsideration of the twentieth-century French appropriation of Hegel. Although it was within the context of French theory, after all, that Hegel became synonomous with totality, teleology, conceptual domination, and the imperialist subject, the French appropriation of Hegel also puts the totalizing and teleological presumptions of Hegel's philosophy into question. Indeed, often the marks of a distinctively "post-Hegelian" position are not easy to distinguish from an appropriative reading of Hegel himself. Kojève's writings are especially pertinent here to the extent that they interrogate the time that emerges after the end of history, thus signaling a closure to teleology that is not precisely a teleological closure, an ending that is more on the lines of a break, interruption, and loss. Although Althusser once termed Kojève's work "silly," he takes seriously Kojève's effort to recast teleology in Hegel as anthropocentrism.[11] Althusser's early reflections on Hegel develop an immanent critique of Kojève's view, arguing that Kojève develops the subjective dimension of negativity to the exclusion of the objective one.[12] The attempt to reduce the workings of negativity to the subjective is bourgeois revisionism, affirming the individual at the expense of his objective situation. And where objectivity returns via Hegel, it is always devoid of its specifically onomic content, which leads it to valorize a philosophically abstracted notion of equality and democracy at the expense of one wrought from the class struggle. To the extent that Kojève's Hegel is read through the lens of the young Marx, and both Hegel and Marx are understood to affirm a subjective dimension of negation, "Kojève's existentialist Marx is a travesty in which Marxists will not recognize their own" (172).

Although Althusser devotes several essays to the reconsideration of Hegel in his *Écrits philosophiques et politiques*, where he offers a critique of Hegelian abstraction and begins through the practice of immanent critique to articulate a totality without a subject, he is quick to insult Hegel and French Hegelianism in particular. He commends Kojève's book with ambivalence: "His book is more than an *Introduction to the Reading of Hegel*: it is the resurrection of a corpse, or, rather, the revelation that Hegel, a thinker dismantled, torn to pieces, trampled underfoot, and betrayed, profoundly haunts and dominates an apostate age" (171). And later, he remarks in the same vein that despite the discrediting of Hegel's philosophy, "this dead god, covered with insults and buried a hundred times over, is rising from the grave" (174). Finally, Althusser not only accuses Hegelian philosophy of providing a philosophical glorification of the bourgeois status quo, but of supplying a revisionism "of a fascist type" (183).

Pierre Macheray's recent book, *Hegel ou Spinoza*,[13] is clearly influenced by Althusser, but takes the critical potential of Hegel's philosophy more seriously.[14] By counterposing Spinoza to Hegel, and by asking how each philosophical position defines the necessary limit of the other, Macheray argues for a dialectical conception of history relieved of the teleological presumption, in which there is a "struggle of tendencies that do not carry in themselves the promise of a resolution . . . a unity of contraries, but without the negation of negation."[15] Moreover, Macheray considers, contra Althusser, the sense of a Hegelian subject that remains irreducible to its ordinary use as a bearer of predicative judgements. The Hegelian subject is one for whom the stable relation between subject and predicate within ordinary grammar becomes undone (248). Thus, as a reader in the Althusserian tradition, Macheray nevertheless yields an interpretation that converges with that of Lebrun and Nancy in that he acknowledges that the subject is only the term for the process that it accomplishes, is nonsubstantial, and one whose illimitability destroys its ordinary grammatical function.

The revision of *Subjects of Desire* that I might have done would have included as well as Derrida's original criticism of the Hegelian concept in "The Pit and the Pyramid," the subsequent revision and restaging of his view in the introduction to Lacoue-Labarthe's *Typographies* and Derrida's own *Glas*.[16] A fuller consideration would also no doubt include a chapter on Luce Irigaray's various engagements with Hegel, especially in "The Eternal Irony of the Community" in *Speculum of the Other Woman*, her reflections on Hegel, kinship and universality in *Sexes et parentés*.[17] One of my future projects will be to consider Frantz Fanon's engagement with Hegel in *Black Skin, White Masks* on the problem of recognition within the dynamics of hierarchical racial exchange. Fanon's treatment of Hegel can be read as an important appropriation of Kojève's thesis of the centrality of desire to the struggle for recognition and the constitution of the subject (and the problematic mimimization of labor as a constitutive condition of recognition).[18]

My interest in the Hegelian legacy was not precisely overcome through the early publication of this book. I have taught courses on Hegel and contemporary theory, and continue to be interested in the way that Hegel is read and misread at the advent, institution, and dissemination of structuralism. In a sense, all of my work remains within the orbit of a certain set of Hegelian questions: What is the relation between desire and recognition, and how is it that the constitution of the subject entails a radical and constitutive relation to alterity?

I am currently at work on a book to be published as part of the Wellek Library Lectures series that centrally engages Hegel's writing on Antigone in the *Phenomenology, The Philosophy of Right*, and the *Aesthetics*. In it I am as much concerned with the way in which Antigone is consistently misread by Hegel as with his provocative way of understanding her criminal act as an eruption of an alternate legality within the sphere of public law. Whether Antigone functions as a subject for Hegel remains a compelling question for me, and raises the question of the political limit of the subject, that is, both the limitations imposed upon subjecthood (who qualifies as one), and the limits of the subject as the point of departure for politics. Hegel remains important here, for his subject does not stay in its place, displaying a critical mobility that may well be useful for further appropriations of Hegel to come. The emergent subject of Hegel's *Phenomenology* is an ek-static one, a subject who constantly finds itself outside itself, and whose periodic expropriations do not lead to a return to a former self. Indeed, the self who comes outside of itself, for whom ek-stasis is a condition of existence, is one for whom no return to self is possible, for whom there is no final recovery from self-loss. The notion of "difference" is similarly misunderstood, I would suggest, when it is understood as contained within or by the subject: the Hegelian subject's encounter with difference is not resolved into identity. Rather, the moment of its "resolution" is finally indistinguishable from the moment of its dispersion; the thinking of this cross-vectored temporality ushers in the Hegelian understanding of infinity and offers a notion of the subject that cannot remain bounded in the face of the world. Misrecognition does not arrive as a distinctively Lacanian corrective to the Hegelian subject, for it is precisely by misrecognition that the Hegelian subject repeatedly suffers its self-loss. Indeed, this is a self constitutively at risk of self-loss. This subject neither has nor suffers its desire, but is the very action of desire as it perpetually displaces the subject. Thus, it is neither precisely a new theory of the subject nor a definitive displacement of the subject that Hegel provides, but rather a definition in displacement, for which there is no final restoration.

Judith Butler
Berkeley, California
August 1998

Notes

1. For an excellent work in intellectual history with a comprehensive bibliography, see Michael S. Roth, *Knowing and History: Appropriations of Hegel in Twentieth-Century France* (Ithaca: Cornell University Press, 1988).

2. For an excellent consideration of the place of Bataille in French Hegelianism, see part 3 of Allan Stoekl, *Agonies of the Intellectual: Commitment, Subjectivity, and the Performative in the Twentieth-Century French Tradition* (Lincoln: University of Nebraska Press, 1992). For an illuminating set of perspectives on Bataille and Kojève, see the special issue of *Parallax*, "Kojève's Paris. Now Bataille" (no. 4, Feb. 1997). See as well Denis Hollier, ed. *The College of Sociology, 1937–39*, (Minneapolis: University of Minnesota Press, 1988).

3. For a clear rendition of this relationship, see Jean Hyppolite, "On the *Logic of Hegel*," in *Studies on Marx and Hegel*, tr. John O'Neill (New York: Basic Books, 1969).

4. David Clarke and Tillotama Rajan, eds., *Intersections: Nineteenth-Century Philosophy and Contemporary Theory* (Albany: SUNY Press, 1995), reprinted in *Hegel passé, Hegel à Venir* (Paris: L'Harmattan, 1995): my *The Psychic Life of Power: Essays in Subjection* (Stanford: Stanford University Press, 1997).

5. The French edition, originally published by Gallimard in 1947, also contains an important appendix that was not translated with the English edition: "L'idée de la mort dans la philosophie de Hegel." The English edition is *Introduction to the Reading of Hegel: Lectures on the Phenomenology of Spirit*, assembled by Raymond Queneau, ed. Allan Bloom, tr. James H. Nichols, Jr. (1969; reprint, Ithaca: Cornell University Press, 1980).

6. For a recent intellectual biography, see Dominique Auffret, *Alexandre Kojève: La philosophie, l'État, la fin de l'Histoire* (Paris: Grasset, 1990).

7. The contingency of the end of history thesis is indicated by Hegel himself at the end of the *Phenomenology of Spirit* when "infinity" exceeds the historical domain, but also when one reads the *Phenomenology* in the context of the *Logic* and the specific temporality of the concept developed there.

8. Lebrun can be seen to extend the provocative insights offered by Alexandre Koyré in his essay "La terminologie hégélienne." See Lebrun, *La patience du concept* (Paris: Gallimard, 1972), p. 18.

9. (Paris: Hachette Littératures, 1997), forthcoming in English by University of Minnesota Press. See also Nancy's earlier work on the speculative sentence, *La Remarque spéculative (un bon mot de Hegel)* (Paris: Éditions Galilée, 1973).

10. See as well the translation of Hegel's "How Common Sense Understands Philosophy" by Jean-Marie Lardic and her commentary, which argues that contingency and the radical disorientation of common sense are central to the meaning of the dialectic: *Comment le sens commun comprend la philosophie suivi de la contingence chez Hegel* (Paris: Actes Sud, 1989).

11. Althusser writes, "Hegelian history is neither biological nor providential nor mechanistic, for these three schemas all entail externality. The negative dimension by virtue of which history constitutes itself through and for itself . . . does not lie outside history, but with the self: the nothingness by means of which history is engendered and then takes possession of itself as it evolves is in history. This nothingness is man." Louis Althusser, *The Spectre of Hegel: Early Writings*, ed. François Matheron, tr. G. M. Goshgarian (London: Verso, 1997), first published in *Écrits philosophiques et politiques. Tome I* (Paris: Stock/IMEC, 1994).

12. Ibid., 171.

13. (Paris: Éditions la Découverte, 1990).

14. See also Jean-Pierre Lefebvre and Pierre Macheray, *Hegel et la société* (Paris: Presses Universitaires de France, 1984). The discussion of Hegel's *Phi-*

losophy of Right in this volume focuses usefully on the inversion of "beginning" and "ending" in the text, confounding usual notions of teleological development.

15. Ibid., my translation, p. 259.

16. I published a brief consideration of Derrida's early views on Hegel as "Response to Joseph Flay's 'Hegel, Derrida, and Bataille's Laughter' " in *Hegel and His Critics: Philosophy in the Aftermath of Hegel*, ed. William Desmond (Albany: SUNY Press, 1989). I highly recommend Tim Walter's book on the idea of "Critique" in Hegel (forthcoming, Stanford University Press) for a consideration of the affinities between Hegel and Derrida as well as Werner Hamacher's *Premises* (Cambridge: Harvard University Press, 1997) and Rodolphe Gasché's *The Tain of the Mirror: Derrida and the Philosophy of Reflection* (Cambridge: Harvard University Press, 1986).

17. Some of my reflections on Irigaray's work will be published in my book on Antigone and contemporary kinship, forthcoming in the Wellek Library Lectures Series, Columbia University Press.

18. On the question of Hegel, race, and recognition, see also Franz Fanon, *Black Skin, White Masks* (New York: Grove Press, 1967); Valentin Mudimbe, *The Surreptitious Speech: Présence Africaine and the Politics of Otherness, 1947–1992* (Chicago: University of Chicago Press, 1992); Shamon Zamir, *Dark Voices* (Chicago: University of Chicago Press, 1994); Paul Gilroy, *The Black Atlantic: Modernity and Double-Consciousness* (Cambridge: Harvard University Press, 1993).

Preface

In Tennessee Williams' *A Streetcar Named Desire* Blanche Dubois describes her journey: "They told me to take a street-car named Desire, and then transfer to one called Cemeteries and ride six blocks and get off at—Elysian Fields!"* When she hears that her present dismal location *is* Elysian Fields, she is sure that the directions she received were wrong. Her predicament is implicitly philosophical. What kind of journey is desire that its direction is so deceptive?

And what kind of vehicle is desire? And does it have other stops before it reaches its mortal destination? This inquiry follows one journey of desire, the travels of a desiring subject who remains nameless and genderless in its abstract universality. We would not be able to recognize this subject in the train station; it cannot be said to exist as an individual. As an abstract structure of human longing, this subject is a conceptual configuration of human agency and purpose whose claim to ontological integrity is successively challenged throughout its travels. Indeed, like Blanche and her journey, the desiring subject follows a narrative of desire, delusion, and defeat, relying on occasional moments of recognition as a source of merely temporary redemption.

Introduced in Hegel's *Phenomenology of Spirit*, this subject's desire is structured by philosophical aims: it wants to know itself, but wants to find within the confines of this self the entirety of the external world; indeed its desire is to discover the entire domain of alterity as a *reflection*

---

* (New York: Signet 1947), p. 15.

[xix]

of itself, not merely to incorporate the world but to externalize and enhance the borders of its very self. Although Kierkegaard wondered aloud whether such a subject might really *exist,* and Marx criticized Hegel's conceit as the product of a mystified idealism, the French reception of Hegel took the theme of *desire* as its point of critical departure and reformulation.

The works of Alexandre Kojève and Jean Hyppolite redescribe Hegel's subject of desire with a more restricted set of philosophical aspirations. For Kojève, the subject is necessarily confined within a post-historical time in which Hegel's metaphysics belongs, at least partially, to the past. For Hyppolite, the subject of desire is a paradoxical agency whose satisfaction is necessarily thwarted by the temporal exigencies of human existence. Jean-Paul Sartre's dualistic ontology signals a break with Hegel's postulated unity of the desiring subject and its world, but desire's necessary dissatisfaction conditions the *imaginary* pursuit of Hegel's ideal. Indeed, for Sartre and for Jacques Lacan, desire's aim is the production and pursuit of imaginary objects and Others. And in the work of Lacan, Gilles Deleuze, and Michel Foucault, Hegel's subject is criticized as itself a wholly imaginary construct. For Lacan, desire no longer designates autonomy, but characterizes pleasure only after it conforms to a repressive law; for Deleuze, desire misdescribes the disunity of affects signified by Nietzsche's will-to-power; and for Foucault, desire is itself historically produced and regulated, and the subject always "subjected." Indeed, the "subject" now appears as the false imposition of an orderly and autonomous self on an experience inherently discontinuous.

The French reception of Hegel may be read as a succession of criticisms against the subject of desire, that Hegelian conceit of a totalizing impulse which, for various reasons, has lost its plausibility. And yet, a close reading of the relevant chapters of the *Phenomenology of Spirit* reveal that Hegel himself was an ironic artist in the construction of this conceit, and that his vision is less "totalizing" than presumed. Further, Hegel's French critics appear to ground their refutations of Hegel in terms which, ironically, work to consolidate Hegel's original position. The subject of desire remains a compelling fiction even for those who claim to have definitively exposed his charades.

This inquiry neither provides an intellectual history of the French reception of Hegel, nor does it serve as a sociology of knowledge concerning twentieth-century French intellectual trends. And it is not the history of a line of influence between the authors considered here. Readers who seek a comprehensive understanding of the works of Kojève or Hyppolite are advised to wait for a different sort of study to appear. This is but the philosophical narrative of a highly influential trope, the tracing of its genesis in Hegel's *Phenomenology of Spirit,* its various reformulations in Kojève and Hyppolite, its persistence as a nostalgic ideal in Sartre and Lacan, and the contemporary efforts to expose its fully fictional status in Deleuze and Foucault. Although the trope often functions where clear references to Hegel are absent, its reemergence is nowhere more provocative than in those contemporary theories which assert that the subject of desire is dead.

Abbreviations Used in the Text and Notes

Michel Foucault

HS   *Histoire de la sexualité: La volonté de savoir (The History of Sexuality* vol. 1, *An Introduction).*

Jean Hyppolite

CE   "The Concept of Existence in the Hegelian Phenomenology."
F   *Figures de la pensée philosophique, I* and *II.*
GS   *Genèse et structure de la Phénoménologie de l'esprit de Hegel (Genesis and Structure of Hegel's "Phenomenology of Spirit.")*

Alexandre Kojève

IH   *Introduction à la lecture de Hegel (Introduction to the Reading of Hegel)*

Jacques Lacan

FFCP *Les Quatre concepts fondamentaux de la psychanalyse (The Four Fundamental Concepts of Psychoanalysis).*

Jean-Paul Sartre

E	*Esquisse d'une théorie des émotions (The Emotions: Outline of a Theory).*
BN	*L'Être et le néant, Essai d'ontologie phénoménologique (Being and Nothingness: An Essay in Phenomenological Ontology).*
FI	*L'Idiot de la famille: Gustave Flaubert de 1821 à 1857 (The Family Idiot/Vol. I).*
PI	*L'Imaginaire: Psychologie phénoménologique de l'imagination (The Psychology of Imagination).*
"I"	"Intentionality: A Fundamental Idea in Husserl's Phenomenology."
SG	*Saint Genet, comédien et martyr (Saint Genet: Actor and Martyr).*
TE	*La Transcendance de l'ego: Esquisse d'une description phénoménologique (The Transcendence of the Ego).*

Subjects of Desire

Introduction

*The greatest poverty is not to live
In a physical world, to feel that one's desire
Is too difficult to tell from despair . . .*
         Wallace Stevens, "Esthétique du Mal"

When philosophers have not dismissed or subdued human desire in their effort to become philosophical, they have tended to discover philosophical truth as the very essence of desire. Whether the strategy is negation or appropriation, the philosophic relation to desire has been imperious and brief. No doubt, the bulk of the Western tradition has sustained skepticism toward the philosophical possibilities of desire, and desire has been figured time and again as philosophy's Other. As immediate, arbitrary, purposeless, and animal, desire is that which requires to be gotten beyond; it threatens to undermine the postures of indifference and dispassion which have in various different modalities conditioned philosophical thinking. To desire the world and to know its meaning and structure have seemed conflicting enterprises, for desire has signified an engagement of limited vision, an appropriation for use, while philosophy in its theoretical purity has presented itself as not needing the world it seeks to know. If philosophers were to desire the world that they investigate, they would fear losing sight of pattern, coherence, generalized and regular truth, and would find instead a world characterized by radical particularism and arbitrary objects, delectable but disarmingly displaced. Desire has thus often signaled philosophy's despair, the impossibility of order, the necessary nausea of appetite.

Because philosophers cannot obliterate desire, they must formulate strategies to silence or control it; in either case, they must, in spite of themselves, desire to do something about desire. Thus, even the negation of desire is always only another one of its modalities. To discover the philosophical promise of desire thus becomes an attractive alternative, a domestication of desire in the name of reason, the promise of a psychic harmony within the philosophical personality. If the philosopher is not *beyond* desire, but a being of *rational* desire who knows what he wants and wants what he knows, then the philosopher emerges as a paradigm of psychic integration. Such a being holds out the promise of an end to psychic disequilibrium, the long-standing split between reason and desire, the otherness of affect, appetite, and longing.

If desire potentially serves the philosophical pursuit of knowledge, if it is a kind of tacit knowledge, or if it can be cultivated to be a single-minded motivating force for knowledge, then in principle there is no necessarily irrational desire, no affective moment that must be renounced for its intrinsic arbitrariness. Over and against a naturalistic understanding of desires as brute and random facts of psychic existence,[1] this model of desire vindicates particular affects as potential bearers of truth, rife with philosophical significance. When desires appear in their random or arbitrary form, they call then to be decoded and deciphered; if desire and significance are presumed to be coextensive, the task becomes that of developing the appropriate hermeneutics of self-reflection to uncover their implicit meaning.

The ideal of an internal integration of reason and desire not only poses an alternative to a naturalistic or positivistic understanding of desire, but promises to expand the very notion of rationality beyond its traditional confines. If desires are essentially philosophical, then we reason in our most spontaneous of yearnings. Reason is no longer restricted to reflective rationality, but characterizes our immediate and impulsive selves. In other words, the immediacy of desire proves to be always already mediated, and we are always much more intelligent in the moment of desire than we immediately know ourselves to be. In the ostensibly prerational experience of desiring some feature of the world, we are always already

[2]

interpreting that world, making philosophical motions, expressing ourselves as philosophical beings.

The philosopher of metaphysical impulses, this being of intelligent desire, is an enticing alternative to the alienated philosopher void of affect. But it seems that we must ask if the model of integration is a viable alternative to the internally bifurcated philosophical soul, or if it is a reformulation of alienation at a more sophisticated level. Can desire be rendered rational, or does it always present a disruption and rupture of the philosophical project? Can philosophy accommodate desire without losing its philosophical character? Does the philosophical appropriation of desire always entail a fabrication of desire in the image of philosophy?

But these questions are too large, and the conclusions that they anticipate too rash. We tread on uncertain ground when we refer too hastily to "philosophy" and "desire" without first showing that these terms bear univocal meanings. We know, of course, that these terms are historicized, that they bear multiple meanings which are only reduced and falsified if we employ them outside of the contexts, philosophical and historical, in which they appear. The question must become, what are the philosophical circumstances that occasion the question of desire? Under what conditions do we ask after the meaning and structure of human desire to understand the nature of philosophy, its limits and possibilities? When does the theme of human desire make philosophical thinking problematic?

Desire has been deemed philosophically dangerous precisely because of its propensity to blur clear vision and foster philosophical myopia, encouraging one to see only what one *wants,* and not what *is.* Desire is too narrow, focused, interested, and engaged. But when philosophy interrogates its own possibilities as *engaged* or practical knowledge, it tends to ask after the philosophical potential of desire. Hence, it is Spinoza's *Ethics* that formulates desire as the essence of man,[2] and Kant's *Critique of Practical Reason* that distinguishes that higher faculty of desire necessary for moral reasoning.[3] When knowledge of philosophical truth becomes a function of living a philosophical life, as is the case in moral philosophy traditionally, the question is necessarily raised, does ought imply can? is moral action supported by human psychology? can philosophical truth be embodied in a psychologically feasible philosophical life? If desire were a principle of irrationality, then an integrated philosophical life would be chimerical, for desire would always oppose this life, undermine its unity,

[3]

disrupt its order. Only if desire—or some form of desire—can be discovered as evincing a moral intentionality, as is the case with Plato's philosophical *eros*,[4] Aristotle's notion of unified desire,[5] Kant's pure will,[6] or Spinoza's *cupiditas,* is the philosophical life, conceived as the pursuit of integrity, still feasible.

The unified subject with its unified philosophical life has served as a necessary psychological premise and normative ideal in moral philosophies since Plato and Aristotle. Without a discrete subject with internally consistent desires, the moral life remains indefinite; if the subject is ambiguous, difficult to locate and properly name, then to whom shall we ascribe this life? And if desires are random or, at best, self-contradictory, then the moral life is either impossible or, when possible, based on repression[7] rather than true autonomy. When moral action is understood as a function of the moral life, then it is not enough to conform to a moral rule, but that rule must be "given to oneself," in the Kantian sense; it must be the product of a moral affect, a desire for the good. Otherwise, morality is an imposition upon a resistant personality, and rather than express the autonomy of the moral subject, it reaffirms the necessity of external authority. Philosophers have time and again wanted to have a love affair with the good, maintaining that the true philosopher is one who spontaneously and easily desires the good, and just as easily translates those desires into good deeds. Whether desire is habituated to pursue the good, as in Aristotle's *Ethics,* or whether the charioteer in Plato's *Phaedrus* has given freer rein to that more spiritual of horses, the vision of a thoroughly moral being has been one who passionately wants what is right. If to act rationally is to act time and again in a consistent way, consistently in accord with what is deemed morally good, then a rational act bespeaks a unified self and a unified life. If a moral agent acts against its desire, it acts from contradiction, opposing desire to reason, undermining the possibility of moral autonomy as a function of a thoroughly integrated moral subject. In such a case, to act morally is always to act from internal division or contradiction.[8]

When we ask, then, what are the philosophical circumstances that occasion the question of human desire, we see that moral philosophy in particular has needed to know whether desire has a moral intentionality, a nascent essence of reason, in order to affirm the possibility of the unified moral subject and the integrated moral life. And yet the questions of

[4]

identity, unity, and integration that moral philosophy raises about the moral being are very often first raised about beings in general; moral psychology thus has assumed a moral ontology, a theory about what a being must be like in order to be capable of moral deliberation and action, in order to lead a moral life and be a moral personality. And it has also assumed a more general ontological scheme in which not only the "unity" or "internal integrity" of the moral subject is conditioned, but the unity and integrity of any being. For in the moral philosophies of most speculative metaphysicians, moral philosophy has exemplified one dimension of metaphysical truth, and the domain of the moral agent has not been ontologically distinct, but rendered as immanent to a more encompassing rational system. Hence, the subject of internal or psychological harmony who is at once—at least potentially—in harmony with the world of objects and others reemerges in various forms in the history of speculative metaphysics. Indeed, the doctrine of internal relations that develops in Aristotle, Spinoza, Leibniz, and Hegel seems to require a discrete human subject who is simultaneously independent of and essentially interrelated to other beings with a similarly ambiguous ontology. In these cases, the unified subject is a theoretical requirement, not only for the moral life, but for the grander effort *to secure a preestablished metaphysical place for the human subject*. For Spinoza and Hegel, the metaphysical place of the human subject is articulated through the immanent rationality of desire, for desire is at once the fundamental striving of the human subject and the mode through which that subject rediscovers or constitutes its necessary metaphysical place. If desire were to escape this grand metaphysical project, if it were to follow its own laws or not to follow any laws at all, the human subject, as a desiring being, would constantly risk metaphysical homelessness and internal fragmentation.

Once again we see that if desire were otherwise, if it did not evince a moral intentionality or metaphysical place, philosophy would be left defenseless against the onset of nihilism and metaphysical dislocation. Indeed, if we consider that the philosophical preoccupation with desire in the twentieth century begins in France with Alexandre Kojève's lectures on Hegel in the 1930's, the question of the metaphysical place and moral efficacy of human subjects is everywhere present. The philosophical narrative of Hegel's reception and reinterpretation in France begins with the self-sufficient yet metaphysically secure Hegelian subject, that omnivorous

[5]

adventurer of the Spirit who turns out, after a series of surprises, to *be* all that he encounters along his dialectical way. The works of Kojève, Jean Hyppolite, and, in certain respects, Jean-Paul Sartre can be understood as so many meditations on the viability of this philosophical ideal. In their readings and overreadings of Hegel, Kojève and Hyppolite question whether the metaphysically ensconsed Hegelian subject is still supportable on the basis of a contemporary historical experience everywhere characterized by dislocation, metaphysical rupture, and the ontological isolation of the human subject. The consideration of desire becomes essential in assessing the historical viability of Hegel's metaphysics, for desire, according to Hegel, is the incessant human effort to overcome external differences, a project to become a self-sufficient subject for whom all things apparently different finally emerge as immanent features of the subject itself. Kojève and Hyppolite represent two moments in the French reappropriation of Hegel, moments that in retrospect prove to be the incipient stages of the dissolution of Hegel's doctrine of internal relations. Both of these commentators ask what constitutes desire's satisfaction, a question that implicitly contains a host of other questions, such as whether the psychic dissonance between reason and desire can be overcome in psychic harmony, and whether external differences among subjects, or between subjects and their worlds, are always capable of being recast as internal features of an internally integrated world. In questioning whether desire can be satisfied, and of what this satisfaction consists, they are asking whether belief in Hegelian harmonies is still possible, whether the subject always circles back to itself and, indeed, whether human striving always delivers the human subject into a metaphysically solicitous world. As Hegel's doctrine of internal relations is successively challenged for its philosophical viability, desire increasingly becomes a principle of the ontological displacement of the human subject, and in its latest stages, in the work of Lacan, Deleuze, and Foucault, desire comes to signify the impossibility of the coherent subject itself.

Twentieth-century French reflections on Hegel have, then, consistently looked to the notion of desire to discover possibilities for revising Hegel's version of the autonomous human subject and the metaphysical doctrine of internal relations that conditions that subject. In Hegel's *Phenomenology of Spirit,* the autonomous subject reconstitutes external difference as an immanent dynamic of itself through a succession of supersessions

(Aufhebungen); it both presupposes and articulates a metaphysical monism, the implicit and final unity of all beings. This metaphysically conditioned subject has a variety of philosophical precedents, and the genealogy of this subject cannot adequately be reconstructed within the confines of this inquiry. My task, then, is to comprehend retrospectively the latest stage of that genealogy, perhaps its last modern moment: the formulation of desire and satisfaction in Hegel's *Phenomenology of Spirit,* its philosophical celebration and reconstruction by some twentieth-century French philosophers, and the incipient moment of Hegel's dissolution in France through the deployment of desire to refute Hegel's metaphysically supported subject.

But how do we move from a philosophically satisfying desire to one that threatens the conventional premises of philosophy itself? What narrative can explain the dissolution of Hegel's doctrine of internal relations, the emergence of ontological rupture, the insurpassability of the negative? How is it that desire, once conceived as the human instance of dialectical reason, becomes that which endangers dialectics, fractures the metaphysically integrated self, and disrupts the internal harmony of the subject and its ontological intimacy with the world? These are the questions that will guide the philosophical story I am trying to tell. But, first, we must know why this story begins where it does. What distinguishes Hegel's brief references to desire? Why do they become the occasion for so much philosophical and antiphilosophical clamor?

Although desire *(Begierde)* is mentioned only occasionally in the *Phenomenology of Spirit,* it is established early on in the text as a permanent principle of self-consciousness. Hegel claims that "self-consciousness in general is Desire" (¶167), by which he means that desire signifies the *reflexivity* of consciousness, the necessity that it become other to itself in order to know itself. As desire, consciousness is outside itself; and as outside itself, consciousness is *self-consciousness.* Clearly, the meaning of this "outside" is yet to be clarified, and becomes a crucial ambiguity in the section "Lordship and Bondage." For introductory purposes, however, it suffices to note that desire is essentially linked with self-knowledge; it is always the desire-for-reflection, the pursuit of identity in what appears to be different. The Hegelian subject cannot know itself instantaneously or immediately, but requires mediation to understand its own structure. The permanent irony of the Hegelian subject consists of this: it requires mediation to know itself, and knows itself only as the very structure of mediation; in effect, what is reflexively grasped when the subject finds itself "outside" itself, reflected there, is this very fact itself, that the subject is a reflexive structure, and that movement out of itself is necessary in order for it to know itself at all.

This fundamental movement of desire, this general structure of con- sciousness' *reflexivity*, not only conditions the subject's knowledgeable pursuit of itself, but of its metaphysical place as well. Indeed, the Hegelian subject only knows itself to the extent that it (re)discovers its metaphysical place; identity and place are coextensive, for Hegelian autonomy depends upon the doctrine of internal relations. This can be seen quite clearly if we consider the sense in which the world "reflects" the subject, for it does not passively reflect the subject as one object reflects the light that ema- nates from another; reflection always presupposes and articulates onto- logical relatedness. In being reflected in and by that piece of world, the subject learns that it shares a common structure with that piece of world, that a prior and constituting relation conditions the possibility of reflec- tion, and that the object of reflection is nothing other than that relation itself. Hence, the subject that encounters an object or Other, or some feature of the world as external and ontologically disparate, is not iden- tical with the subject that discovers itself reflected in and by those osten- sibly external phenomena. In other words, before mediated self-reflection is achieved, the subject knows itself to be a more limited, less autonomous being than it potentially is. In discovering that reflection is possible, and that every reflection reveals a relation constitutive of the subject, a way in which it is integrally related to the world that it previously did not understand, the subject thus cultivates a more expanded conception of its place. Importantly, the Hegelian subject is not a self-identical subject who travels smugly from one ontological place to another; it *is* its travels, and *is* every place in which it finds itself.

Insofar as desire is this principle of consciousness' reflexivity, desire can be said to be satisfied when a relation to something external to consciousness is discovered to be constitutive of the subject itself. On the other hand, desire's dissatisfaction always signifies ontological rupture, the insurpassability of external difference. But according to the "ontolog- ical optimism"[9] of the *Phenomenology,* the Hegelian subject expands in the course of its adventure through alterity; it internalizes the world that

[8]

it desires, and expands to encompass, to be, what it initially confronts as other to itself. The final satisfaction of desire is the discovery of substance as subject, the experience of the world as everywhere confirming that subject's sense of immanent metaphysical place.

From a phenomenological perspective we must understand this journey of desire as something found in experience; the philosophical problem of desire must be something that the experience of desire itself tacitly poses, not only a problem imposed upon desire from some philosophical position abstracted from the experience itself. This conception no doubt sounds questionable, for what would it mean for desire itself to pose a question, much less to pose it tacitly? In what sense can we understand desire to speak, and to speak quietly at that? For Hegel's presentation of desire to be phenomenological, the desiring subject must experience what it seeks to know, its experience must take on the shape of a pursuit of knowledge, and its various philosophical pursuits must become manifest in forms of life. If desire is a tacit pursuit of identity, then the experience of desire must be a way of posing the problem of identity; when we desire, we pose the question of the metaphysical place of human identity—in some pre-linguistic form—and in the satisfaction of desire, the question is answered for us. In effect, desire is an interrogative mode of being, a corporeal questioning of identity and place. But what privileges desire as this impulsive and corporeal mode of metaphysical questioning?

Hyppolite suggests that desire is "the power of the negative in human life" ("CE" 27). Conceived as a lack, a being-without, desire initially signifies negativity; as the pursuit of substance, desire thus implicitly raises the question of whether human negativity, that which constitutes its ontological difference, can be resolved into an encompassing network of being. Human desire articulates the subject's relationship to that which is *not* itself, that which is different, strange, novel, awaited, absent, lost. And the satisfaction of desire is the transformation of difference into identity: the discovery of the strange and novel as familiar, the arrival of the awaited, the reemergence of what has been absent or lost. Thus, human desire is a way of thematizing the problem of negativity; it is the negative principle of human life, its ontological status as a lack in pursuit of being—Plato's vision in the *Symposium*. But desire is also the mode in which consciousness makes its own negativity into an explicit object of reflection, something to be labored upon and worked through. In effect, we read

[9]

our negativity in the objects and others we desire; as desirable, detestable, solicitous, or rejecting, these emotional facts of the world mirror our ontological insufficiency in Hegelian terms; they show us the negativity that we are, and engage us with the promise of plenitude or the threat of reaffirming our nothingness.[10] Whatever the emotional permutation of desire, we are, in virtue of desire, posing the question of final destination. And for Hegel, in posing the question, we presume the possibility of an answer, a satisfaction, an ultimate arrival.

But perhaps I have once again moved too quickly, for what, after all, does *arrival* mean in Hegelian terms? Insofar as the subject is engaged in the act of reproducing the totality of relations that constitute its identity, it is involved in the "labor of the negative," and, as negative, this subject cannot wholly identify with an encompassing plenitude. Insofar as the negative cannot be harnessed within the wider circumference of being, the subject cannot find a final satisfaction for desire. Hyppolite argues that although Hegel insists that "the truth is the whole," it is not clear that this whole, this totality, can be reproduced by the existing subject through a limited set of determinate acts. In the case of the *Phenomenology,* the Absolute is achieved when the history of the journeying subject is reconstituted as immanent to the subject itself, but the moment of this reconstitution does not escape the history itself, and neither is this history reproducible in a single moment.[11] The subjective constitution of the Absolute thus takes place through a series of acts which are, in principle, infinite; the phenomenological task of reproducing that history is necessary as long as the subject exists in time, that is, as long as new moments of experience call for integration into that subject's identity. Moreover, new experience does not augment an existing subject, but occasions an entirely new narrative of the subject itself, a new point of view from which the narrative must be retold.

The openness of the *Phenomenology's* narrative suggests the impossibility of metaphysical closure within experience. Hegel reiterates this claim in various ways in the *Logic,*[12] in the *Philosophy of History,* and in various sections of *The History of Philosophy.* In this last work, Hegel's criticisms of Spinoza highlight Hegel's own skepticism toward metaphysical closure. Spinoza is charged with erecting a metaphysical system that excludes the negativity of self-consciousness, that aspect of human life that precludes its final assimilation into Being:

This negative self-conscious moment, the movement of knowledge . . . is lacking in the content of Spinoza's philosophy. . . . the negation is only present as Nothing. . . . we do not find its movement, its Becoming and Being. . . . Self-consciousness is born into this ocean, dripping with the water thereof, i.e., never coming to absolute selfhood."[14]

Spinoza's ostensible failure to include human negativity within his metaphysical system proves relevant to my purpose here inasmuch as Spinoza's notion of desire *(cupiditas)*, the human *conatus* and principle of rational self-actualization, prefigures Hegel's own notion of desire. For Hegel, however, reason is understood as reflexive, and self-actualization requires the negative work of self-constitution. For both, desire serves the purposes of articulating and reaffirming a metaphysical monism, but Hegel's criticism of Spinoza's exclusion of consciousness's own negativity suggest a way of understanding Hegel's original contribution to the philosophical formulation of desire.

For Spinoza, desire is a modality of substance and is distinguished as the fundamental modality of human existence: "Desire is the essence of man" or "the endeavour to persist in one's own being."[15] Further, desire is not a merely corporeal impulse, for "desire is appetite with consciousness thereof." Spinoza can be understood to rehabilitate Aristotle's project in *De Anima*, where appetite and mind are but two dimensions of the same. While for Aristotle, "that which moves . . . is a single faculty of appetite" and "As it is, mind is never producing movement without appetite,"[16] for Spinoza, "the decrees of the mind are nothing but the appetites themselves."[17] One refers, then, to "appetites" when one regards the human monad from the perspective of its corporeal life, and to "the will" when we regard this selfsame being from the perspective of reason, but neither perspective comprehends the entirety of this being. Hence, for Spinoza, desire is the term given to the simultaneity of appetite and will, the name they are given when the corporeal and the mental aspects are taken as two dimensions of an integral being.[18]

Hegel clearly applauds Spinoza's monistic refutation of the Cartesian mind/body dualism, even as it applies to a theory of psychic organization. In Spinoza's criticism of Descartes, Hegel sees the incipient moments of a dialectical theory of identity: "With Descartes corporeality and the thinking 'I' are altogether independent Beings; this independence of the two extremes is done away with in Spinozism by their becoming moments

[11]

of the one absolute being. This expression signifies that Being must be grasped as the unity of opposites."[19]

For Spinoza, however, thought and appetite are different aspects of the human *conatus,* that endeavor to persist in its own being, which in turn must be understood as one of Substance's many attributes. The self-actualizing process of Substance multiplies and differentiates itself among all existence, becoming an internally differentiated monistic principle. This one Substance, this all-pervasive self-actualizing or self-realizing agency, is specified and instanced in the human monad as *desire.* For Hegel, Spinoza serves as a significant philosphical precedent for promoting a metaphysical monism capable of internal differentiation; the vision of an all-pervasive Substance as an agency of differentiation nears Hegel's own vision of the Absolute; hence, for Hegel "to be a follower of Spinoza is the essential commencement of all philosophy."[20] And yet Substance is overdetermined in Hegel's view, precisely because it fails to come into a dynamic interplay with the human subject; in effect, Substance does too much work, and human self-consciousness remains sadly unemployed. As Hegel explains it, "with Spinoza there is too much God."[21]

Hegel's *Phenomenology* can be read as an effort to relocate the Absolute as a principle originating in human consciousness as well, thus recasting the Absolute as having two complementary but equally necessary sources. Spinoza's metaphysics takes the point of view of the completed system as its starting point, but Hegel's *Phenomenology* poses the question of how this system is known, and how the knower comes to know himself as part of this system. In other words, Hegel wants to know how the movement of human knowledge, the negativity of self-consciousness, comes to be understood as necessary for the constitution of the system itself and, further, how the necessity of human negativity confirms the impossibility of that system's completion and closure. As Werner Marx explains, "for Spinoza, substance was the absolute or *causa sui.* By contrast, at the onset of the 'new spirit,' made explicit for Hegel in idealist philosophizing since Kant, philosophy began to see the Absolute, no longer in substance, but in the power of self-consciousness, in the subject."[22] Hegel charges Spinoza with failing to understand the negative power of thinking, regarding his own thought as a mere expression of some more powerful agency. Appropiating agency for himself, Hegel conceives substance itself as posited and moved by thinking.[23] In terms that curiously anticipate the charges Kierkegaard will level against Hegel, Hegel charges Spinoza with "lacking a firm grasp on the individual," failing to understand the role of the knowing subject in the constitution of metaphysical knowledge; with Spinoza, "thought has only the signification of the universal, not of self-consciousness."[24]

Hegel's anthropocentric reorientation of Spinoza's monism results in a reformulation of Spinoza's notion of self-actualization. The journeying subject of the *Phenomenology* also seeks its own actualization, but finds that this does not happen without the paradoxical assistance of negativity. The human subject does not exhibit greater potency through an unobstructed expression of selfhood, but requires obstruction, as it were, in order to gain reflection of itself in its environment, recognition of itself by Others. Hence, actualization only occurs to the extent that the subject confronts what is different from itself, and therein discovers a more enhanced version of itself. The negative thus becomes essential to self-actualization, and the human subject must suffer its own loss of identity again and again in order to realize its fullest sense of self. But once again, can this full self be found, and does Hegel's introduction of essential negativity effectively preclude the possibility of achieving full selfhood consonant with completed metaphysical knowledge? Can the living human subject reconstitute every external relation as internal, and simultaneously achieve adequacy to itself and its world? Is the ideal of substance recast as subject merely that, a regulative ideal which one longs for and suffers under but never appropriates existentially? If this is the case, has Hegel then created the notion of a subject as a perpetual striving? Does Hegel then return us to Fichte for whom yearning *(Sehnsucht)*[25] is the inevitable existential condition of human beings, or can satisfaction still have a meaning for us?

Although Hegel is often categorized as the philosopher of totality, of systematic completeness and self-sufficient autonomy, it is not clear that the metaphysical totality he defends is a finite system. Indeed, the abiding paradox of Hegel's metaphysics seems to consist in the openness of this ostensibly all-inclusive system. For a metaphysics to be simultaneously complete and infinite means that infinity must be included in the system itself, but "inclusion" as a spatial relation is a poor way of describing the relationship of the infinite to the system itself. To be able to think Hegel's absolute, the infinite and the systematic at once, is to think beyond spatial categories, to think the essence of time as Becoming.[26] But if the Absolute is not a principle of spatial stasis, if it is a temporal modality, the internal complexity of temporality itself, then satisfaction no longer carries the meaning of finality, stasis, closure. Although some post-Hegelians tend to criticize Hegel as a philosopher of totality and metaphysical closure, Kojève and Hyppolite, in very different ways, interpret Hegel as pursuing the Absolute in the indefinite movement of time, of history, of the various permutations of Becoming in which negativity is neither resolved nor negated, but sustained in a progressive and open adventure of Spirit.

It may well seem that Kojève and Hyppolite are reinventing Hegel, or reading him selectively for their own philosophical purposes, but this is a question to be textually pursued. What lies in the balance, however, is the question of whether desire's satisfaction signifies a kind of death in life,[27] whether satisfaction is life's closure or its openness, and whether satisfaction, conceived as the achievement of moral and metaphysical autonomy and an immanent sense of "place," is desirable after all. Has Hegel answered his own criticism of Spinoza in his own philosophical system, or is he also guilty of silencing the power of the negative?

Whether the ideal of a static identification of substance and subject is Hegel's own, or one falsely attributed to him, this final synthesis proves illusory for twentieth-century French readers of Hegel. Hyppolite interprets Hegel's absolute as the structure of temporality itself; Kojève, as the meaning of historical agency and efficacy. Although Sartre is more often viewed as a student of Husserl's phenomenological program, his ontology can nevertheless be viewed as a disintegrated Hegelianism. For Sartre, consciousness is a permanent source of negation, and human desire is understood as the "vain passion" which informs all of intentional consciousness. The absolute noncoincidence of for-itself and in-itself in *Being and Nothingness* has the effect of dissolving this idealized Hegelian synthesis altogether.

Although Derrida and other critics of the "metaphysics of presence" have argued that Hegel's revisionist followers (Kojève and Hyppolite) as well as his metaphysical critics (Sartre, Heidegger) are still within the orbit of a philosophical death wish for a final and static metaphysical identity, the history of Hegel's reception and reconstruction in France proves to be more internally complex when analyzed in detail. That analysis forms the bulk of my purpose here. Derrida's suggestion, however, is well taken, for it seems that philosophers who accept the metaphysical promise of desire, as well as those who meditate endlessly on the failure of that promise, remain entranced by an image of finality and self-identity which is itself a kind of death. The criticisms waged against Hegel by Lacan insist upon the psychoanalytic inevitability of dissatisfaction, while Deleuze and Foucault, through recourse to Nietzsche, take issue with the entire Hegelian emphasis on negativity and offer a version of desire based on excess and plenitude rather than lack. For Lacan, Hegel suffers from Cartesian innocence; for Deleuze and Foucault, Hegel exemplifies slave morality and the lifeless dependence on the principle of identity. The question may seem to be, is Hegelianism in its metaphysical mode a death-bent enterprise? But perhaps that is too strong, for the relationship between desire and metaphysics proves to be a complicated history, one to be only partially narrated here. In the context of the French reception of Hegel, we will inquire into the metaphysics of desire, the metaphysical defense against desire, and lastly the post-metaphysical discourse on desire.

My narrative is thus formed in four parts: (1) the metaphysical defense of/against desire in Hegel's *Phenomenology of Spirit;* (2) the revision of Hegelian desire by Kojève and Hyppolite to exemplify the human subject as a mode of Becoming, internally nonidentical; (3) Sartre's post-Hegelian nostalgia for a self-identical subject, and his version of desire as a vain metaphysical striving; and (4) the post-Hegelian critique of the metaphysical discourse on desire in a selective reading of Lacan, Deleuze, and Foucault. My task is to trace the latest stage of philosophy's quarrel with the life of impulse, the philosophical effort to domesticate desire as an instance of metaphysical place, the struggle to come to terms with desire as a principle of metaphysical dislocation and psychic dissonance, and the effort to deploy desire to dislocate and defeat the metaphysics of identity. Throughout my inquiry I will be concerned with the dissolution of Hegelianism as well as the peculiar forms of its insistent reemergence, its reformulation, and its inadvertent reappearance even when subject to its most vehement opposition. Indeed, we will see the degree to which opposition keeps desire alive.

I

Desire, Rhetoric, and Recognition in Hegel's Phenomenology of Spirit

The sun by day and the gods revealed are familiar sights
Shaping the countenance which, by ancients named "one and all,"
Has filled to the brim with free satisfaction the reticent heart,
And first and alone is the source of gratified desire.

Hölderlin, "Bread and Wine"

A consideration of desire in the *Phenomenology of Spirit* requires a preliminary turn to the larger problem of how philosophical themes are introduced and "argued" within the terms of this sometimes tortuous text. I place the verb "argue" within quotations, not to dismiss the kind of argumentation that Hegel pursues, but to draw attention to the idiosyncrasy of its form. After all, the *Phenomenology of Spirit* is a *Bildungsroman*,[1] an optimistic narrative of adventure and edification, a pilgrimage of the spirit, and upon immediate scrutiny, it is unclear how Hegel's narrative structure argues the metaphysical case he wants to make. Moreover, Hegel's sentence structure seems to defy the laws of grammar and to test the ontological imagination beyond its usual bounds. His sentences begin with subjects that turn out to be interchangeable with their objects

[17]

or to pivot on verbs that are swiftly negated or inverted in supporting clauses. When "is" is the verb at the core of any claim, it rarely carries a familiar burden of predication, but becomes transitive in an unfamiliar and foreboding sense, affirming the inherent movement in "being," disrupting the ontological assumptions that ordinary language usage lulls us into making.

The rhetorical inversion of Hegelian sentences as well as the narrative structure of the text as a whole convey the elusive nature of both the grammatical and human subject. Against the Understanding's compulsion to fix the grammatical subject into a univocal and static signifier, Hegel's sentences indicate that the subject can only be understood in its movement. When Hegel states, "Substance is Subject," the "is" carries the burden of "becomes," where becoming is not a unilinear but a cyclical process. Hence, we read the sentence wrong if we rely on the ontological assumptions of linear reading, for the "is" is a nodal point of the interpenetration of both "Substance" and "Subject"; each *is* itself only to the extent that it *is* the other because, for Hegel, self-identity is only rendered actual to the extent that it is mediated through that which is different. To read the sentence right would mean to read it cyclically, or to bring to bear the variety of partial meanings it permits on any given reading. Hence, it is not just that substance is being clarified, or that the subject is being defined, but the very meaning of the copula is itself being expressed as a locus of movement and plurivocity.

The grammatical subject is, thus, never self-identical, but is always and only itself in its reflexive movement; the sentence does not consist of grammatical elements that reflect or otherwise indicate corresponding ontological entities. The sentence calls to be taken as a whole, and in turn indicates the wider textual context in which it itself is to be taken. But the way in which this context is "indicated" is less referential than rhetorical; Hegel's sentences *enact* the meanings that they convey; indeed, they show that what "is" only is to the extent that it is *enacted*. Hegelian sentences are read with difficulty, for their meaning is not immediately given or known; they call to be reread, read with different intonations and grammatical emphases. Like a line of poetry that stops us and forces us to consider that the *way* in which it is said is essential to *what* it is saying, Hegel's sentences rhetorically call attention to themselves. The discrete and static words on the page deceive us only momentarily into

[18]

thinking that discrete and static meanings will be released by our reading. If we refuse to give up the expectation that univocal meanings linearly arranged will unfold from the words at hand, we will find Hegel confused, unwieldy, unnecessarily dense. But if we question the presumptions of the Understanding that the prose asks us to, we will experience the incessant movement of the sentence that constitutes its meaning.

Hegel's sentences are never completed in that they never offer up "what is meant" in some final and digestible form. "Substance is Subject" suggests not only what substance is, what the subject is, and what the meaning of the copula is, but also that no ratiocination of possible meanings could capture all of the meanings that the sentence suggests. All three terms signify indefinitely inasmuch as each calls for continual concretization and revision. To know the meaning of that sentence is to know the meaning of Hegel's system, and that meaning cannot be known once and for all by any living subject. Hence, Hegel's sentences send us forth, as it were, into a journey of knowledge; they indicate what is not being expressed, what must be explored for any given expression to acquire meaning. As sentential narratives, they are cyclical and progressive at once, reflecting and enacting the movement of consciousness by which they might be comprehended. Because Hegel's rhetoric defies our expectations of a linear and definite philosophical presentation, it initially obstructs us (no one reads Hegel quickly), but once we have reflected upon the assumptions that Hegel wants to release us from, the rhetoric initiates us into a consciousness of irreducibly multiple meanings which continuously determine each other. This multiplicity of meanings is not static, according to Hegel, but is the essence of becoming, of movement itself.[2] In reading for multiple meanings, for plurivocity, ambiguity, and metaphor in the general sense, we experience concretely the inherent movement of dialectical thinking, the essential alteration of reality. And we also come to understand the role of our own consciousness in constituting this reality inasmuch as the text must be read to have its meaning enacted.

This last point is made especially clear in the *Phenomenology*, which is specifically concerned with the point of view of the human subject. Like the grammatical subject of Hegel's metaphysical remarks, the human subject is never simply and immediately there. As soon as we get a grammatical indication of his location, he travels forth and becomes

[19]

something different from what he was when we first got wind of it.*
More than the rhetorical strategy of Hegel's sentential narratives, the
organizing narrative structure of the *Phenomenology* narrows the distance
between philosophical form and content. Hegel's narrative is designed to
seduce the reader, to exploit his need to find himself in the text he is
reading. The *Phenomenology* requires and effects the imaginative identification of the reader with the traveling subject so that reading becomes
a philosophically instructive form of travel.

Identifying with Hegel's protagonist is no easy matter. We begin the
Phenomenology with a sense that the main character has not yet arrived.
There is action and deliberation, but no recognizable agent. Our immediate impulse is to look more closely to discern this absent subject in the
wings; we are poised for his arrival. As the narrative progresses beyond
the "this" and the "that," the various deceptions of immediate truth, we
realize slowly that this subject will not arrive all at once, but will offer
choice morsels of himself, gestures, shadows, garments strewn along the
way, and that this "waiting for the subject," much like attending Godot,
is the comic, even burlesque, dimension of Hegel's *Phenomenology*. Moreover, we discover that simply waiting is not what is expected of us, for
this narrative does not progress rationally unless we participate in thinking
through the logical necessity of every transition. The narrative purports
to develop inexorably, so we must test the necessity of its every move.

Although Hegel's *Bildungsroman* does not address his reader directly,
as does Diderot's *Jacques le fataliste*,[3] the narrative strategy of the *Phenomenology* is to implicate the reader indirectly and systematically. We
do not merely witness the journey of some other philosophical agent, but
we ourselves are invited on stage to perform the crucial scene changes. At
the close of the *Phenomenology*, the philosopher is no longer "Other" to
ourselves, for that distinction would announce an "outside" to that ostensibly all-inclusive unity. Indeed, we recognize *ourselves* as the subjects
we have been waiting for inasmuch as we gradually constitute the perspective by which we recognize our history, our mode of becoming,
through the *Phenomenology* itself.

* Although Hegel's subject is a fictive personage, and clearly without recognizable gender,
I will refer to this fiction as "he." This procedure ought not to be taken as an identification
of the universal with the masculine, but is intended to avoid an unwieldy grammatical
situation.

[20]

Thus, the *Phenomenology* is not only a narrative about a journeying counsciousness, but is the journey itself. The narrative discloses and enacts a strategy for appropriating philosophical truth; it sets the ontological stage in a variety of ways, compels our belief in the reality of that staged scene, encourages our identification with the emergent subject that the scene includes, and then asks us to suffer the inevitable failure of that subject's quest for identity within the confines of that scene. The subject fails—and we, imaginatively, with him—precisely because he took seriously the ontological commitments that the scene required; hence, his demise is revealed again and again as a function of a tragic blindness, although, for Hegel, tragic events are never decisive. There is little time for grief in the *Phenomenology* because renewal is always so close at hand. What seems like tragic blindness turns out to be more like the comic myopia of Mr. Magoo whose automobile careening through the neighbor's chicken coop always seems to land on all four wheels. Like such miraculously resilient characters of the Saturday morning cartoon, Hegel's protagonists always reassemble themselves, prepare a new scene, enter the stage armed with a new set of ontological insights—and fail again. As readers, we have no other narrative option but to join in this bumpy ride, for we cannot anticipate this journey without embarking on it ourselves. Time and again the *Phenomenology* compels our belief in an ontological scene, a picture of what the world is like and where the Absolute can be found, only to reveal that picture finally as a systematically induced deception.

It makes no more sense for the reader to reject the particular configurations of the world that the *Phenomenology* offers than it would to refuse to accept a novel as true. Hegel's provisional scenes, the stage of self-certainty, the struggle for recognition, the dialectic of lord and bondsman, are instructive fictions, ways of organizing the world which prove to be too limited to satisfy the subject's desire to discover itself as substance. These scenes are thus consistently undermined by that which they unwittingly exclude, and are forced to reassemble as more complicated arrangements, now including that which brought the previous scene to dissolution. As readers who accept each scene as true, we identify imaginatively, but every effort at identification is finally subverted. What initially compels our belief turns out to be a false premise, but this falsehood immediately indicates a truer and more inclusive premise by

[21]

which it might be replaced. Hegel's subject does not rest easily with any partial conception of its relationship with the world of substance, and every exclusionary ontological commitment engenders a "return of the repressed." Hegel's subject suffers no permanent bout of bad faith or debilitating repression of what is real. Every deception immediately releases a broader conception of truth by which it might be transcended. This subject journeys with compulsive metaphysical honesty toward his ultimate dialectical harmony with the world. No matter how many times his world dissolves, he remains infinitely capable of reassembling another world; he suffers the negative, but is never wholly engulfed by it. Indeed, suffering only enhances his synthetic powers. The negative is always and only useful—never debilitating in any final sense. Hegel's subject is thus a fiction of infinite capability, a romantic traveler who only learns from what he experiences, who, because infinitely self-replenishing, is never devastated beyond repair.

The dramatic metaphysical hope of Hegel's subject prompted Kierkegaard to ask whether such a person might really be said to exist. After all, how do we account for the relentless desire not merely to survive but to profit from suffering, illness, loss? For Hegel, this desire is presuppositional, so that a metaphysical finesse obscures the existential and psychological difficulties at work. But how often does suffering prompt the reconstruction of a world on yet firmer ground, and how often does suffering simply erode whatever ground there is, producing anxiety about the very possibility of a coherent world? Clearly, Hegel's subject has a very fine director working for him, one who monitors those scene changes carefully and makes sure that every transition is survived. But as Kierkegaard once asked about existence, "where is the director? I should like to have a word with him."[4]

If we accept Kierkegaard's existential critique of Hegel's subject, what becomes of the *Phenomenology's* claim to be experiential truth? If Hegel's subject is fictional, can he perhaps still have a meaning for us? Consider that the narrative of the *Phenomenology* is a series of deceptions which prove to be the *via negativa* of philosophical truth, that these successive fictions form the history of a consciousness which, in turn, constitutes its substance, the circle of its being. The deceptive pursuit of the Absolute is not a vain "running around in circles," but a progressive cycle which reveals every deception as permitting some grander act of synthesis, an insight into yet more regions of interrelated reality. The substance that is known, and which the subject *is,* is thus an all-encompassing web of interrelations, the dynamism of life itself, and, consequently, the principle that all specific determinations are not what they appear to be. And yet, as beings who must be cultivated to the absolute standpoint, we begin with the determinate, the particular, and the immediate, and treat it as if it were absolute, and then learn through that misplaced certainty that the Absolute is broader and more internally complicated that we originally thought. The history of these deceptions is a progressive one inasmuch as we understand how these deceptions imply each other as necessary consequences, and that together they reveal that the *insufficiency* of any given relationship to the Absolute is the basis of its *interdependence* on other relationships, so that the history of deception is, finally, the unity of internal relations which is the Absolute. Absolute truth in the *Phenomenology* is thus something like the dramatic integrity of a comedy of errors. In Nietzsche's comparable view, " 'Truth': this, according to my way of thinking, does not necessarily denote the antithesis of error, but in the most fundamental cases only the posture of various errors in relation to one another."[5]

In this sense, the *Phenomenology* is a study in fiction-making which shows the essential role of fiction and false belief in the quest for philosophical truth. According to such a reading, the fictional status of Hegel's subject takes on a new set of possible meanings. We might read this subject as a trope for the hyperbolic impulse itself, that frantic and overdetermined pursuit of the Absolute which *creates* that place when it cannot be found, which projects it endlessly and is constantly "foiled" by its own projection. As a being of metaphysical desires, the human subject is prone to fiction, to tell himself the lies that he needs to live.[6] Reading Hegel in this Nietzschean fashion, we can take the *Phenomenology* as a study of desire and deception, the systematic pursuit and misidentification of the Absolute, a constant process of inversion which never reaches ultimate closure. The subject becomes a locus of ever more sophisticated forms of deception, and thus learns about ever more insidious appearances of the Absolute which turn out to be partial, fictional, and false. Hence, if Hegel's subject cannot be located in existence, perhaps we ought not to be surprised at his fictional reality. Like Don Quixote, Hegel's subject is an impossible identity who pursues reality in systematically mistaken ways.

As readers of his text, accepting time and again the terms of his journey, we indulge in the same exorbitant desires; we become makers of fiction who cannot sustain belief in our creations, who wake to their unreality, but only to dream more shrewdly the next time.

The Ontology of Desire

Hegel's explicit discussion of desire begins in the section, "The Truth of Self-Certainty," which initiates the transition between consciousness and self-consciousness. The appearance of desire at this juncture is curious, for if the progress of the *Phenomenology* is impelled by desire, why does desire emerge as an explicit theme only in the fourth chapter of the text? Indeed, what does it mean that desire "appears" at a given stage in the *Phenomenology* at all?

Desire *appears,* but the moment of appearance is not necessarily the initial moment of its efficacy. In a sense, nothing comes into existence *ex nihilo* for Hegel; everything comes into explicit form from a potential or implicit state; indeed, everything has, in a sense, been there all along. "Appearance" is but one explicit or actual moment in the development of a phenomenon. In the *Phenomenology,* a given phenomenon appears in the context of a given configuration of the world. In the case of desire, we must ask, what kind of world makes desire possible? What must the world be like for desire to exist?

When we ask after the conditions or features of the world that make desire possible, we are not asking a preliminary question which, once answered, will allow us to continue the investigation with ease. Nor is it the Kantian inquiry into the transcendental conditions of desire's appearance. For Hegel, the preconditions of desire are the object of the inquiry itself, for desire in its articulation always thematizes the conditions of its own existence. When we ask, what is desire "after," we can give a partial answer: the illumination of its own opacity, the expression of that aspect of the world that brought it into being. This is part of what is meant by the *reflexivity* that desire is said to embody and enact. Eventually, the reflexivity enacted by desire will be identical with absolute knowledge itself. As Stanley Rosen remarks, "In analytical terms, part of the self is encountered outside oneself; the desire to assimilate the desire of the

Other is thus an effort to grasp analytically the preanalytic or indeterminate structure of absolute reflection."[7] Desire is *intentional* in that it is always desire *of* or *for* a given object or Other, but it is also *reflexive* in the sense that desire is a modality in which the subject is both discovered and enhanced. The conditions that give rise to desire, the metaphysics of internal relations, are at the same time what desire seeks to articulate, render explicit, so that desire is a tacit pursuit of metaphysical knowledge, the human way that such knowledge "speaks."

At the juncture in the *Phenomenology* where desire emerges as a central theme, we are in the midst of a quandary. The subject has not arrived, but a predecessor is on the scene: consciousness. Consciousness is marked by its assumption that the sensuous and perceptual world it encounters is fundamentally different from itself. The "world" it encounters is a natural world, spatiotemporally organized, exhibiting discrete empirical objects. Consciousness contemplates this world, convinced that it is the Absolute and that it is external, or ontologically different from, itself. The sensuous and perceptual world is self-generating and self-subsisting; it has no need of consciousness. Consciousness finds itself in exile from the Absolute, believing its own powers of apprehending the world to be unrelated to that world. Consciousness here is pure intentional enthrallment with the world, but is not identified with the world, and in no way determines the truth or objective existence of that world. A paradox arises within this stage of experience because the fact remains that the sensuous and perceptual world is *delineated in* consciousness, and this delineation suggests that consciousness itself participates in the determination of that world's truth. This may not seem initially clear, but when we consider that the sensuous and perceptual world only *becomes actual* or determinate through its mediation in alterity, we recognize that consciousness is this Other which reflects and, thus, actualizes the truth of that world. Seen from this point of view, consciousness all of a sudden returns from its exile and now plays a major ontological role in determining Absolute reality. This sudden reorganization of the world requires a revision of basic concepts: what must consciousness be like if it "mediates" the world, and what meaning can we give to "alterity" and "actualization"? How did the dissolution of this particular world give rise to edifying philosophical insights?

The role of externalization and alterity in the determination of something as true is made clear partially through the introduction of the notion of Force. Appearing in the final section of Part 1 of "The Truth of Self-Certainty," Force is said to prefigure the Concept *(Begriff)*, a mode of consciousness which, Hegel argues, permits one to "think antithesis within the thesis itself" (¶ 160). Force is essential to the transition from consciousness to self-consciousness because it posits the externality of the world of sensuous and perceptual reality as one that is essentially related to consciousness itself; in effect, Force posits externalization as a necessary moment of thought. In order that consciousness complete its own intentional requirement to think "something," it must become *determinate* thought: it must be a thought "of" something external to itself, and, in turn, become determined by that external something. Hence, by thinking a particular thing, thinking itself becomes particularized, becomes a given *mode* of thought. Thought that remains a purely inner phenomenon is not truly thought at all; it must be related to something outside itself in order to gain an actualized and determinate reality as consciousness. The notion of Force thus distinguishes the inner and outer "moments" of thought inasmuch as Force is a constant movement between an inner reality and a determinate manifestation; in effect, Force is the compulsion that a nascent reality exhibits to find a determinate manifestation for itself—Hegel's reformulation of Spinoza's *conatus*. Force characterizes relations in the physical world as well as within consciousness itself, and thus becomes the ontological basis of consciousness' bond with the sensuous and perceptual world that it initially encountered as ontologically disparate from itself. This compulsion to externalize prefigures the work of the Concept itself which, in Charles Taylor's words, "is the Idea of necessity which necessarily posits its own external manifestation."[8]

Force is that which impels an inner reality to gain determinate form, but it is also that which frustrates the absorption of that inner reality into determinate form. In other words, Force sustains a tension between that which appears and that which does not appear, and in this sense is different from other principles of teleological development. The notion of "inner difference" or the unity of opposites which is so central to Hegel's mode of dialectical thinking is enhanced through the notion of Force. It is not the drive toward determinate shape that would bring all nascent reality to explicit potency, but rather the constant process of giving and superseding determinate form. In a brief discussion of gravity,

[26]

Hegel claims that without the notion of Force, or inner difference, we might have to think of space and time as only contingently related to one another: "But through the Notion of inner difference, these unlike and indifferent moments, space and time, etc. are a difference which is no difference, or only a difference of what is selfsame, and its essence is unity. As positive and negative they stimulate each other into activity, and their being is rather to posit themselves as not-being and to suspend themselves in the unity. The two distinguished moments both subsist; they are implicit and are opposite in themselves, i.e., each is the opposite of itself; each has its 'other' within it and they are only one unity"[10] (¶ 161).

The "unity" of the phenomenon impelled by Force is not a static unity, but *movement,* incessant and dialectical. The Absolute cannot be identified with the determinate objects of the spatiotemporal world, the *res extensa* of sensuous and perceptual reality; there is always something that is beyond the determinate, some operative negativity, that accounts for the genesis of determinate form as well as for its eventual dissolution. The notion of Force confirms that there is something that does not appear, but that is nevertheless crucial to any given appearance; moreover, it indicates that reality is not coextensive with appearance, but always sustains and is sustained by a hidden dimension. In order to think the object of experience that the sensuous and perceptual world offers up to consciousness, we must relinquish faith in the kind of thinking that can take only determinate beings as its objects; conceptual thinking must replace Understanding, for only the former can think the movement between opposites. The Understanding consistently mistakes stasis for truth, and can only understand movement as a series of discrete moments, not as the vital unity of moments that imply each other endlessly and do not appear simultaneously. The Understanding cannot grasp movement itself; it is always prone to fix its object in a present tense which purports to present exhaustively the full reality of the object at hand. Because consciousness reaches its most sophisticated development in the Understanding, it proves incapable of the kind of thinking that the phenomenon of Force calls upon it to make. In the explication of Force, consciousness proves to be interminably partial; it always indicates a negativity that it itself cannot grasp. Self-consciousness arises, then, as the effort to think inner difference, the mutual implication of opposites, as constitutive of the object itself. Self-consciousness thus portends to conceptualize Force,

[27]

and Life itself, defined as the constitution and dissolution of shape. Self-consciousness is not the momentary act of a discrete consciousness attending an opposing and discrete world, but a cognitive experience taking place in a developing sense of time; it is, in turn, able to grasp the temporal life of the object itself. Consciousness could think determinate being, but could not think the process of determination and indetermination that is Life itself; it could not think change.

Self-consciousness thus emerges as a kind of knowing that is at once a mode of becoming; it is suffered, dramatized, enacted. Consciousness gives rise to self-consciousness in the bungled attempt to *explain* what it knows: "Appearance, or the play of Forces, already displays infinity . . . this absolute unrest of pure movement, but it is as an *'explanation'* that it first freely stands forth; and in being finally an object for consciousness, as *that which it is,* consciousness is thus self-consciousness" (¶ 163). Force can be explained as a series of isolated phenomena, but the interrelation between them will never satisfactorily be explained. If this explanation is executed from the point of view of consciousness, it will only be a fracturing of the moments of Force; gravity can be analytically separated from positive and negative electricity, and distance and attraction can be similarly scrutinized in isolation, but the phenomenon itself will be lost, or presented as a lifeless series of internally unrelated attributes. The Understanding lacks reflexivity, and so cannot understand how consciousness' own difference from that which it scrutinizes is itself part of the phenomenon under investigation. Hence, it cannot extrapolate from this experience of "constitutive difference" to the object under investigation in order to know how the play of Forces holds together in the temporalized unity of the phenomenon. And so consciousness fumbles to explain Force, listing the moments of the play of Forces, listing them again, trying to force a synthesis from a series, but lacking the proper cognitive tools. And yet this failed explanation reveals an unexpected clue to the proper formulation of the phenomenon. As an "Explanation," the Understanding comes to be determinately manifest in material form; there is consciousness itself sprawled on the page, formed in letters and words, existing, materially, outside itself. In recognizing the authorship of that explanation, consciousness becomes aware of itself for the first time. No longer enthralled intentionally with a world that ostensibly monopolized reality, consciousness discovers its own reflexivity; it has become other to itself, and knows itself as such: "The reason why explaining affords so much self-satisfaction is just because in it consciousness is, so to speak, communing directly with itself, enjoying only itself; although it seems to be busy with something else" (¶ 163).

Consciousness thus relinquishes itself as consciousness in the process of explaining what it knows. By the time the Explanation is over, neither consciousness nor the object it seeks to explain are the same. The process of Explanation transforms the two poles of experience it was meant to mediate. No longer a tool in the hands of a consciousness intact, Explanation becomes a curious kind of agent that turns on its user and shakes his identity. The object of Explanation becomes curiously ambiguous as well; in being explained, the object is revealed as having certain properties that consciousness itself can elucidate. But what the object reveals, and what consciousness contributes, remain indistinguishable, for the only route to the object is through the Explanation itself, so that we cannot appeal to the object what exists outside this explanation in order to see to what extent the Explanation adequately expresses the object itself. Indeed, the object itself is no different from the object-as-explained; it exists in the form of the Explanation which has become its actuality. Consciousness is thus faced with an unanticipated ambiguity, for it finds itself in the terms of an explanation which is "of" the object of experience; it is both itself and the object under investigation. And if it exists in this double sense, then it must be part of the world it investigates. Consciousness thus learns that what exists in itself also exists in its alterity. This principle allows it to grasp the phenomenon of Force, but also, as an inadvertent discovery, to grasp itself as essentially reflexive. Moreover, it comes to understand that its own reflexivity means that it is constitutive of the reality that it investigates:

I distinguish myself from myself, and in doing so, I am directly aware that what is distinguished from myself in not different from me. I, the self-same being, repel myself from myself; but what is posited as distinct from me, or as unlike me, is immediately, in being so distinguished, not a distinction for me. It is true that consciousness of an "other," of an object in general, is itself necessarily self-consciousness, a reflectedness-into-self, consciousness of itself in its otherness. (¶ 164)

In distinguishing something as different from consciousness, consciousness makes a determination of something negative. In *stating* "that is not

[29]

me," a positive reality is born. The fact of the statement seems to undermine the content of the statement, for the statement effects a linguistic
relationship between the "I" and the reality that is "other." Clearly, this
reality which is ostensibly different from the consciousness that announces
itself here is not *so* different that it eludes linguistic reference altogether.
Consciousness knows it well enough to negate it, and this piece of "not
me" has a linguistic place within the world of consciousness itself. Hence,
the question arises, what does it mean to affirm through language that
which one seeks to negate? What kind of curious negation is this that
lives on in language as an affirmation?

When Hegel's emergent subject, here understood as the mode of consciousness, states or explains its fundamental difference from the world,
the mode in which that explanation is made contradicts the explicit
intention and content of the explanation. As that which must express
what it knows in language, i.e., that which must externalize its knowledge
in linguistic form, consciousness is "of" the world, in the sense that it
appears in the world. Hence, if consciousness seeks to explain its ontological difference from the world, it can only contradict itself in the
process. And yet the rhetoric of Explanation does not completely make a
fool of the consciousness that seeks to articulate its ontological distinction.
Consciousness *is* different from the sensuous and perceptual world that
it encounters, but this difference is not an external one; rather, consciousness is internally related to that which it seeks to know, a necessary
moment in the hermeneutical circle in which the investigator is implicated
in the object of investigation.

The encounter with ostensible ontological disparity and the discovery
that interrelatedness exists after all is, here as elsewhere in the *Phenomenology,* effected in the transition from reading literally to reading
rhetorically. When the Hegelian subject states or enacts or otherwise
externalizes its conviction that it is absolutely other to this or that aspect
of the world, the very process of externalizing that conviction works to
undermine it, and, eventually, proves that the opposite is true. In stating
or dramatizing its truth, negation gains a home in the world, and thus is
transformed from an indeterminate negation to a determinate one, one
that exists as a moment in a web of interrelatedness, one that has a place.

Significantly, Hegel relies on the rhetorical meanings of linguistic explanation in effecting the transition between consciousness and self-con-

sciousness. Inasmuch as self-consciousness is characterized by reflexivity, i.e., the capacity to relate to itself, this is conditioned by the power of articulation. Moreover, it is not that articulation offers forth a "content" which is then reflected upon by a consciousness doggedly watching from an ontological elsewhere, but consciousness reveals itself as *an articulated phenomenon,* that which only becomes itself *as* articulation. Once articulated, this consciousness is no longer appropriately called by that name, for it has rhetorically refuted the conditions of ontological disparity which that name denoted. In becoming articulated, consciousness becomes itself, but, in classical Hegelian parlance, it does this only by becoming another. In this instance, that Other, which is, yes, its fullest self, is self-consciousness.

The movement of this transition is a *rhetorical* movement; the insight that is finally revealed is first enacted without self-awareness, and it is only once that enactment is completed, the Explanation stated and finished, that consciousness takes a look at this product and recognizes itself as its author. The purpose of the Explanation no longer matters, for consciousness has made an unexpected and more significant discovery: it has the capacity to recognize itself, it is a reflexive structure, and it inhabits a place in the world. As external, consciousness is "other" to itself, which means that it is that which is generally understood as "other" to itself, namely, the world; hence, the inverse of this statement of identity is also true: consciousness of the world is always simply consciousness of itself in its alterity. The rhetorical movement of the transition thus reaffirms the principle of identity, the ontological place of difference, the supporting web of internal relations.

As a rhetorical agency, the Hegelian subject always knows more than it thinks it knows, and by reading itself rhetorically, i.e., reading the meanings it unwittingly *enacts* against those it explicitly *intends,* it recovers ever greater dimensions of its own identity. Rhetoric is thus the condition of deception and of illumination, the way in which the subject is always beyond itself, meaning what it does not necessarily intend but nevertheless externalizes, then reads, and finally recovers for itself.

The rhetorical drama of Explanation we have been following is recapitulated on a more concrete level in the drama of desire. The problem of consciousness, we will remember, is how to conceptualize its relationship with the sensuous and perceptual world. As the advanced form of Un-

[31]

derstanding, consciousness could delineate the features or "moments" of this world, but could not effect a unity with that world. In effect, consciousness has only a theoretical experience of its object, a notion of what it must be like, but the sensuous and perceptual world remains remote, conjectured, experientially unknown. In the transition to self-consciousness, we are told to expect the following: "the Notion of the object is superseded in the actual object, or the first, immediate presentation of the object is superseded in experience: certainty gives place to truth" *(die Gewissheit ging in der Wahrheit verloren)* (¶ 166).

How then does the sensuous and perceptual world become an experience for self-consciousness, or, in even stronger terms, how is this world experienced *as* self-consciousness? In ¶ 167, the *Phenomenology* begins to answer this question for us by calling on the experience of *desire* as the mode in which self-consciousness requires that sensuous and perceptual world. Hegel introduces the notion of desire casually, at the end of a complicated explanation, as if it were something we should already understand. The problem under consideration is how to make the sensuous and perceptual world a difference that is no difference, that is, how to recapitulate this world as a feature of self-consciousness itself. We have seen that "explaining" the world went part of the way in doing the trick, but the solution there seemed too abstract:

With the first moment, self-consciousness is in the form of consciousness, and the whole expanse of the sensuous world is preserved for it, but at the same time only as connected with the second moment, the unity of self-consciousness with itself; and hence the sensuous world is for it an enduring existence which, however, is only *appearance,* or a difference which, in itself, is no difference. This antithesis of appearance and its truth has, however, for its essence only the truth, viz, the unity must become essential to self-consciousness, i.e. self-consciousness is Desire in general. (¶ 167)

In the "first moment" or primary thesis—roughly Part 1 of the *Phenomenology*—the sensuous world endures as appearance. But what kind of appearance is this? It is, we learn, ostensibly different from a reality or essence, but then this distinction turns out not to hold: it is "difference which, in itself, is no difference." Consciousness has learned through its powers of explanation that it appears to hold the truth of the opposing world, yet a new disparity arises, namely, that between the *appearance* of that world as external and unreachable, and its *truth* which is evidenced in consciousness' well-wrought Explanation. In order to overcome this particular distinction between appearance and truth, this sensuous and perceptual world must become "unified" with consciousness in some way; if this unity is to take place, and one of the terms of this unity is the sensuous world, then it makes sense to assume that self-consciousness itself must have a sensuous expression. And that the sensuous articulation of self-consciousness "is Desire in general."

The German word for desire, *Begierde*, suggests animal appetite rather than the anthropocentric sense conveyed by the French *le désir* and the English *desire*.[9] Introduced at this juncture in the text, the term clearly acquires the meaning of animal hunger; the sensuous and perceptual world is desired in the sense that it is required for consumption and is the means for the reproduction of life. As we follow the textual development of desire, we learn that human desire is distinguished from animal desire in virtue of its reflexivity, its tacit philosophical project, and its rhetorical possibilities. At this point, however, we are equipped only with the insights that Force and Explanation have provided us; we understand *movement* as the play of Forces, and Explanation as the necessary *alterity* of consciousness itself. Predictably enough, the experience of desire initially appears as a synthesis of movement and alterity.

In desiring some feature of the world, self-consciousness effects the unity with the world that consciousness could only effect theoretically and inadvertently. As an explicit desire for some aspect of the world, self-consciousness not only appropriates the rhetorical accomplishment of consciousness, but follows the syllogism through, as it were, and becomes the sensuous enactment of this unity. Hence, desire becomes the sensuous articulation of a sensuous object which is simultaneously a reflexive pursuit of self-consciousness itself. Immediately following Hegel's remark that "self-consciousness is Desire in general," Hegel explains the ambiguity of the project of desire:

Consciousness, as self-consciousness, henceforth has a double object, that of sense-certainty and perception, which however for self-consciousness has the character of a negative; and the second, viz, itself, which is the true *essence*, and is present in the first instance only as opposed to the first object.(¶ 167)

Desire is here described in terms of its ambiguous intentional aims, but these two aims are also developmental stages of consciousness: the first

[33]

aim, the object of sense-certainty and perception, is the conventional object of consciousness, a relationship we have already examined; the second aim, consciousness' reflexive pursuit of itself, is also already known, for that is what we found in the drama of Explanation. Hence, desire is always desire for something other which, in turn, is always a desire for a more expanded version of the subject. The "immediate object . . . of sense-certainty and perception" appears as "a negative" because it is *not* consciousness. And yet self-consciousness seeks to articulate or thematize itself, and in this "first instance" or initial phase of desire's development, the pursuit of alterity and the pursuit of oneself seem in stark opposition. In effect, we have learned the lessons of Force and Explanation, but at this point we can only embody these lessons as an internal paradox. Insofar as we desire, we desire in two mutually exclusive ways; in desiring something else, we lose ourselves, and in desiring ourselves, we lose the world. At this stage in the dramatization of desire, unacceptable impoverishment seems to be its consequence; either as narcissism or as enthrallment with an object, desire is at odds with itself, contradictory and dissatisfied.

Desire has a "double-object," and, therefore, becomes a source of deception when a single univocal aim becomes the object of "true desire." And yet there is motivation for overcoming this paradoxical situation, for the confrontation with the object of sense-certainty and perception is intrinsically dissatisfying. That object is "other," absolutely different, signifying nothing for consciousness except its own ontological limitations. Otherness incites self-consciousness, occasions its articulation as desire, but is also the source of suffering for this emergent subject. Self-consciousness is thus additionally defined by Hegel as "essentially the return from otherness" (¶ 167), in which case desire, as the expression of self-consciousness, is a constant effort to overcome the appearance of ontological disparity between consciousness and its world. This disparity initially appears as insurmountable, and this alleged insurmountability pervades the naive experience of our metaphysical traveler; it is a primary phenomenological given, but one that is gradually dissolved through the efforts of desire. In effect, desire does not alter ontological difference, but provides an alternate mode of conceptualizing this disparity, a conceptualization that permits the revelation of that disparity in its proper, more fully developed, ontological organization. The world of desire, the countervailing world of consciousness, must not be annihilated, but reconceived and rediscovered as constitutive of self-consciousness. This is effected through an enhanced understanding of "difference." The negative relation that adheres between the emerging subject and its world not only differentiates, but *binds*. Consciousness is *not* the object of its desire, but this negation is a *determinate* negation, for that object is prefigured by desire, and desire is essentially transformed by that object; in effect, this negation is constitutive of desire itself. In seeking its own return from otherness, desire implicitly attempts to recast absolute difference as determinate negation, to reconcile difference within a unity of experience in which negation is revealed as a relation that mediates. Desire can thus be said to reveal negation as constitutive of experience itself.

We can see, then, that the ontological primacy of negation is both enacted and revealed by desire, that the negation can only be understood as essential to experience through a consideration of the *reflexivity* of self-consciousness. Insofar as all external relations are transformed into internal—or double—relations through the mediated self-reflection of Hegel's emerging subject, all indeterminate negations or ruptures in the ontology of experience are rediscovered as determinate negations, differences that are contained within the ontological integrity of experience. In that desire always emerges as a confrontation with a difference that appears ontologically disparate, and is, further, an effort to overcome this disparity through disclosing a mode of interrelatedness which has hitherto remained opaque, it seems fair to conclude that desire is always thematizing—and rendering actual—the ontological preconditions of its own emergence. Whereas the initial confrontation with otherness enforces a sense of limitation on consciousness, the satisfaction of desire reveals a more capable self, one that is able to admit its interdependence, and thereby gain a more expanded and expansive identity.

But what is meant by satisfaction? We have learned that Hegel's subject desires the object of sense-certainty and perception, and that this desire incorporates the two projects characteristic of Force and Explanation. At first, these two projects appear at odds, and it seems that the subject can only pursue the object or itself, but never both at once. In an attempt to reconcile this paradox, consciousness sets the paradox into movement. The objects of desire are no longer understood as static and ontologically self-sufficient, but are reconceived as so many *shapes* of Life, where Life is defined as the incessant consolidation and dissolution of shape. The "play of Force" is thus recast onto the field of objects at a more sophisticated level of ontological organization.

The concept of Life appears, then, to reconcile the moments of determinateness and negativity which, conceived from a static point of view, appeared only paradoxically related. Indeed, this unity is constitutive of Life: "the simple substance of Life is the splitting up of itself into shapes and at the same time the dissolution of these existent differences . . . life . . . is just as much an imparting of shape as a supersession of it" (¶ 171). At this point Hegel's subject concludes that the proper object of desire is Life, and subscribes to a primitive form of pantheism which attributes creative powers to the objective world. Excluded from this dialectic of vitalism, the subject views this active world from a distance that signals its relapse into ontological exile. This subject desires Life, but as one who is himself incapable of living, so that desire is mixed with pathos, the inevitable melancholy which attends the knowledge of irretraversible distance. Conceived here as an initial stage of self-consciousness, the subject is wise to Life without being "of" it.

This form of estrangement is reminiscent of the Emily Dickinson poem beginning, "I cannot live with You—It would be Life—And Life is over there—." Like the irony of that poetic voice which so intimately disavows its own proximity to the living, so Hegel's melancholic self-consciousness vitally refutes any claim to Life. This subject does not yet know its own "livelihood," its capacity to create and dissolve shape, and, in fact, does not gain that knowledge until the end of the section "Lordship and Bondage"; indeed, the bondsman exists as a "lifeless thing" until he labors on objects that reflect his creative powers. At this juncture, however, the subject is out of work, like a meditative Faust whose sadness turns to frustration and, finally, to destructive envy.[10] Life here appears as a monolith, self-sufficient and impervious, and human desire, a futile and humiliating enterprise. Like Fichte's notion of human reality as an intrinsically insatiable *Sehnsucht* or longing, so desire at this moment in the *Phenomenology* is a constant reminder of the uselessness of human endeavors. Desire is vacuity, a pure for-itself, the "useless passion" which will later appear in Sartre's *Being and Nothingness*.

Either our traveling subject has forgotten his lessons, or he no longer knows how to sustain his new-found identity as a mediating agent in this encounter with Life. Both are doubtless true, difficulty begetting forget-fulness. Because this hapless agency does not participate in the Life that he desires, he seems not to consider himself a living being, and so desire becomes the experience of a kind of death in life, an isolated moment of non-being, what Emily Dickinson's speaker refers to as "my Right of Frost–Death's privilege . . ." Experiencing itself as an essential poverty, self-consciousness becomes a vacuum that must consume Life in order to gain some temporary reality for itself. This subject does not sit with its identity as a static nothingness in the midst of being; indeed, it seems unable to bear the stasis of its own negativity. Thus, without intentionally challenging the presumption of ontological exile, this agent sets its own negativity into motion, becoming an agent of nothingness, an actor whose role is to negate. Thematizing the presumed conditions of its own identity, this subject dramatizes its despair. Instead of a dead being, it becomes an agency of death.

This reflexive appropriation of the conditions of its own identity results in an *enactment* of negativity which, predictably, has paradoxical rhetor-ical consequences. As an effort to negate, consuming desire seeks to annihilate the independence of some living object (it cannot negate Life in the general sense, so restricts itself to some determinate manifestation of the enemy). By negating *this* living object, rendering this object as nothing, self-consciousness comes to view the object as no longer existing, and accounts for its vanishing from existence in terms of its own actions. Thus, self-consciousness recognizes *itself* as the agency of accomplish-ment; certain of the nothingness of this object, self-consciousness explic-itly affirms that this nothingness is *for itself* the truth of this object. The ontological roles are thus inverted. Through destroying the living object, self-consciousness gives itself positive form as an agency of destruction. Regarding its own agency in this accomplished act, self-consciousness becomes certain of its own reality once again. The lessons gleaned from the drama of Explanation are thus recapitulated in the scene of consuming desire.

Having destroyed an independently living object, self-consciousness now knows itself as an agency of destruction. Its certainty of itself is, of course, dependent on that object that once was and now no longer is. As the effort to consume or destroy life, desire proves to be essentially related to Life, even if only in the mode of negation. The experience of consuming

[37]

desire makes explicit the mediated relationship of self-consciousness and its object once again, for the experience of desire cannot furnish self-certainty without first relating to an independent object. In effect, a destructive agent has no identity without a world to be destroyed; thus, this being who, convinced of his exile from Life, endeavors to destroy all living things, ends up paradoxically dramatizing his essential dependence on the world of the living.

As a destructive or consuming agency, self-consciousness as desire essays to gain reality through the consumption of a living thing. The reality that it gains, however, is different from the reality that it intended to appropriate: having assumed that the object monopolized Life, this agency sought to consume the object and appropriate Life as an attribute that could be easily transferred from the object to self-consciousness. Now this same agency realizes that having negated the object, it still retains a dependency on that object; moreover, that determinate living object is not the same as Life itself, and so a potentially infinite number of living objects must be negated for self-consciousness to gain the monopoly on Life that it seeks, and this project soon appears endless and futile. Self-consciousness thus concludes that Life and living objects cannot be fully assimilated, that desire must find some new form, that it must develop from destruction to a recognition of the insurpassibility of other living things: "In this satisfaction . . . experience makes it aware that the object has its own independence. . . . It is in fact something other than self-consciousness which is the essence of Desire; and through this experience self-consciousness has realized its own truth" (¶ 175).

The project of consuming desire is itself conditioned by a prior ontological assumption which casts self-consciousness in the role of a pure vacuity, external and unrelated to substantive being. This scheme is disrupted through the dramatization of destruction inasmuch as desire once again determines itself as a positive reality through its own determinate acts. Desire is thus revealed as a *negating negativity,* no longer a lifeless and isolated nothingness. As an active or generative negation, desire is once again articulated as a determinate reality. And insofar as desire in this general sense is self-consciousness, we discover at yet another level of experience the *reflexivity* of self-consciousness as that which dramatizes itself, and the *intentionality* of self-consciousness—the insurpassibility of otherness: "Desire and the self-certainty obtained in its gratification are conditioned by the object, for self-certainty comes from superseding this other; in order that this supersession can take place, there must be this other" (¶ 175).

We saw the intentional enthrallment characteristic of consciousness, and here we see it recapitulated as a mediating structure of self-consciousness. As the experience of desire, self-consciousness sustains a necessarily ambiguous relation to that which is other to itself. Desire is always desire "for" something other than self-consciousness (even when what is desired is the obliteration of the other, it is "the obliteration of the other" which remains its intentional object). Moreover, the intentionality of desire is always also informed by its reflexive project; desire always reveals the desiring agent as intrinsically other to itself: self-consciousness is an *ekstatic* being, outside itself, in search of self-recovery. The proliferation of objects of desire affirm for self-consciousness the persistent realm of alterity. In order for desire to gain determinate reality, it must continually pursue an indefinite domain of alterity; the reflexive experience of desire is only possible in and through the experience of desirable things. The conclusion drawn by self-consciousness that the world of objects is not consumable in its entirety has an unexpected inverse conclusion: desire requires this endless proliferation of alterity in order to stay alive as desire, as a desire that not only wants life, but *is living*. If the domain of living things could be consumed, desire would, paradoxically, *lose* its life; it would be a quiescent satiety, an end to the negative generativity that is self-consciousness. This agency that once assumed that a counterposing world of being monopolized Life, that "Life is over there," now distrusts self-identical being as death itself, and safeguards its own negativity as the source of its own perpetual life.

The drama of consuming desire proves to be not wholly satisfying. As self-consciousness eats its way through the world, it realizes that this mode of contending with difference is exceedingly tiresome. For a while, this ravenous agent figures that ultimately the domain of external objects will all be consumed, but Life proves to be more prolific than expected, and instead of gradually eliminating the domain of alterity, self-consciousness confronts the infinity of determinate objects and, accordingly, the infinite insatiability of desire. As the constant activity of negation, desire never successfully thematizes itself in and through a given object, for that object is always vanishing into the stomach of desire, as it were, and so

[39]

vanishes self-consciousness' own experience of itself. Self-consciousness knows itself as that which consumes alterity, but it only knows this indirectly, inferring from the absence of an object its own power of agency. Now convinced of its own status as a living being, self-consciousness becomes weary of its own vanishing act, and comes to wonder whether it might not reconcile Life with some more permanent sense of self. Endeavoring to escape the fate of a purely transient self, self-consciousness develops the notion of a being like itself which might remain independent and offer a more stable experience of reflexivity than the consumption of natural objects could provide. The intentional object of desire thus alters from the infinity of natural objects to the finite Other:

> It is in fact something other than self-consciousness that is the essence of Desire; and through this experience self-consciousness has realized its truth. But at the same time it is no less absolutely *for itself*, and it is so only by superseding the object; and it must experience its satisfaction, for it is the truth. On account of the independence of the object, therefore, *it can achieve satisfaction only when the object effects the negation within itself* [my emphasis]; and it must carry out this negation of itself in itself, for it is *in itself* the negative, and must be *for* the other what it *is*. Since the object is in its own self negation, and in being so is at the same time independent, it is consciousness. (¶ 175)

When Hegel claims that something "other than self-consciousness" must be the essence of desire, he seems to be relying on the previously drawn conclusion that for desire the realm of alterity is insurpassable. And yet the very next sentence casts doubt on this initial claim: "at the same time it [self-consciousness] is no less absolutely *for itself*." The question then emerges, how are we to understand self-consciousness as essentially realized in otherness, and yet as absolutely for itself? What kind of "otherness" must self-consciousness find such that self-realization mediated by this Other results in self-recovery? If desire is realized in otherness, and this otherness reflects itself, then the otherness that desire seeks must be *another self-consciousness*. Hence, the only true satisfaction for desire is to be found in an object that mirrors the reflexive structure of desire itself. The externality of the independent object can only be overcome if intrinsic to that externality is a self-negating or reflexive structure: "on account of the independence of the object, therefore, it can achieve satisfaction only when the object effects the negation within itself."

[40]

We might well question whether self-consciousness is the kind of phenomenon that fits this requirement exclusively. Hegel tells us that negation is specified in self-consciousness as "absolute negation" (¶ 178), which distinguishes self-consciousness from other phenomena that embody negation in other ways. Apart from absolute negation, which is equivalently referred to as "Desire" or "negation in another self-consciousness," there is negation as a determinateness or apparent externality, and negation as "the inorganic universal nature of Life," the dynamic of consolidating and dissolving shape already considered (¶ 178). In absolute negation, we find negation operating as the essence and final actualization of a given reality. Like Spinoza's definition of desire as a "final end," [11] Hegel here characterizes the negativity of desire as the final, fully realized form of self-consciousness. To understand this correctly, we must not assume that negation is nothingness; on the contrary, as a differentiating relation that mediates the terms that initially counter each other, negation, understood in the sense of *Aufhebung,* cancels, preserves, and transcends the apparent differences it interrelates. As the final realization of self-consciousness, negation is a principle of absolute mediation, an infinitely capable subject that is its interrelations with all apparently different phenomena. The human capacity for negation is privileged inasmuch as the work of negation can be thematized and appropriated by the negating agency itself; indeed, thematization and appropriation become essential moments of "the labour of the negative," the work of discovering relations where there seemed to be none. Hence, Hegel claims that only in self-consciousness do we find a "universal independent nature in which negation is present as absolute negation." In the following paragraph, Hegel elaborates: "the immediate 'I' "—the other self-consciousness that is the object of desire—"is itself absolute mediation, it *is* only as a supersession of the independent object, in other words, it is Desire" (¶ 176).

For desire to enact absolute negation, it must find a way to embody absolute negation as an object of experience; and if it *is* absolute negation, it must, therefore, duplicate itself as the object of desire. Only through its duplication as an Other can desire be rendered explicit, realized as its own final end: "a self-consciousness exists *for a self-consciousness.* Only so is it in fact self-consciousness; for only in this way does the unity of itself in its otherness become explicit for it" (¶ 177).

In "The Truth of Self-Certainty," this other self-consciousness is imagined as the logically appropriate object of desire, but not until the following section, "Lordship and Bondage," do we meet such an Other, and only in the course of that section do we become convinced of the necessity of its existence. We have understood desire as the effort of a disembodied consciousness to acquire reality from an ostensibly disparate world of substance, and we have altered our notion of human agency to fit the reflexive requirements of self-consciousness. As a sensuous articulation of consciousness, desire discloses self-consciousness as that which participates in what it investigates. Desire thus constantly widens its intentional aims and thereby expands the domain of reflexivity which it indicates and enacts. Indeed, from Force to Explanation, to the consumption of Life, we have gained insight into the ever widening circumference of reflexivity that constitutes the emerging subject of the *Phenomenology*. In this last dramatic moment, we learn that this subject not only consumes its world, that the mediation of difference is not only the internalization of otherness, but also the externalization of the subject. These two moments of assimilation and projection are part of the same movement, that ever-widening circumference of reality which, in Hegel's words, "unifies" subject and substance, those two related but independent moments which condition the irreducible ambiguity of this emerging identity. Desire is this subject's necessarily ambiguous movement toward the world, consumption and externalization, appropriation and dispersal; the "Life" of the subject is the constant consolidation and dissolution of itself. As desire becomes desire-for-another-desire, this subject hopes to get a self-sustaining picture of himself, an independent embodiment of negation that will reflect his own powers of absolute negation. This subject no doubt expects that this is the end of the journey, that to know oneself as "absolute negation" is to recognize one's own self-sufficiency, the unity of independence—explicit reality—and negativity that one is. But at this point this subject's vision is too narrow, for he mistakenly restricts his dependence to the world of natural objects, and does not anticipate his dependence on the self-consciousness he will meet. He shows no understanding of human embodiment, and he surely underestimates the complexity and consequences of what it means to be reflected in and by another emerging subject. Vain and headstrong, this subject once again travels swiftly toward defeat.

[42]

Bodily Paradoxes: Lordship and Bondage

An infernal love . . . aims at subjugating a freedom in order to take shelter in it from the world.—Sartre, *Saint Genet*

Desire is *aufgehoben* in "Lordship and Bondage"; it is canceled yet preserved, which is to say that it is transformed into a more internally complicated mode of human striving. Viewed as the least sophisticated project of self-consciousness, desire is sometimes dismissed as no longer having an ontological role to play in this section;[12] it may be said to be supplanted by the struggle for recognition and the dialectic of lord and bondsman, but the meaning of "supplanted" must be critically attended. As long as we are still within the experience of self-consciousness, and "Desire in general" is its essential character, then the drama of recognition and labor must be seen as permutations of desire; indeed, what we witness in this chapter is the gradual specification of desire: self-consciousness as desire *in particular.* The notion of desire loses its reified character as an abstract universal, and becomes situated in terms of an embodied identity. For Hegel, labor is "inhibited desire" (¶ 195), and recognition becomes the more sophisticated form of reflection that promises to satisfy desire.

The above argument is in some sense superfluous, for it is not finally appropriate to consider whether desire, conceived as some independent agency, is *aufgehoben* or superseded in "Lordship and Bondage." The action of supersession is not applied to desire as a force externally imposed upon a discrete agent; desire is nothing other than the action of supersession itself. Moreover, what it means to "supersede" a given externality itself changes and develops throughout the *Phenomenology,* and *Aufhebung* is only the abstract and logical term for a developing set of experiences which dramatize the negation of difference and thereby posit/reveal ever more encompassing unities or interrelations. The concrete meaning of *Aufhebung* is here understood as the developing sequence: consuming desire, desire for recognition, desire for another's desire. Hence, in asking whether desire is still operative in "Lordship and Bondage," we misunderstand the operative force in the *Phenomenology* at large, its logical motor, as it were, which, embodied by human subjects, is desire itself. The sophistication of desire's intentional aims is at once the enhancement

[43]

of human conceptual powers, the ever-expanding capacity to discern identity in difference, to expand the hermeneutical circle of Hegel's traveling metaphysician.

In "The Truth of Self-Certainty" we learn that through the experience of desire self-consciousness discovers itself as "essentially negative." Moreover, we come to see how the "difference" between consciousness and its object becomes the ground for a new identity. The effort of desire to appropriate an object, and through that appropriation to assert its own identity, reveals self-consciousness as that which must relate itself to another being in order to become itself. The gradual yet insistent effort of Hegel's journeying subject in the *Phenomenology of Spirit* never relinquishes this project to relate itself to externality in order to rediscover itself as more inclusive being. The insurpassability of externality implies the permanence of desire. In this sense, insofar as Hegel's subject never achieves a static union with externality, it is hopelessly beyond its own grasp, although it retains as its highest aim the thorough comprehension of itself. This thoroughgoing self-determination is the ideal of integrity toward which self-consciousness strives, and this striving is denoted by desire.

On the one hand, we concede that desire alone will never achieve this total self-comprehension for desire alone is the consumption of objects, and we have seen how consumption fails effectively to assimilate externality. On the other hand, we need to ask whether speaking of "desire alone" in Hegel's view makes any sense. After all, desire revealed an implicit intentional aim, namely, to disclose and enact a common ontological structure with the world. Hence, despite the alleged object of desire, i.e., "this piece of fruit," or its more general aim, "the consumption of this brute being which poses as other to me," desire has at base a metaphysical project which, while requiring determinate objects, transcends them as well, i.e., to effect a unity with the realm of externality which both preserves that realm and renders it into a reflection of self-consciousness. The dissatisfaction of desire implies that something *would* satisfy desire, that this something is missing, and that a consideration of the inadequacies of the mode of consumption will provide the criteria for a satisfying object. In the turn to another self-consciousness as a possible object of satisfaction, we can see that it is not desire itself that is superseded, but a *peculiar form* of desire, and that the aim of self-consciousness, even as it leaves the section on self-certainty, is still the satisfaction of desire.

Desire does not merely survive into the section "Lordship and Bondage," but remains essential to the ever-expanding project of negation that structures the *Phenomenology*. Because desire is the principle of self-consciousness' reflexivity or inner difference, and because it has as its highest aim the assimilation of all external relations into relations of inner difference, desire forms the experiential basis for the project of the *Phenomenology* at large. Desire and its satisfaction constitute the first and final moments of the philosophical pursuit of self-knowledge (¶ 165). In this regard, the metaphysical project that informs the entire project of *Geist* finds its original and final measure in the criteria desire sets forth for its satisfaction. Hence, to claim that desire is simply an unsophisticated form of knowing and being in Hegel's system is to misread the standard of truth that governs the *Phenomenology* generally; the gradual sophistication of desire—the expanding inclusiveness of its intentional aims— is the principle of progress in the *Phenomenology*.

Stanley Rosen, a student of Kojève's, argues that desire is the basis of both historical progress and the development of philosophical self-reflection; he places Hegel among those modern philosophers who stress the primacy of desire in human development:

In the tradition of such modern philosophers as Machiavelli and Hobbes, [Hegel] recognizes desire as the "engine" of world-history (thereby uniting the Platonic Eros with the directedness of historical development). The spirit first knows itself as subjective feeling. When feeling is localized externally, or given an objective status, spirit divides itself into inner and outer world. We become alienated from ourselves or regard our true self as contained in the object outside us, which we desire to assimilate. Desire is thus fundamentally desire for myself, or for my interior essence from which I have become detached. The struggle to satisfy my desires leads to the development of individual consciousness. Since others desire the same things, this struggle is also the origin of the family, the state, and, in general, of world-history.[13]

As Rosen suggests, the dramatic education of Hegel's journeying subject consists of a series of self-alienations which prompt a revision of the subject itself.[14] Every confrontation with an external reality is at once an alienation of the subject; difference threatens the subject with annihilation until the subject can discover that difference as an essential moment of itself. In the section "Lordship and Bondage," Hegel's emergent subject confronts another self-consciousness, and immediately concludes that it, the initial subject, has lost itself. Desire remains defeated until it can find a way of revealing that other subject as essential to its own identity; this way is forged through the struggle for recognition.

The previous section on self-certainty provides a theoretical understanding of the necessity of the Other. Self-consciousness needed to understand itself as self-negation, as a self-determining being. The Other was distinguished from other objects in that it was like the first self-consciousness—an independently subsisting being who exhibited the principle of self-negation. Discovering this Other self-consciousness appears in that section to be the only way that the initial self-consciousness can regard its own essential structure rendered explicit. The task of "Lordship and Bondage" is to demonstrate how this process is effected in experience. The reflection of the subject in and through the Other is achieved through the process of reciprocal recognition, and this recognition proves to be—in the terms of that section—the satisfaction of desire. Our task, then, is to understand the project of desire—the negation and assimilation of otherness and the concomitant expansion of the proper domain of the subject—in the encounter with another subject with a structurally identical set of aims.

The transition from "The Truth of Self-Certainty" to "Lordship and Bondage" is a curious one in that the former section conjectures the existence of the Other as an adequate object for self-consciousness' desire in *theoretical* terms. And yet the progress of the *Phenomenology* is ostensibly necessitated by knowledge gained from experience. The first paragraph of "Lordship and Bondage" reiterates this theoretical conclusion, asserting prior to its demonstration that "self-consciousness exists in and for itself when, and by the fact that, it so exists for another; that is, it exists only in being acknowledged [*anerkannt*]" (¶ 178). Because we cannot expect that self-consciousness has certain knowledge of its own requirements before these requirements are made clear in experience, we are forced to regard the emergence of the Other in the following paragraph as puzzling: "Self-consciousness is faced by another self-consciousness" (¶ 179)—but why? And why has it not happened earlier? Why did the journeying subject of the *Phenomenology* begin its journey alone, and why was its confrontation with the sensuous and perceptual world previous to its confrontation with an Other?

[46]

As I noted in my earlier discussion of the "appearance" of desire, the development of the *Phenomenology* suggests that the reader must make a strict distinction between the *appearance* of a given entity and its conceptual reality. The appearance of the Other must be understood as an emergence into explicit reality which has hitherto remained an implicit or nascent being. Before its actual appearance, the Other remains opaque, but not for that reason without reality. Coming into existence—or explicit appearance—is never, for Hegel, a creation *ex nihilo*, but is, rather, a moment in the development of a Concept *(Begriff)*. The Other is revealed as an essential structure of all experience in the course of the *Phenomenology;* indeed, there can be no experience outside the context of inter-subjectivity. Hence, even as the *Phenomenology* claims to be an experience of the genesis of *Geist,* it is a fictive experience created by and through the text, and must be understood as an experience uniquely philosophical—a sustained inverted world—which delineates in the terms of its own temporality the structures that condition and inform historical experience as we know it.[15]

To say, then, that the Other appears is not to claim that the initial self-consciousness discovers a phenomenon that previously had no ontological status; rather, it is only now that the Other becomes explicit in virtue of its centrality to the initial self-consciousness' pursuit of an identity that encompasses the world. The Other becomes the general object of desire.

The optimism that characterized the closure of "The Truth of Self-Certainty" and the opening paragraph of "Lordship and Bondage" is a function of the purely conceptual nature of the conclusion that mutual recognition is a possible and gratifying object for desire; this possibility, however, must be dramatized in order to be known. Self-consciousness begins this struggle in ¶ 179 where it discovers that the structural similarity of the Other is not an immediate occasion for deriving an adequate reflection of itself in the Other; indeed, the first experience of the Other's similarity is that of *self-loss.*

Self-consciousness is faced by another self-consciousness; it has come *out of itself.* This has a two-fold significance: first, it has lost itself, for it finds itself as an *other* being; secondly, in doing so it has superseded the other, for it does not see the other as an essential being, but in the other sees its own self. (¶ 178)[16]

The initial self-consciousness seeks to have itself reflected in the other self-consciousness, but finds itself not merely reflected, but wholly absorbed. The initial self-consciousness no longer seeks to consume the Other, as it sought to consume objects, *but is instead consumed by the Other*. Self-consciousness comes out of itself when faced with the Other, where *"ausser sich"* in German not only denotes coming out of oneself, but ecstasy as well as anger.[17] The intentional and reflexive relations to the Other are temporarily lost, and self-consciousness is convinced that the Other has occupied its own essence—self-negation—stolen it even, and in this sense self-consciousness finds itself besieged by the Other. In one respect, self-consciousness discovers that the self-negating principle of self-consciousness itself is a detachable attribute, one that might be extricated from the particular embodiment that the initial self-conscious-ness is. And insofar as self-negation is its own essence, self-consciousness concludes that essence and embodiment are only contingently related, that the same essence might inhabit different embodiments at different times. That self-consciousness can find its own essential principle embod-ied *elsewhere* appears as a frightening and even angering experience. And yet the ambiguity of *"ausser sich sein"* suggests that the externality that self-consciousness is now seen to inhabit is not wholly external: in desiring the Other, self-consciousness discovers itself as ecstatic being, a being that has it in itself to become other to itself, which, through the self-surpassing principle of desire, *gives itself up* to the Other even as it charges that the Other has somehow appropriated it. The ambiguity of gift and appropri-ation characterizes the initial encounter with the Other, and transforms this meeting of two desires into a struggle (*Kampf*).[18]

The first lesson gleaned from the encounter with the Other is that of the essential ambiguity of self-consciousness' externalization. Self-con-sciousness seeks a reflection of its own identity through the Other, but finds instead the enslaving and engulfing potential of the Other. As desire for a comprehensive identity, self-consciousness initially expects the Other to be a passive medium of reflection for itself; the Other will mirror itself since the Other is like itself. Perhaps extrapolating from its experience with objects, self-consciousness naively expects that the Other will be passive like objects, and differ only insofar as it can reflect self-conscious-ness' structure. Apparently, this initial self-consciousness did not take seriously enough the extent to which the Other is, indeed, *like* itself, i.e., a principle of *active* negation, and so is scandalized by the independent freedom of the Other. The independence that was to be a passive reflection

[48]

of the initial self-consciousness is now conceived as an externality which safeguards freedom within the Other, a situation considered threatening by the first self-consciousness who viewed freedom as its own exclusive property.

Self-consciousness' anger—the way in which it is *"ausser sich"*—does not proceed directly from the perceptual experience described above, but as a consequence of its own ecstatic involvement with the Other. The Other embodies its freedom because the initial self-consciousness has forfeited its freedom to the Other. Desire is here understood as ecstatic self-sacrifice, which is in direct contradiction to the overriding project of desire, i.e., to attain an ever more capable identity. Desire thus founders on contradiction, and becomes a passion divided against itself. Striving to become coextensive with the world, an autonomous being that finds itself everywhere reflected in the world, self-consciousness discovers that implicit in its own identity as a desiring being is the necessity of being claimed by another.

The initial encounter with the Other is thus a narcissistic project which fails through an inability to recognize the Other's freedom. This failure of recognition is itself conditioned by the view of the Other's externality as encapsulating, a view that presupposes that the ecstatic involvement of the first self-consciousness is necessarily self-annihilating. The philosophical assumption of this experience is that freedom is an exclusive characteristic of the individual, and that it can inhabit a particular embodiment only as that embodiment's exclusive property. Thus, insofar as it is the body of the Other that is seen to lay claim to freedom, it is that body that must be destroyed. Only through the death of the Other will the initial self-consciousness retrieve its claim to autonomy.

The quandary conditioning the struggle of life and death is that of having to choose between ecstatic and self-determining existence. Not only the bodily exteriority of the Other offends the initial self-consciousness, but its own estrangement from itself. This estrangement is not to be understood solely in terms of the fact of the Other as an independent freedom, but also as *the self-estrangement implicit in the experience of desire.* As an intentional movement, desire tends to eclipse the self that is its origin. Enthralled with its object, the desiring self can only regard itself as estranged. As a movement outside of itself, desire becomes an act of willful self-estrangement even as its overriding project is to establish a more inclusive self. Thus, the effort to overcome the Other is simultaneously an effort to overcome self-consciousness' own otherness to itself.

The ambiguity of the otherness self-consciousness seeks to overcome forms the central theme of "Lordship and Bondage," and it becomes clear that any reflexive relation that self-consciousness seeks to have is itself only possible through an intentional relation to an Other; it can overcome its own self-alienation only through overcoming the externality of the Other's self-consciousness:

It must supersede this otherness of itself. This is the supersession of the first ambiguity, and is therefore itself a second ambiguity. First, it must proceed to supersede the *other* independent being in order thereby to become certain of *itself* as the essential being; secondly, in so doing it proceeds to supersede its *own* self, for this other is itself. (¶ 180)

The experiential meaning of "supersession" or "overcoming" in the above reveals itself as *recognition (Anerkennung)*. The initial self-consciousness can only retrieve itself from its ecstatic involvement with the Other insofar as it recognizes the Other as also in the process of retrieving itself from its own estrangement in desire. Self-consciousness' predicament, that of having to choose between ecstatic and self-determining existence, is seen to be the predicament of the Other as well. This similarity between the two self-consciousnesses ultimately proves to be the basis of their harmonious interdependence, the discovery of each that "as consciousness, it does indeed *come out of itself,* yet, though out of itself, is at the same time kept back within itself, is *for itself,* and the self outside it, is for *it*. It is aware that it at once is, and is not, another consciousness" (¶ 184). Recognition, once achieved, affirms the ambiguity of self-consciousness as both ecstatic and self-determining. The process of recognition reveals that the self-consciousness which is self-estranged, unrecognizable to itself, is still the author of its own experience: "there is nothing in it of which it is itself not the origin" (¶ 182). When the Other is viewed as the same as the subject, and this subject understands his own act of recognition as having brought the Other into explicitness, then the self is also revealed as the author of the Other. As it becomes clear that the same truths hold true of the Other's relationship to the self, the Other is also viewed as the author of the subject. Desire here loses its character as a purely consumptive activity, and becomes characterized by the ambiguity of an exchange in which two self-consciousnesses affirm their respective autonomy (independence) and alienation (otherness).

The life and death struggle appears as a necessary dramatic move for a self-consciousness that assumes that the Other's embodiment is primarily responsible for thwarting self-consciousness' pursuit of its own identity. Here corporeality everywhere signifies limitation, and the body which once seemed to condition freedom's concrete determination now requires annihilation in order for that freedom to be retrieved. The corporeal externality of each to the other presents itself as an insurpassable barrier, and seems to imply that each subject can be certain only of his own determinate life, but never can get beyond his own life to be certain of the life of the Other. Determinate life itself becomes suspect in this predicament; it thwarts self-consciousness' project to transcend its own particularity and discover itself as the essence of objects and Others in the world. The effort to annihilate the Other is originally motivated by the desire of the initial self-consciousness to present itself as a "pure abstraction"; it seeks to break its dependence on the Other and, hence, prove "that it is not attached to any specific *existence,* not to the individuality common to existence as such, that is, not attached to life" (¶ 187). And yet in order to disenthrall itself from the enslaving externality of the Other, this self-consciousness must stake its own life in the process. The project of "pure abstraction" is quickly foiled as it becomes clear that without determinate existence the initial self-consciousness would never live to see the identity after which it strives. Moreover, the death of the Other would deprive self-consciousness of the explicit recognition it requires.

The life and death struggle is a crucial section in the *Phenomenology's* development of the notion of autonomy; as Hegel claims, "the individual who has not risked his life may well be recognized as a *person,* but he has not attained to the truth of this recognition as an independent self-consciousness" (¶ 187). Although determinate life is a necessary precondition for the project of self-consciousness, desire is never satisfied when it is merely the desire to live. In order to discover itself as a negative or self-surpassing being, self-consciousness must do more than merely live; it must transcend the immediacy of pure life. It cannot stay content with the "first nature" into which it is born, but must engage itself in the creation of a "second nature" which establishes the self, not merely as a presupposition or a point of view, but as an achievement of its own making. Autonomy can be achieved only through relinquishing an enslavement to life.[19]

The life and death struggle is an extension of self-consciousness' initial project to gain unity with the Other, and to find its own identity through the Other. Insofar as the effort to obliterate the Other is a mutual or "two-fold action" (¶ 187), each self-consciousness seeks to destroy the determinate boundaries that exist between them; they seek to destroy each other's bodies. Violence to the Other appears as the most efficient route by which to nullify the Other's body. And insofar as both individuals seek to rid themselves of their dependence on determinate existence, and release the pure freedom which they view as trapped within corporeality, each seeks to merge with the Other as the abstract principle of freedom, "absolute abstraction" (¶ 186), pure being-for-self.

Thus, the life and death struggle is a continuation of the erotic that introduces Hegel's chapter; it is desire once again transformed to destruction, a project that assumes that true freedom exists only beyond the body. Whereas destructive desire in its first appearance sought to internalize otherness into a self-sufficient body, this second appearance of destructive desire endeavors to overcome bodily life altogether, i.e., to become an abstract identity without corporeal needs. Endeavoring to rid the Other of its determinate life, each self-consciousness engages in an anti-corporeal erotic which endeavors to prove in vain that the body is the ultimate limit to freedom, rather than its necessary ground and mediation.

The dynamic of lord and bondsman emerges as an extenuation of the desire to annihilate, but, because annihilation would undermine the project altogether by taking away *life,* this desire is held in check. Domination, the relation that replaces the urge to kill, must be understood as the effort to annihilate within the context of life. The Other must now *live its own death.* Rather than become an indeterminate nothingness through death, the Other must now prove its essential nothingness *in life.* The Other which was at first captivating, now becomes that which must be captured, subdued, contained. Angered at having been captivated by the Other, self-consciousness in pursuit of its own absolute freedom forces this Other to annihilate its own freedom and thus affirm the illusion that the Other is an unfree body, a lifeless instrument.

[52]

The lord's reflexive relation must be understood as an internalization of the intentional relation it had toward the Other in the life and death struggle. Self-consciousness' original effort to annihilate the body of the Other entailed the staking of its own bodily life. In dramatizing annihilation, this subject learns that annihilation can be dramatized, that is, given a living form; moreover, the fear and trembling accompanying the risking of his own life teaches him the relief of abstraction. Terror gives rise to dissociation. The lord cannot deny his body through suicide, so he proceeds *to embody his denial*. This internalization of an intentional relation, i.e., its transformation into a reflexive one, itself engenders a new intentional one: the reflexive project of disembodiment becomes linked to the domination of the Other. The lord cannot get rid of the body once and for all—this was the lesson of the life and death struggle. And yet he retains the project of becoming a pure, disembodied "I," a freedom unfettered by particularity and determinate existence, a universal and abstract identity. He still acts on the philosophical assumption that freedom and bodily life are not essential to one another, except that bodily life appears to be a precondition of freedom. But freedom does not, in the tacit view of the lord, require bodily life for its concrete expression and determination. For the lord, bodily life must be taken care of, but just as well by an Other, for the body is not part of his *own* project of identity. The lord's identity is essentially beyond the body; he gains illusory confirmation for this view by requiring the Other to *be* the body that he endeavors *not* to be.

The lord appears at the outset to live as a desire without needs; significantly, the lord is said to "enjoy" (*"im Genusse sich zu befriedigen"*) the fruits of the bondsman's labor, where enjoyment implies a passive reception and consumption of something other to self-consciousness, as distinct from desire which requires an active principle of negation (¶ 190). The lord desires without having to negate the thing desired, except in the impoverished sense of consuming it; the bondsman, through working on the thing, embodies the principle of negation as an active and creative principle, and thus inadvertently dramatizes that he is more than a mere body, and that the body itself is an *embodying* or expressive medium for the project of a self-determining identity. Through the experience of work, the body is revealed as an essential expression of freedom. And insofar as the bondsman works to create goods that sustain life, the bondsman also

[53]

demonstrates that desire—rather than expressing a freedom *from* needs—can find fulfillment through the satisfaction of needs. Indeed, insofar as the bondsman creates a reflection of himself through his labor on products, he triumphs as the freedom that, through finding itself expressed in determinate existence (through physical labor on physical things), has found some semblance of recognition for himself as a self-determining agent. And although the lord endeavors to be free of the need for physical life, he can sustain this illusory project only through developing a need for the bondsman. As needed by the lord, the bondsman discovers his action as efficacious. The lord's need thus confirms the bondsman as more than a body; it affirms him indirectly as a laboring freedom. It provides *indirect recognition* of the bondsman's power of self-determination.

At the outset of the struggle of lord and bondsman we know that self-consciousness' desire is, at its most general articulation, a desire to discover itself as an all-inclusive identity, and also a desire *to live*. Desire must arrange for its satisfaction within the context of life, for death is the end of desire, a negativity which, except in the imaginary realms of Augustine's or Dante's hells, cannot be sustained. Desire is coextensive with life, with the realm of otherness, and with Others. Whatever the ultimate satisfaction for desire, we know at this stage that certain preconditions must first be met. We also know from our introductory remarks on Hegel that whatever exists as a precondition of desire serves also as an intentional aim of desire's articulation. The lord acknowledges with reservation and self-deception that he is, indeed, tied to life. Life appears as a necessary precondition for the satisfaction of desire. The bondsman asserts this precondition as the proper end of desire; acting in the face of the fear of death (¶ 194), the bondsman asserts the desire to live.

Both the posture of the lord and the posture of the bondsman can be seen as configurations of death in life, as death-bent desires emerging in the shadows of more explicit desires to die. Domination and enslavement are thus defenses against life within the context of life; they emerge in the spirit of nostalgia over the failed effort to die. In this sense, domination and enslavement are projects of despair, what Kierkegaard termed the despair of not being able to die.[20] Life or determinate existence requires the sustained interrelationship of physical existence and the cultivation of identity. As such, it requires the maintenance of the body in conjunction with the project of autonomous freedom.

[54]

The lord and the bondsman turn against life in different ways, but both resist the synthesis of corporeality and freedom, a synthesis that alone is constitutive of human life; the lord lives in dread of his body, while the bondsman lives in dread of freedom. The dissolution of their antagonism paves the way for an embodied pursuit of freedom, a desire to live in the fullest sense. "Life" in this mediated sense is not a merely physical enduring—that was seen as a posture of death in life in the case of the bondsman. The desire to live in the full sense is rendered synonymous with the desire to attain a more capable identity through reciprocal recognition. Hence, the desire to live is demonstrated here not merely as the *precondition* of the pursuit of a self-determining identity, but as its highest achievement. Desire that seeks to rediscover substance as subject is the desire to become the whole of life. Desire is thus always an implicit struggle against the easier routes of death; domination and enslavement are metaphors for death *in life*, the presence of contradictions, that keep one from wanting life enough.[21]

The dialectic of lord and bondsman is implicitly a struggle with the generalized problem of life. The division of labor between lord and bondsman presupposes a discrepancy between the desire to live and the desire to be free. The lord, displeased with the prospect of having to live, delegates the task to the bondsman. The bondsman takes to working on things, fashioning them into products for human consumption. For the lord, life appears as material exigency, as a limit to his project of abstraction. The lord's desire to be beyond life (the intentionality of his desire) reveals a desire to be beyond desire (the reflexivity of his desire). He does not relish the dialectic of want and satisfaction; his sole project is to remain sated and, hence, to banish desire and its possibilities.

The bondsman, delegated the task of trafficking with life, is originally cast as a mere thing, "the consciousness for which thinghood is the essential characteristic" (¶ 190), but this role did not accommodate the repetitive dimension of having to live. The bondsman cannot merely exist as a thing and yet endeavor to live; in fact, the inorganic quality of things is constitutive of their deathlike dimension. Life is not, as the lord assumed, a merely material and, hence, limiting precondition of self-consciousness. It is a task that demands to be taken up again and again. The bondsman cannot be identified with the *Naturwüchsigkeit* of the things he works upon, precisely because work turns out to be the negation of naturalness: "through his service he rids himself of his attachment to natural existence in every single detail; and gets rid of it by working on it" (¶ 194). The labor of the bondsman emerges as a truncated form of desire: he exhibits the principle of active negation, but does not wholly view himself as the author of his actions; he still works for the lord rather than for himself. In the case of the bondsman, the desire to live, specified as the desire to create the goods to live, cannot become integrated with the desire to be free until he relinquishes his shackles through disobedience and the attendant fear of death.

The division of tasks between lord and bondsman can be seen to explicate two different yet related projects of dissatisfied desire. The lord implicitly restricts desire to the consumption of ready-made goods and thus substitutes the satisfaction of desire for the entirety of the process. The bondsman exemplifies the dimension of desire missing from the lord's implicit account; his is a project of survival and activity encompassed by the meaning of labor. The lord's project of disembodiment becomes, ironically, a posture of greed; distanced from the physical world, yet requiring it to live, the lord becomes a passive consumer who, despite his privilege, can never be satisfied.

The lord's project to be beyond need becomes itself a pressing and relentless need; and his requirement to remain always sated ties him irrevocably to particularity and his own body, a tie he originally sought to break. And the bondsman, consigned to the realm of particularity, discovers through laboring on natural things his own capacity to transform the brutely given world into a reflection of his own self. The lord becomes schooled in the lessons of life, while the bondsman becomes schooled in freedom. And the gradual inversion of their initial roles offers lessons in the general structure and meaning of desire.

The project or desire to live and the project or desire to gain autonomous identity can be integrated only in the desire that explicitly takes account of need. The denial of need alienates self-consciousness from itself, and is a key way in which self-consciousness renders part of itself as an externality. As long as need is considered to be a contingency or piece of affective facticity, self-consciousness remains split off from itself, and the possibility of attaining an integrated self is foreclosed. When the satisfaction of needs becomes integrated into the pursuit of identity, we find that needs are but the alienated forms of desire; the need to live, formulated as such, affirms the view of life as mere exigency, and confirms the faulty distinction between the desire to live and the desire to achieve a self-determining identity. When needs are owned, they are experienced as desire.

Desire requires as well the transformation of the particularity of the natural world (the lived body as well as natural objects) into reflections of human activity; desire must become expressed through labor, for desire must give shape or form to the natural world in order to find itself reflected there (¶195). Giving form is thus the external determination of desire; in order to find satisfaction, i.e., recognition for itself, desire must give way to creative work. Desire is not wholly canceled through work of this kind, but work is "desire held in check, fleetingness staved off; in other words, work forms and shapes the thing. *The negative relation to the object becomes its form* and something permanent, because it is precisely for the worker that the object has independence" (¶ 195; my emphasis).

The negating or appropriative function of desire is no longer to be construed as consumption, the ecstatic enthrallment with another, nor domination, but as the re-creation of natural objects into reflections of their maker. Desire is to find its satisfaction, the reflection of itself as a self-determining and determinate existence, through effecting a human genesis of the external world. The externality of the world is negated through becoming transformed into a creation of human will. Self-consciousness is to attain to a godlike authorship of the world, "a universal formative activity," not "master over some things, but . . . over the universal power and the whole of objective being" (¶ 196).

I have argued that desire always maintains a reflexive as well as an intentional structure; I must now add that desire's intentionality is twofold: desire is always linked with the problem of recognition of and by another self-consciousness, and desire is always an effort to negate/transform the natural world. The realm of sensuous and perceptual reality relinquished in the discovery of the Other as a self-negating independence is here resurrected in new form. Mutual recognition only becomes possible in the context of a shared orientation toward *the material world*. Self-consciousness is mediated not only through another self-consciousness, but each recognizes the other in virtue of the form each gives to the world. Hence, we are recognized not merely for the form we inhabit in the world (our various embodiments), but for the forms we create of the world (our

[57]

works); our bodies are but transient expressions of our freedom, while our works shield our freedom in their very structure.

Hegel begins "Lordship and Bondage" with the claim that "self-consciousness exists in and for itself when, and by the fact that, it so exists for another; that is, it exists only in being acknowledged [*als ein Anerkanntes*]" (¶ 178). But what is it that the other recognizes us *as?* The answer is, as a *desiring* being: "Self-consciousness is Desire in general" (¶ 167). We have seen that desire is a polyvalent structure, a movement to establish an identity coextensive with the world. Hegel's discussion of labor begins to show us how the world of substance becomes recast as the world of the subject. Desire as a transformation of the natural world is simultaneously the transformation of its own natural self into an embodied freedom. And yet, these transformations cannot occur outside of an historically constituted intersubjectivity which mediates the relation to nature and to the self. True subjectivities come to flourish only in communities that provide for reciprocal recognition, for we do not come to ourselves through work alone, but through the acknowledging look of the Other who confirms us.

At the close of "Lordship and Bondage" we have the sense that the life of self-consciousness is slowly drawing to an end. With the possibility of mutual recognition, we see the beginnings of Spirit or *Geist*, that collective identity which signifies yet a different set of ontological presumptions. The subject of Hegel's *Phenomenology* emerges not only as a mode of intentional enthrallment and the reflexive pursuit of identity, but as a desire that requires Others for its satisfaction and for its own constitution as an intersubjective being. In the effort to gain reflection of itself through the recognition of and by the Other, this subject discovers its dependency not only as one of many attributes, but as its very self. This interdependence, this new subject, is still desire, but one that seeks metaphysical satisfaction through the articulation of the subject's historical place in a given community.

This reformulation of desire as the articulation of historical identity and historical place forms the philosophical starting point of Alexandre Kojève's introduction of Hegel into twentieth-century French intellectual life. In effect, Kojève halts the *Phenomenology* at the end of "Lordship and Bondage," and retells Hegel's narrative from the point of view of that struggling individual on the brink of collective identity. Kojève's subject retains all the metaphysical impulses of his Hegelian precursor, but is tempered by a Marxian distrust of Hegel's idealism. Hence, self-consciousness emerges decades later in the French language as an historical actor requiring recognition by Others, and fully expecting his sense of immanent metaphysical place to be confirmed therein. In seeking to historicize the metaphysical plan of Hegel's traveler, Kojève unwittingly introduces the possibility that historical action and metaphysical satisfaction may not imply each other mutually. Indeed, as Hegel's subject makes his way across the border into France, and into the twentieth century, we will see that the question of historical agency and historical experience will come to challenge that subject's well-planned itinerary. Indeed, without his progressive journey, it will become unclear whether the traveler himself can survive.

2

Historical Desires:
The French Reception of Hegel

*Desire is at the base of Self-Consciousness, i.e. of a truly human
existence (and therefore—in the end—of philosophical existence).*
Alexandre Kojève, *Introduction to the Reading of Hegel*

As late as 1931 Alexandre Koyré reported in the *Revue d'histoire de la
philosophie*[1] that Hegel studies in France were practically nonexistent.
With the exception of Jean Wahl's *Le Malheur de la conscience dans la
philosophie de Hegel*, published in 1929, no major French commentary
on Hegel claimed any intellectual popularity in France.[2] By 1946, however, the situation of Hegel studies in France had changed considerably:
in that year Merleau-Ponty was to claim in the preface to his *Phenomenology of Perception* that "all the great philosophical ideas of the past
century—the philosophies of Marx and Nietzsche, phenomenology, German existentialism, and psychoanalysis—had their beginnings in Hegel."[3]
Although we may reasonably question Merleau-Ponty's exuberant val-
uation of Hegel's influence, the more significant inquiry is into the intellectual climate that made such exuberance possible. Indeed, the intense
interest in Hegel during the 1930s and 1940s in France appealed to widely
shared and long-suppressed intellectual and political needs. In *Force and
Circumstance* Simone de Beauvoir recalls that she turned to Hegel in 1945

[61]

at Hyppolite's urging: "we had discovered the reality and weight of history; now we were wondering about its meaning."[4] By 1961 Koyré, in a postscript to a reprinted version of his 1931 review of French Hegel studies, remarked that Hegel's presence in academic life had "changed beyond recognition."[5]

If my inquiry were to enter the domain of the sociology of knowledge, I might then ask after the historical conditions of world war in Europe which precipitated the enthusiastic turn to Hegel during this period.[6] My question, however, concerns the significance of the theme of desire appropriated from the *Phenomenology of Spirit:* what view of subjectivity and history did Hegel's concept of desire afford the writers of this period? In the case of Kojève, Hegel provided a context for an inquiry into certain philosophical questions relevant to the times: the problem of human action, the creation of meaning, the social conditions necessary for the constitution of historically responsible subjectivities. The *Phenomenology's* vision of an active and creating subjectivity, a journeying subject empowered by the work of negation, served as a source of hope during these years of political and personal crisis. Hegel provided a way to discern reason in the negative, that is, to derive the transformative potential from every experience of defeat. The destruction of institutions and ways of life, the mass annihilation and sacrifice of human life, revealed the contingency of existence in brutal and indisputable terms. Hence, the turn to Hegel can be seen as an effort to excise ambiguity from the experience of negation.

The ontological principle of negation made itself known historically during these times as a principle of destruction, and yet Hegel's *Phenomenology* provided a way to understand negation as a creative principle as well. The negative is also human freedom, human desire, the possibility to create anew; the nothingness to which human life had been consigned was thus at once the possibility of its renewal. The nonactual is at once the entire realm of possibility. The negative showed itself in Hegelian terms not merely as death, but as a sustained possibility of *becoming.* As a being that also embodies negativity, the human being was revealed as able to endure the negative precisely because he could assimilate and recapitulate negation in the form of free action.

[62]

Kojève: Desire and Historical Agency

Kojève's lectures on Hegel are both commentaries and original works of philosophy. His appropriation of the theme of desire is, accordingly, an elucidation of Hegel's concept as well as a theory that stands independently of Hegel. Taking seriously Hegel's claim that the object of philosophical analysis is itself partially constituted by the analysis itself, Kojève analyzes Hegel not as an historical figure with a wholly independent existence but, rather, as a partner in a hermeneutical encounter in which both parties are transformed from their original positions. Hegel's text is not a wholly independent system of meanings to which Kojève's commentary endeavors to be faithful. Hegel's text is itself transformed by the particular historical interpretations it endures; indeed, the commentaries are extensions of the text, they *are* the text in its modern life.

Kojève's peculiarly modern appropriation of Hegel's doctrine of desire occasions the questions of what in Hegel survives into the twentieth century and what is lost. Hegel's claim that desire presupposes and reveals a common ontological bond between the subject and its world requires that we accept a prior set of ontological relations which structure and unify various subjectivities with one another and with the world that they confront. This presupposition of ontological harmonies that subsist in and among the intersubjective and natural worlds is difficult to reconcile with the various experiences of *disjunction* which emerge as insurpassable in the twentieth century. Kojève writes from a consciousness of human mortality that suggests that human life participates in a peculiar and unique ontological situation that distinguishes it from the natural world and that also establishes the differences among individual lives as negative relations that cannot be wholly superseded in a collective identity. Kojève's refusal of Hegel's postulation of an ontological unity that conditions and resolves all experiences of difference between individuals and between individuals and the external world is the condition of his own original theorizing. By rejecting the premise of ontological harmony, Kojève is free to extend Hegel's doctrine of negation. The experience of desire becomes crucial for Kojève's reading of Hegel precisely because desire thematizes the differences between independent subjects and the differ-

[63]

ences between subjects and their worlds. Indeed, desire becomes a permanent and universal feature of all human life, as well as the condition for historical action. Hegel's *Phenomenology* becomes for Kojève the occasion of an *anthropology* of historical experience in which desire's transformation into action, and action's aim of universal recognition, become the salient features of all historical agency.

Kojève's reading of Hegel is clearly influenced by the early Marx's recapitulation of Hegelian views of action and work. Although inspired by the newly discovered manuscripts of 1844, Kojève sought in Hegel a more fundamental theory of action, labor, and historical progress than he found in Marx. Reversing the Marxist trend to view Hegel as wrong-side-up, Kojève argued that Hegel provided an anthropology of historical life (*IH* 72–73), alienating the essential features of human existence which necessitate the continual re-creation of social and historical worlds. Kojève traced Marx's theory of class struggle to Hegel's discussion of lord and bondsman in the *Phenomenology,* and although Marx viewed class struggle as the dynamic proper to capitalist society, Kojève generalized his conclusion, claiming that the struggle for recognition forms the dynamic principle of all historical progress. Although influenced by Marx, Kojève appears exclusively concerned with the early Marx: the theory of labor as the essential activity of human beings, the theory of alienation, the necessity of transforming the natural and intersubjective worlds in order to fulfill essential human projects. The early Marx, as opposed to the Marx of *Capital* or the *Grundrisse,* accepted an anthropological view of human labor, that is, a view that enforced the universal and invariant features of labor as an essential human activity.

Kojève found the basis of an anthropological view of human action and labor in the fourth chapter of the *Phenomenology.* Indeed, one might argue that the *Phenomenology* stops with Chapter 4 for Kojève, for it is there that the structures of desire, action, recognition, and reciprocity are revealed as the conditions for historical life universally. For Kojève, the *Phenomenology* achieves the *telos* of Western culture insofar as it occasions the beginning of an anthropocentric understanding of historical life. Kojève's claim that all post-Hegelian thought inhabits a posthistorical time attests to this achievement. Insofar as Kojève and his readers live post-historically, they live without the hope that philosophy will reveal new truths concerning the human situation. The telos of history was to reveal the structures that make history possible. Modernity is thus, for Kojève, no longer concerned with unlodging the teleological plan that is the historical cunning of reason; modernity is characterized by historical action on the part of individuals, an action less determined than free. The end to teleological history is the beginning of human action governed by a self-determining telos. In this sense, the end of history is the beginning of a truly anthropocentric universe. In Kojève's words, it is the revelation of "Man" or, perhaps more descriptively, of human subjectivity.

Kojève appears to reverse the order of significance that the *Phenomenology* establishes between human desires and a larger metaphysical order. For Kojève, Hegel's metaphysical categories find their consummate expression in human ontology; the categories of Being, Becoming, and Negation are synthesized in human action. Action that is truly human transforms (negates) that which is brutally given (Being) into a reflection and extenuation of the human agent (Becoming). In a 1941 review of the contemporary significance of Hegel, Mikel Dufrenne wrote that for Kojève, "what is ontologically considered as negativity, and metaphysically considered as time [is] phenomenologically considered as human action."[7] For Kojève, then, the perspective of human agency gave concrete expression to Hegel's entire system; indeed, the *Logic* was to be understood as gaining its concrete meaning only in the context of human action. In this sense, Chapter 4 of the *Phenomenology* becomes the central moment in Hegel's entire system. Kojève went so far as to claim that Hegel's entire theological speculations ought to be understood as a theory of human action (*IH* 258–59).

In order to maintain the centrality of the human perspective in Hegel's system, Kojève rejected the panlogistic interpretation of Hegel's view of nature. Indeed, in order to safeguard reason as the sole property of human beings, Kojève had to read Hegel's doctrine of the dialectic of nature either as mistaken or as requiring the contributing presence of a human consciousness.[8] Kojève introduces desire in the *Introduction to the Reading of Hegel* as designating the ontological difference between human and purely natural beings. In particular, Kojève distinguishes human consciousness as something more than a simple identity, that is, as the kind of being that only becomes itself through *expression*. Reformulating the

[65]

drama of Explanation found in the *Phenomenology,* Kojève argues that human consciousness remains indistinguishable from animal consciousness until it asserts its reflexivity in the form of self-expression.

In Kojève's view, prior to its self-constituting expression, human consciousness is like animal consciousness, *absorbed* in the objects outside itself; this absorption is termed "contemplation" by Kojève. The self learns nothing about itself in contemplation for "the man who contemplates is 'absorbed' in what he contemplates; the 'knowing subject' 'loses' himself in the object that is known." As opposed to a contemplation that cannot afford the experience of self-constitution or self-knowledge, Kojève distinguishes *desire* as the only mode through which the human subject can express and know itself. Desire distinguishes human subjects as reflexive structures; it is the condition of self-externalization and self-understanding. Desire is "the origin of the 'I' revealed by speech"; desire prompts the linguistic subject into self-reference: "desire constitutes that being as I and reveals it as such by moving it to say 'I' " (*IH* 3).

Through referring to the role of self-expression in desire, Kojève builds upon Hegel's notion that desire both forms and reveals subjectivity. For Kojève, desire motivates the formation of a distinct sense of agency. In order to achieve what one desires, one formulates desires in speech or expresses them in some other way, for expression is the instrumental medium through which we appeal to Others. Expression is also the way in which we *determine* our desires, not simply in the sense of "give concrete expression to," but also in the sense of "give direction to." Desires are not contingently related to their expression, as if wholly formed prior to their expression; desire is essentially a desire-for-determination; desire strives for concrete expression as part of its satisfaction. Moreover, the determination of a desire as a concrete desire-for-something necessitates the determination of the self. In the formulation "I desire x," the "I" emerges as if by accident; subjectivity is unwittingly created and discovered through the concrete expression of desire.

Kojève argues that animal desire does not achieve self-reflection through desire, whereas for human desire, satisfaction and self-reflection are indissolubly linked. Human desire does presuppose animal desire insofar as the latter constitutes the organic possibility of the former; animal desire is the necessary but insufficient condition for human desire. Biological life, according to Kojève, can never constitute the meaning of human desire, because human desire is less an organic given than the negation or transformation of what is organically given; it is the vehicle through which consciousness constructs itself from a biological into a nonbiological, i.e., distinctively human, being. Contrary to the common belief that desire is itself a manifestation of biological necessity, Kojève inverts this relation and claims that desire is the transcendence of biology insofar as biology is conceived as a set of fixed natural laws.[9]

Kojève views nature as a set of brutally given facts, governed by the principle of simple identity, displaying no dialectical possibilities, and, hence, in stark contrast to the life of consciousness. Desire is thus non-natural insofar as it exhibits a structure of reflexivity or internal negation that natural phenomena lack. The subject is created through the experience of desire and is, in this sense, a non-natural self. The subject does not precede his desires and then glean from his desires a reflection of a ready-made self; on the contrary, the subject is essentially defined through what it desires. Through desiring a certain kind of object, the subject posits itself unwittingly as a certain kind of being. In other words, Kojève's subject is an essentially intentional structure; the subject *is* its desire for its object or Other; the identity of the subject is to be found in the intentionality of its desire.

For Kojève, the proper aim of desire is the transformation of natural givens into reflections of human consciousness, for only through taking this process of transformation as its object can desire manifest itself as the transformative power that it is. In Kojève's view, "desire is a function of its food" (*IH* 4), so that if a subject were to remain content with desiring natural objects alone, his desire would remain a purely natural desire; he would not evince the "transcendence" implicit in human desire: "The I created by the active satisfaction of such a Desire will have the same nature as the things toward which that Desire is directed; it will be a 'thingish' I, a merely living I, an animal I" (*IH* 5).

Kojève gives emphasis to the transition between "The Truth of Self-Certainty" and "Lordship and Bondage" as the development of desire's intentional aims from objects to Others. Interpreting Hegel's contention that desire is conditioned by its object, Kojève views the transition between these chapters as signifying the cultivation of desire into a "transcendent" or non-natural capacity. Arguing that desire takes on specific forms according to the kind of object it encounters and pursues, Kojève rejects the suggestion that an inexorable logic necessitates the transformation of desire into a satisfactory synthesis of self and world. There is nothing intrinsic to desire, no inner teleology, that would itself create the anthropogenesis of the world that Hegel views as desire's ultimate satisfaction. Desire is itself dependent upon the availability of a proper historical community to express its own transformative potential. Desire's satisfaction, then, is not secured through ontological necessity, but is itself context-bound, dependent upon an historical situation that provides for the expression of desire's transformative potential.

In Kojève's view, desire only becomes truly human, fully transformative, when it takes on a non-natural object, namely, another human consciousness. Only in the context of another consciousness, a being for whom reflexivity or inner negation is constitutive, can the initial consciousness manifest its own negativity, i.e., its own transcendence of natural life: "Desire directed toward another Desire, taken as Desire, will create, by the negating and assimilating action that satisfies it, an I essentially different from the animal 'I' " (*IH* 5).

The act of reciprocal exchange that constitutes the two subjectivities in their transcendence is that of recognition. The initial consciousness does not contemplate itself reflected in the Other; the passivity of contemplation is supplanted by the activity of desire. Kojève explains the movement of desire in search of recognition as an active negation: "this 'I' . . . will be 'negating-negativity,' " and "since Desire is realized as action negating the given, the very being of this I will be action" (*IH* 5). Recognition of one consciousness by another takes effect within a shared orientation toward the material world; the context of work (the negation of the natural world) occasions the process of recognition (the negation of the Other's naturalness). Work that exemplifies human being as transcending the natural and which occasions the recognition of Others is termed *historical action*. As the efficacious transformation of biological or natural givens, historical action is the mode through which the world of substance is recast as the world of the subject. Confronting the natural world, the historical agent takes it up, marks it with the signature of consciousness and sets it forth in the social world to be seen. This process is evident in the creation of a material work, in the linguistic expression of a reality, in the opening up of dialogue with other human beings: historical action is possible within the spheres of interaction and production alike.

[68]

Kojève's anthropocentrism leads him to view desire as a negating activity which founds all historical life. Desire cannot be overcome precisely because human subjectivity is the permanent foundation of historical life; action does not indicate a prior and more inclusive reality as its ground— action *is* the ground of history, the constituting act by which history emerges as nature transformed. Desire is thus a kind of negation that is not resolved into a more inclusive conception of being; desire indicates an ontological difference between consciousness and its world which, for Kojève, *cannot* be overcome.

Kojève's formulation of desire as a permanent activity of negation permits a modern conception of desire freed from the implicit teleological claims of Hegel's view in the *Phenomenology*. Kojève views desire as a "revealed nothingness" (*IH* 5), a negative or negating intentionality without a preestablished teleological structure. The various routes of desire are conditioned by the social world confronting desire, but the specific routes that desire pursues are in no sense prearranged. Human desire thus indicates a set of options for Kojève. The dissolution of Hegel's harmonious ontology, the scheme whereby negation is continuously superseded by a more encompassing version of being, allows for the formulation of desire as an expression of freedom.

Posting negation as a permanent feature of historical life proves central to articulating subjectivity as constituting and constituted by desire. For Kojève, desire does not—as it does for Hegel—discover its pre-given commonality with the world through an affirmation of itself as a sensuous medium. In Kojève's view, the sensuous aspect of human identity is precisely what calls for transcendence, what desire seeks to negate. Recalling the lord's project of abstraction, desire is, for Kojève, an idealizing project; it endeavors to determine human agency as transcendent of natural life. In this way, Kojève's formulation of desire avows the insurpassability of subjectivity; the ultimate project of desire is less a dialectical assimilation of subjectivity to the world, and the world to subjectivity, than a unilateral action upon the world in which consciousness instates itself as the generator of historical reality.

For Hegel, desire is a negating activity that both distinguishes and binds consciousness and its world, whereas for Kojève, desire is a negating activity through which consciousness is related externally, yet efficaciously, to the world. Rather than *revealing* the mutually constitutive dimensions of subject and substance as ontological *presuppositions* of their encounter, Kojève asserts consciousness as *creating* its relation to the world through its transformative action.

Kojève clearly questions the pre-given "place" of the human subject, and argues in an existential vein that whatever place there is, is a place *created* by that subject. Yet, by viewing desire as non-natural, as a transcendence of the purely sensuous, this "place" remains a metaphysical abstraction rather than a concrete existential situation, and Kojève deprives his position of an *embodied* understanding of desire. His subject becomes an abstract creator, the paradigm for the philosophical thinker himself; negation is less an embodied pursuit than an effort to become a pure freedom. Moreover, Kojève's rejection of Hegel's positive linkage of self-consciousness' sensuousness with the sensuousness of the world implies a radical disjunction between human consciousness and the natural world which deprives human reality of a natural or sensuous expression. Kojève's distinction between the sensuous and the "truly human" involves him in an idealist position which recreates the paradox of determinateness and freedom that Hegel seemed to overcome in the *Phenomenology*. I turn to the problematic features of this position first in order to clarify the relation between the sensuous and desire and in order to lay the groundwork for Kojève's view of desire as manifesting human existence in its temporality and freedom.

Kojève's reading of the "Lordship and Bondage" section underscores his difference from Hegel on the problem of the sensuous. In Hegel's chapter the bondsman discovers that he is not a thing-like creature, but a dynamic, living being capable of negation. The bondsman experiences himself as an embodied actor, one who also thirsts for life. Although the bondsman confronts his freedom from natural constraints through the negating activity of his labor, he rediscovers the "natural" aspect of his existence as a *medium* of self-reflection. The body which once signified his enslavement comes to appear as the essential precondition and instrument of his freedom. In this respect the bondsman prefigures the synthesis of determinateness and freedom that *Geist* subsequently comes to represent. In the larger terms of the text, substance is recast as subject through the reconciliation of determinate life and absolute freedom.

Kojève's reading of this section stops before the reconciliation of determinate life and freedom is introduced through the concept of *Geist*, and neither does he acknowledge the bondsman's body as a medium of expression. Instead, Kojève argues that the lesson of the section is that negating action consists of a transcendence of the natural and determinate. The paradox of consciousness and the body remains a dynamic and constitutive paradox. The fate of human reality is "not to be what it is (as static and given being; as natural being, as 'innate character') and to be (that is, to become) what it is not" (*IH* 5). In this formulation, prefiguring the Sartrian view of the paradoxical unity of the in-itself and for-itself, Kojève underscores his view of consciousness as that which *transcends* rather than unites with nature. The project of subjectivity is to overcome all positivity that includes the "inner nature" or apparently fixed features of consciousness itself: "in its very becoming this I is intentional becoming, deliberate evolution, conscious and voluntary progress; it is the act of transcending the given that is given to it and that it itself is" (*IH* 5).

Kojève's normative view, that desire must become manifest as a thoroughgoing experience of "conscious and voluntary progress" implies that all claims regarding innate drives or natural teleologies to human affectivity must be dismissed as mistaken. Insofar as the givenness of an agent's own biological life is to be transformed into a creation of will, Kojève is proposing that desire be regarded as an instrument of freedom. The reification of desire as a natural phenomenon is, then, the arbitrary restriction of desire to certain ends, and the unjustifiable elevation of those ends to a natural or necessary status. As an expression of freedom, desire becomes a kind of choice.

Kojève's view of the paradoxical ontological situation of human beings—not to be what it is (nature), and to be what it is not (consciousness or negation)—has the consequence that human beings are necessarily projected into time. The human "I" is a continual surpassing of itself, an anticipation of the being that it is not yet, as well as an anticipation of the nothingness that will emerge from whatever it at any moment happens to be: "the very being of this I will be becoming, and the universal form of this being will be not space, but time" (*IH* 5). Desire is a nothingness that is essentially temporalized: it is a "revealed nothingness" or an "unreal emptiness" which intends its own fulfillment, and, through this intending, creates a temporal future. In Kojève's view, the experience of time is conditioned by the various projects instituted by human agents;

time, like the Heideggerian notion of temporality, is relative to the human orientation through which it is experienced. By "time," Kojève means *lived time,* the experience of time conditioned by the way agents, through their hopes, fears, and memories, create a specific experience of future, present, and past. The experience of desire, in particular, gives rise to futurity: "the movement engendered by the Future is the movement that arises from desire" (*IH* 134).

In keeping with Kojève's rejection of "natural being" as irrelevant to human consciousness, he relinquishes natural time for a human temporality essentially structured by desire and its intended fulfillment. Unsatisfied desire is an absence that circumscribes the kind of presence by which it might relinquish itself as absence. Insofar as it posits itself as a determinate emptiness, i.e., as empty *of* some specific object or Other, it is itself a kind of presence: it is "the presence of an absence of reality" (*IH* 134); in effect, this absence "knows" what it is missing. It is the tacit knowledge of *anticipation.* The anticipation of fulfillment gives rise to the concrete experience of futurity. Desire thus reveals the essential temporality of human beings.

Kojève's theory of the lived experience of time suggests an existential alternative to the *Phenomenology's* approach to temporality. I suggested earlier that the *Phenomenology* makes use of a fictive temporality in order to demonstrate the development of appearances into their all-encompassing Concept. That certain figures of consciousness "appear" at some juncture in this development does not mean that they come into being; rather, their opacity must also be regarded as an essential moment of their being. In effect, it is only from the human perspective that appearances pass in and out of being. In effect, every moment of negation is ultimately revealed to be contained within a unity that has been there implicitly all along. The progression of the *Phenomenology* consists of the gradual development of the point of view of the journeying subject into that of the comprehensive absolute.

Kojève appears to reject the possibility of an absolute point of view, restricting his account of desire and historical action within the confines of the lived experience of a finite subject. In effect, he keeps our traveling subject from widening the circumference of his metaphysical reality. Kojève does not view himself, however, as rejecting or even revising Hegel; he argues that Hegel's position is rightly represented in his own. Rather than enter into a debate over whether Kojève's interpretation is correct, suffice it to say that Kojève asserts the ontological primacy of individuality over collectivity, and also maintains that Hegel's *Phenomenology,* despite the appearance of Christ at the closure, is a tract in atheism.[10] Whether Kojève rewrites Hegel or simply brings into relief a possible reading of Hegel, the point remains that Kojève asserts the perspective of lived experience as the necessary context in which to analyze desire and temporality. For Kojève, human action is the highest incarnation of the Absolute, so that the experience of lived time is vindicated over and against the fictive temporality of the *Phenomenology's* development. According to this latter view, lived temporality could only be regarded as a mere appearance within the overarching framework of Hegel's ontological unity: hence, the temporal experience of desire moving beyond itself toward an object (and thereby opening up a future for itself), turns out to be a perspective essentially deceived. The movement of desire reveals itself as a movement internal to the all-encompassing dance of subject and substance, "a bachanallian revel" (¶ 13) to be sure, but one in which every movement returns to its original place.

Kojève's view implies that temporality gains its meaning only through the concrete acts through which it is engendered. Anticipating a future that is not-yet, the desiring agent does not come to find that the not-yet has always been; rather, desire *creates* the not-yet through an orientation toward an absent object. Desire, for Kojève, no longer reveals a pre-given structure of temporal progression within an overarching unity, but institutes temporality *ex nihilo*. The ecstatic character of desire, then, is not resolved into a more inclusive form of self-relatedness, but desire remains truly outside itself. Desire in the form of anticipation (the negation of the present, the desire for the not-yet) reveals the ambiguous "place" of subjectivity, as neither here nor there, but spanning both; anticipation discloses subjectivity as a being projected into time and as a being who projects time. That temporality gains its meaning through subjective experience alone is underscored by Kojève in his essay, "A Note on Eternity, Time, and the Concept": "we have seen that the presence of Time in the real World is called Desire" (*IH* 137).

In this same article Kojève refers to Hegel's comment in his Jena lectures that "Geist ist Zeit."[11] This formulation is echoed in the preface to the *Phenomenology:* "die Zeit ist der daseiende Begriff selbst" (¶ 46). This "time in the real world" is the experience of projected possibilities implicit in desire which distinguishes *human* desire. Time arises through human "projects" which manifest the idealizing function of desire:

Time (that is, historical Time, with the rhythm: Future Past Present) *is* Man in his empirical—that is, spatial—integral reality: Time is the History of Man in the World. And, indeed, without Man there would be no Time in the World. . . . To be sure, the animal, too, has desires, and it acts in terms of those desires, by negating the real: it eats and drinks, just like man. But the animal's desires are natural; they are directed toward what *is,* and hence they are *determined* by what is; the negating action that is effected in terms of *these* desires, therefore, cannot *essentially* negate, it cannot change the *essence* of what is. Being remains identical to itself, and thus it is *Space,* and not Time. . . . Man, on the other hand, essentially transforms the World by negating action of his (struggles) and his Work. Action which arises from *non*-natural human Desire toward another Desire—that is, toward something which does not exist really in the natural world *(IH* 138).

The desire of another individual serves as the condition for the experience of futurity; hence, reciprocal recognition and temporality are, for Kojève, essentially related. To recognize another means to relate to the other's *possibilities,* implicit in which is a sense of futurity, i.e., the conception of what the Other can become. Only when we relate to others as natural beings do we assert a purely present relation to them; only by acknowledging them as consciousness, i.e., as negativities, beings who are not yet what they are, do we relate to them as truly human: "desire . . . is directed toward an entity that does not exist and has not existed in the real natural World. Only then can the movement be said to be engendered by the Future, for the Future is precisely what does not (yet) exist and has not (already) existed" *(IH* 134).

The Other is distinguished from natural beings insofar as the Other is capable of futurity and is, thus, a nonactual being in terms of the present. And yet the Other comes into being as a social being to the extent that he is recognized, and this recognition follows upon the performance of transformative acts. Insofar as desire achieves this second-order being through recognition, the pure futurity that was desire is transformed into "History" or equivalently, "human acts accomplished with a view to social Recognition" *(IH* 135).

The transformation of desire into a social identity constitutes the structure of the act by which history emerges from nature. Defined as a "hole" in existence, or occasionally, as "the absence of Being" *(IH* 135), desire is conceived as a negating intentionality which seeks social reality through reciprocal recognition. Unrecognized, desire lacks positive being; recognized, desire achieves a being that is second nature, the creation of a community of reciprocally recognizing desires. Without the world of Others, desire and the personal agency it introduces would have no reality: "only in speaking of a 'recognized' human reality can the term human be used to state a truth in the strict and full sense of the term. For only in this case can one reveal a reality in speech" (*IH* 9).

History is defined by Kojève in normative terms; it is not merely a set of events, but, rather, a set of *projects* which effectively transform naturally given being into social constructions. History is a set of *acts* in which an idea or possibility is realized, something is created from nothing, anthropogenesis succeeds. In a formulation that breaks with the monism of Hegel's Concept, which prefigures Sartre's view of negation as pure creation, Kojève argues that

the profound basis of Hegelian anthropology is formed by this idea that Man is not a Being that *is* in an eternal identity to itself in Space, but a Nothingness that *nihilates* as Time in spatial Being, through the negation or transformation of the given, starting from an idea or ideal that does *not* yet *exist*, that is still nothingness (a "project")—through negation that is called the *Action (Tat)* of Fighting and of Work *(Kampf und Arbeit).* (*IH* 48)

In Kojève's reading of the *Phenomenology,* the traveling subject achieves his most sophisticated form as an historical agent. Moreover, there are certain markedly ahistorical features about this historical agency, namely, his relentless "nothingness," the structure of his action, the ideal of recognition. The extent to which Kojève's revision of Hegel results in both an *anthropology* and a normative ideal of *anthropogenesis* suggests that the subject's travels have, in effect, come to an end. As a posthistorical agent, one whose historical formation has been concluded, Kojève's subject no longer requires a dialectical narrative to reveal his own historicity. Narrative history is already over, and the subject who emerges from that history enacts an anthropogenesis, a reproduction of substance as subject, from the point of view of the bondsman emerging into collective identity, that is, from the viewpoint of the end of Chapter 4. As a subject for whom progressive history is over, Kojève's historical agent is expressed, not through an omniscient narrative, but in the words of the first-person singular. Its word becomes its deed, the linguistic creation of the subject itself, a creation *ex nihilo.*

We can see that the narrative strategy of the *Phenomenology* is necessitated by the doctrine of internal relations, that web of constitutive relations which always remains partially hidden, and which requires a temporalized presentation to be grasped in its integrity. Kojève, on the other hand, has no need of metaphysical narrative, because the "becoming" of his traveler is self-generated. Indeed, the traveler has ceased his travels altogether, set up shop in the environs of ontological exile, and shown Hegel, as it were, that contrary to the argument of the *Phenomenology*, an efficacious subjectivity can emerge from such soil. Kojève's subject lacks the irony of Hegel's incessantly myopic traveler; he is no longer mocked by the metaphysical domain which seemed always to exceed his understanding. On the contrary, Kojève's subject is less comic than heroic, exemplifying the efficacy of transformative action, affirming autonomy as true accomplishment, no longer as a comic moment of inflated self-appraisal. Hence, when Kojève's historical agent speaks, the nothingness of his self is articulated and then ensconced in the being of the audible utterance, his own desire thereby giving birth to himself. The subject is "not what is" only to the extent that the generating silence remains concealed, and must continually be renewed, but this internal non-coincidence of the subject is only efficaciously vital and never comic. The reason is that this subject knows itself as this non-coincidence, and is not fooled by a limited version of its own identity. This is a subject alarmingly intact, self-serious, no longer displacing the Absolute, but claiming it now as its very self.

Kojève clearly attributes freedom to his historical agent in ways that Hegel would have dismissed as metaphysically ill-informed. For Kojève, desire is an active negation which is not resolved into a more inclusive conception of reality, but is, rather, a free project in pursuit of recognition and, consequently, historical reality. At first glance, this conception of the desiring agent as a "voluntary progress" might seem paradoxical in light of Kojève's other claim that "all human Desire . . . is finally a function of the desire for recognition" (*IH* 7). Although voluntary, human desire manifests a choice which ultimately gains its meaning from within a domain of existing conventions of recognition. In other words, in desire, choice is manifest in the kind of recognition one seeks, but it remains outside of the limits of choice to avoid recognition altogether.

Although Hegel closes the preface to the *Phenomenology* with an admonishment that "the individual must all the more forget himself, as the nature of Science implies and requires" (¶ 72), Kojève argues that social

[76]

recognition is always directed toward the individual's value. Indeed, for Kojève, the kind of action which satisfies human desire is that in which one is "recognized in (one's) human value, on (one's) reality as a human individual." For Kojève, all human value is individual value, and "all Desire is desire for a value" (*IH* 6).

Recognition does not have the effect of assimilating the individual into a more inclusive community; following the tradition of classical liberalism, Kojève views recognition as a process in which individuals form communities, but these communities facilitate the development of individuality and not its transcendence. The difficulty of achieving this state of reciprocal recognition is exemplified for Kojève in historical strife. Every individual agent desires recognition of his value from all other individuals in the community; as long as some individuals do not recognize an Other, they view him as a natural or thing-like being and exclude him from the human community. Domination arises as a self-contradictory effort to achieve recognition in this context. For Kojève, the desire for domination is derivative of the desire for universal recognition, but the strategies of the oppressor—the lord—guarantee the failure of the project. The lord may attempt to impose his individual will upon the bondsmen who depend on him, but this imposition can never elicit the recognition that the lord requires: the lord does not value those by which he aspires to be recognized so that their recognition cannot be received by him as a human recognition.

The satisfaction of desire, for Kojève, which is simultaneously the development of individuality, requires the universalization of reciprocal recognition, i.e., a universally instituted egalitarianism of social value. The struggle for recognition which has produced a conflict of interests throughout history can be fully overcome only through the emergence of a radical democracy. Conversely, this kind of egalitarianism would imply the complete recognition of individual values, the satisfaction and social integration of desires:

Man can only truly be "satisfied," History can end, only in and by the formation of a society, of a State, in which the strictly particular, personal, individual value of each is recognized as such; and in which the universal value of the State is recognized and realized by . . . all the Particulars. (*IH* 58)

Although Kojève claims that it is the essence of Hegel's system that he explicates through his analysis, it seems clear that he has, in fact, restricted his analysis to certain central themes of the *Phenomenology,* and provided a peculiarly modern elaboration of these themes. Kojève clearly accepts the modern liberal conception of individual desire as the foundation of the social and political world. Although a good many Hegel scholars view individual desire as transcended in and through the concept of *Geist,* Kojève clearly sees the ideal Hegelian society as one that maintains a dialectical mediation of individuality and collectivity. In fact, collective life appears to gain its final measure and legitimation in proving capable of recognizing *individual* desires.

Kojève's brand of democratic Marxism does not, however, rely on the Hobbesian view of the conflict of desires without reinterpreting that doctrine. In line with Hegel, Kojève views the conflict of individual desires not as a natural state of affairs but as one which implies its own super-session through a universally accepted social order resting on principles of reciprocal recognition. Moreover, individuality itself is not to be under-stood strictly in terms of individual desire, for desire creates a distinctively *human* subjectivity through recognition of and by another desire; indi-viduality gains its own full expression and satisfaction only through a validated participation in the social sphere. As distinct from the Hobbes-ian view, society does not arise as an artificial construct in order to arbitrate between naturally hostile desires, but society provides for the articulation and satisfaction of desire. Accordingly, the political com-munity does not recognize individual wills which, strictly speaking, exist prior to the state apparatus of recognition; rather, recognition itself fa-cilitates the constitution of true individuals, truly human subjectivities, which is the ultimate aim of desire. The end of history, the satisfaction of desire, consists in the successful recognition of each individual by every other.

Kojève's reading of Hegel through the natural law tradition results in a theory that values individuality more than Hegel's original theory does. His acceptance of the subjective point of view permits him an analysis of desire in terms of the structures of freedom and temporality that desire presupposes and enacts. And yet the distinction between consciousness and nature that pervades his view leads him to promote desire as a disembodied pursuit; desire is a negation, but one that is unsupported by a corporeal life. Kojève's references to desiring agents as "negations" and "nothingnesses" suffer from an abstractness that has philosophical consequences. Hegel's argument that the pursuit of recognition must take place within life remains true: the body is not merely the precondition for desire, but its essential medium as well; inasmuch as desire seeks to be beyond nature, it seeks to be beyond life as well. I turn to Hyppolite in an effort to reconsider the paradox of determinateness and freedom which still troubles the Hegelian formulation of desire. Is the heroic subject still possible? Does it make sense to understand desire as a disembodied generativity, or is this a contradiction in terms which no Hegelian synthesis can resolve? What would it mean to accept the existential transvaluation of Hegel's subject, but to place him in the midst of life, an embodied being intrinsically related to the natural world? If we take even more seriously the finitude of this subject, then how will his desire and his action be further circumscribed? If Kojève's project of anthropogenesis proves impossible, does this subject, once comic, then heroic, now become a *tragic* figure?

Hyppolite: Desire, Transience, and the Absolute

In the modern human world, the tragic never seems to disappear. We can well perceive that human existence, in its precariousness, is jeopardized, but we are not sure, as Hegel was, that this coincides with the rational. This coincidence is once again a kind of optimism that we can no longer postulate.—Jean Hyppolite, "The Phenomenon of 'Universal Recognition' in Human Experience"

Hyppolite initiated his own studies of Hegel in part to continue and revise Kojève's effort to ground Hegelianism in a post-historical time. By bringing to bear the *Logic* and the *Early Theological Writings* on the *Phenomenology of Spirit,* however, Hyppolite sought to escape the anthropocentric biases of Kojève's heroic narrative of the human spirit. Kojève's subject appeared as an omnipotent actor on the historical scene, guilty of metaphysical grandstanding as the generating agency of both history and time. In Hyppolite's view, the demise of teleological history necessitated the further circumscription of the Hegelian subject: even the grandest historical actors are not freed of the temporal exigencies that attend any human life; heroism inevitably has its demise. The

Hegelian traveler who once relied on the metaphysics of internal relations becomes for Kojève the historical actor solely responsible for creating interrelations, and in Hyppolite, this subject becomes even less sure of its place. Indeed, its "place" turns out to be its "time," the temporal basis of its identity, the necessary anxiety of its life.

Most of Hyppolite's reflections on the *Phenomenology* are to be found in his monumental commentary on the text, *Genèse et structure de la Phénoménologie de l'esprit,* published in 1946 in France, following the gradual publication of his translation of the *Phenomenology* in 1939–1942. The title itself suggests the philosophical problem to be pursued: that the *Phenomenology* permits an analysis in terms of its "genesis and structure" suggests that Hegel's narrative requires yet another conceptual schema by which to be properly understood. Throughout the commentary, Hyppolite argues that phenomenological presumptions regarding the progressive movement of history and the satisfaction of the subject are historically conditioned ideas. Hence, only from a perspective beyond the *Phenomenology* do the historical origins of the text become clear. This very claim, however, is a result of the "structure" of the *Phenomenology* itself: the privilege of the retrospective point of view as the most wise, the most all-encompassing, the one that can discern the condition that makes any given unified picture of the world break into dissension and dissolve. In effect, Hyppolite makes use of the principle of retrospective wisdom to criticize the *Phenomenology* for its presumptions of progressivity, elaborating the reflexive structure of Hegel's narrative transitions to effect a transition beyond the *Phenomenology* itself. That the *Phenomenology* requires a commentary at all indicates the problem of reading this text within an historical experience that can no longer support the optimism of Hegel's ever-buoyant narrative. To question the teleological model of history, and still to remain an Hegelian, one must find the posthistorical prefigured in the text itself. Kojève finds this experience of modernity embodied in the slave who, shaken with terror, flees from the body to a life of dissociated abstraction and becomes the philosophical craftsman, carving out history and metaphysical truth in a single act. Hyppolite stops Hegel's phenomenological narrative further back, at the moment of Life and the infinite labor of desire.

Hyppolite is quite clear that desire can have no consequence within the finite life of the individual that is not further desire, that an ultimate satisfaction is impossible, that human negativity is never successfully integrated into a higher-order identity. The infinity of desire is referred to in "The Truth of Self-Certainty," and is implicitly affirmed in the *Logic* and *Early Theological Writings;* indeed, the experience of infinite desire is not only the "posthistorical" moment within the *Phenomenology,* but the incipient modernism of Hegel's metaphysical notion of the Absolute.

Hyppolite's rehabilitation of time as a monistic absolute suggests an alternative to Kojève's ontological dualism. For Kojève, the human and natural worlds were ontologically distinct domains; for Hyppolite, the common structure of time serves as a monistic principle which governs in both worlds. Although Hyppolite claims to be "in agreement with Kojève in his effort to recognize all of the existential resonances in Hegel's work" (F 239), he clearly thought that Kojève failed to take account of some key existential themes. Kojève interprets negation as the transformative action that marks the natural world with a human signature; Hyppolite extends the domain of negation, arguing that human subjects are negativity inasmuch as they are temporal beings comported toward death. Kojève's figure of the historical actor implicitly denies the existential facts of temporality. Although Kojève criticizes the notion of teleological history, he has not cured himself of the belief in a *telos* to human existence. Hence, for Kojève, the teleological view of history is less rejected than internalized as a potential feature of an individual life; the "end" of existence is found in the narrative of a life that makes universal history every time its own action engages worldwide recognition. Hyppolite suggests that this "end" or set of ends are only momentary achievements, and that the "momentary" status of these accomplishments remains unanalyzed in Kojève's theory. In this way Kojève refuses to think through the consequences of a posthistorical time, the experience of temporality without relief, the thought of time as the essence of Life.

According to Hyppolite, Kojève's almost exclusive emphasis on the *Phenomenology* necessitates the restrictive anthropocentrism of his view:

The *Phenomenology* would be the epic of the human spirit coming to the end of its history, of the working of negativity. In becoming conscious of this history, Hegel's philosophy, consummated in the present, would be absolute knowledge. (F 237)

Negativity, however, is found not only in the historical self-constitution of the *Phenomenology's* subject, but in the thinking of difference which,

[81]

for Hyppolite, is the function of time and constitutes the being of Life. He writes,

I believe that Kojève's interpretation is too exclusively anthropological. For Hegel, absolute knowledge is no more a theology than it is an anthropology. It is the discovery of the speculative, of a thought of being which appears through man and history, the absolute revelation. It seems to me that it is this sense of speculative thought which is opposed by Kojève's purely anthropological interpretation. (*F* 241)

Hyppolite distinguishes two tendencies in Hegel's work, one that begins with the point of view of the subject and one that begins, as it were, with the point of view of substance, the "adventure of being," the subject-less sojourn of metaphysics. In an essay entitled "Notes on the Preface to the *Phenomenology of Spirit:* The Absolute is Subject," he writes:

According to us, there are two complementary and nearly irreconcilable aspects to Hegelian thought: 1) there is the thought of history, the concrete human adventure, and this constitutes itself through taking account of this experience; 2) there is also the adventure of Being—Hegel speaks of the Absolute—and not only of man, which is why it is speculative, absolute knowledge, beyond history, becoming, and temporality. (*F* 334–35)

Although this speculative knowledge of the absolute is "beyond history, becoming, and temporality," it is only accessible to a human consciousness through its own temporal life. *Life* is the speculative element that is understood through human temporality, but that transcends human temporality as well, essential to logical and natural relationships apart from any relationship to human reality. Hence, Hyppolite does not ask after the being of "man," but after the being of "life"; through this return to Life, the imparting and dissolution of shape, Hyppolite finds the absolute as both dynamic and thoroughly monistic.

As speculative rather than anthropological, Hyppolite's notion of time is opposed to Kojève's postulation of time as *created* by the various "projects" of human agents. For Hyppolite, time constitutes human reality as an *ek-static* enterprise, a mode of permanent self-estrangement. Living in time, human beings are necessarily other to themselves, not only because they cannot inhabit memory and anticipation at once, but because time itself is necessarily beyond their control; indeed, time is less a human creation than the necessary limit on all human creativity, the inevitable transience of all human creations. While for Kojève, the absolute is found

[82]

in properly historical acts, for Hyppolite, it is found in a temporality which inevitably reveals these acts as less than absolute. Kojève appears to forget the key Hegelian lesson of the *Phenomenology* that Life is a matter of necessary repetition. Indeed, Kojève's view of History seems opposed to time; historical deeds and works are meant to stay time, to elevate the human spirit beyond the futility of animal life to the permanence of the historical world. And if history is understood as a realm of permanence, then history itself must be opposed to time. Kojève admits as much, arguing that the truly human task is to transform time into History, to resolve transience into durable forms. In this sense, Kojève has elevated the wisdom of the bondsman to an absolute task, for the bondsman learned that in the creation of a work, "desire is held in check" and "transience is staved off" (¶ 195). For Hyppolite, such an actor who, through his acts, lifts himself out of time, is a lifeless being, a being turned against life. Hyppolite emphasizes that intrinsic to life is the dissolution of form as well as its reconstitution. Hence, for Hyppolite, the absolute is not an achievement as such, but the dialectic of achievement and loss, the perpetual noncoincidence of beings and, in the human sphere, the permanence of desire, the inevitability of transience.

Hyppolite understands his own project as less a rewriting of Hegel than an elaboration of some underrepresented Hegelian themes. The interpretation of absolute knowledge as the thought of *time* is a case in point:

Absolute knowledge does not really exist; it is not beyond becoming in a supervening intelligible or suprasensible realm. In turn, this becoming is not an effect of dispersal, lacking connection; it is an unprecedented teleology, an adventure of sense, where the moments conjoin and separate like the moments of time: "Time is the Concept which is there . . . it is the disquiet of life and the process of absolute distinction." (*F* 335)

Hyppolite's interpretation of absolute knowledge as the "disquiet of life" aligns Hegel more closely with Kierkegaard. Following Jean Wahl's argument that Hegel's *Early Theological Writings* evince a Kierkegaardian view of the Absolute as paradox, Hyppolite argues that Hegel's effort "to think pure life through" is a paradoxical venture, like Kierkegaard's "thought of existence" ("CE").[12] According to Hyppolite, the Hegelian thinker who attempts to think the absolute, the truth that structures all things, must learn to think time itself, and this thought is of necessity an experience of anxiety, placelessness, inevitable transience. Hence, to think the absolute is to engage both a knowledge of temporality and a temporal experience of this truth; in effect, the truth of time must be suffered to be known.

In the introduction to this commentary, Hyppolite reconstructs Hegel's efforts throughout the Jena period to effect a conceptual synthesis between the being of man and the being of life. In *Early Theological Writings,* Hegel rejected the possibility of a *rational* movement between the finite perspective of the human knower and the infinity of the world. In the *System der Sittlichkeit* he argued that only a *religious* movement could effect this transition. And in his essay, *Natural Law,* he outlined the kind of transcendent intuition that alone could grasp the finite and the infinite within a single movement of consciousness. That Hegel later developed the Concept as a rational comprehension of the infinite is not, according to Hyppolite, a thorough break with his earlier claims concerning the limits of reason. Reason accommodates rather than replaces religion and intuition. Hyppolite argues:

If later, in the *Logic,* [Hegel] managed to express in rational form an intuition of the very being of life or of the self, which he earlier declared could not be thought through, we should not conclude from this that nothing remains of the first intuition, the kernal from which his whole system developed. (*GS* 147)

Even in the *Logic,* according to Hyppolite, the Concept is tied to the notion of infinity such that conceptual knowing must itself be a continuous process rather than a determinate act or set of acts. The telos of conceptual knowing is not the resolution of Becoming in and through an enhanced conception of Being, but, rather, the discovery that this enhanced conception of Being is nothing other than continuous Becoming. Being, no longer conceived as simple identity, is identity-in-difference, or, equivalently, self-relatedness through time. Identity does not "contain" difference as if some spatial relation adhered between the two; identity is now defined as flux itself, the perpetual "disquiet" of the self. Commenting on the preface to the *Phenomenology,* Hyppolite writes, "the Absolute is always unstable and disquieted, that in which the tendency, the impulse, has not disappeared behind the achieved result . . . the Absolute is always an instance of alteration, is always a departure, and adventure" (*E* 333). The identification of the being of man and the being of life is made possible through a common *groundlessness,* the loss of a stationary metaphysical place. Thus, Hegel's metaphysical subject is no longer understood as ensconced in a metaphysical place, but is now revealed as modern, anxious, perpetually dislocated: "this being of life is not substance but rather the disquiet of the self" (*GS* 149).

Although Hyppolite is concerned with infinite desire and Life, themes that are introduced before the section on lordship and bondage, it is clear that for him these earlier categories provide an explanation for the latter. The "disquiet" of the self, its experience of time, is exacerbated through the experience of the Other. Indeed, it is only as a social being that this subject learns that Life is essential to its own projects (the Life and Death Struggle) and that the fear of death initiates individuation (the willingness to risk its Life). As the necessity of repetition and the dialectic of form and formlessness, Life is the dialectical notion of time. The knowledge of death enforces this subject's knowledge of limited time. But in the encounter with the Other, this subject learns that it does not exist all at once, but is alternately lost and then recovered: "This life is disquiet, the disquiet of the self which has lost itself and finds itself again in its alterity. Yet the self never coincides with itself, for it is always other in order to be itself." (*GS* 250)

No longer convinced of the coincidence of subject and substance, Hyppolite here avows their infinite non-coincidence, and affirms this non-coincidence (of each to the other, and each to itself) as their common situation. The absolute mediation of the self and its alterity is no longer conceived as a feasible project, and Hyppolite confirms that alterity always exceeds the self, as the self exceeds alterity. Hyppolite understands this non-coincidence or dis-quiet at the heart of being as implicit in Hegel's notion of the infinite, the priority of Becoming over Being, i.e., the reconceptualization of Being as a movement of Becoming. Reciprocal desire appears to approach this thought of the infinite. Hence, Hyppolite confirms the identity of desire and Conceptual thinking by claiming that desire is an "absolute impulse"[13]:

The concept is omnipotence; it is omnipotence only through manifesting itself and affirming itself in its other. It is the universal which appears in the soul of the particular and determines itself completely in it as the negation of the negation, or as genuine specificity. Or, in yet other words, it is love, which presupposes duality so as continually to surpass it . . . the concept is nothing else than the self which remains itself in its alteration, the self which exists only in this self-becoming. (*GS* 147)

The development of reciprocal desire is toward the ever-expanding autonomy of each partner. "Desire is conditioned by a necessary otherness" (*GS* 162), and yet this otherness is surpassed every time that one self-consciousness discovers the Other not as a limit to freedom but as its very condition. Concretely, the meaning of this paradox will only become clear in the Sartrian dialectic of self and Other, but we can begin to extrapolate its meaning here. This constant transformation of the Other from a source of danger into a promise of liberation is effected through a transvaluation of the Other's body. The self and Other do not observe each other, documenting the mental events that occur in the course of their transaction; they desire one another, for it is only through desire that the exteriority of the Other, the body, becomes itself expressive of freedom. Desire's project is to find the exteriority of the Other suffused by and with the Other's freedom. Desire is the expressiveness of the body, freedom made manifest. The alterity of the Other is softened, if not overcome, as the body gives life to consciousness, as the body becomes the paradoxical being that maintains and expresses negation. In this sense desire is the embodiment of freedom, and reciprocal desire initiates an infinite exchange.

The ontological project pursued by desire for Hyppolite takes its bearings within Hegel's own formulation, but strays from the presumption that the absolute can be discerned as a coincidence of the rational and the real. Hyppolite continues to assert that desire seeks to discover itself as ontologically joined with its world, but qualifies this claim through asserting this ontological dis-juncture as the being of time. Hyppolite maintains that "the most profound aim of desire is to find itself as a being," not as determinate or positive but as a being internally negated, a temporalized and paradoxical being. Hyppolite steeps himself in Hegel's own contentions in the *Logic:* "If we ordinarily say of Spirit that it is, that it has a being, that it is a thing, a specific entity, we do not thereby mean that we can see it or hold it or stumble against it. But we do make such statements" (*GS* 167).[14] For Hyppolite, the kind of being that informs both consciousness and life in general, and that characterizes desire, "is not merely a positive reality, a *Dasein* which disappears and dies absolutely, crushed by what exceeds it and remains external to it; it also is that which at the heart of this positive reality negates itself and maintains itself in that negation" (*GS* 166).

Self-surpassing or internal negation requires a reciprocal relation of recognition between selves. The aim of desire, according to Hyppolite, "the vocation of man—to find himself in being, to make himself be," is an aim "realized only in the relation between self-consciousness" (*GS* 167). Recognition conditions the "recovery" of the self from alterity, and thus facilitates the project of autonomy. The more fully recovered this self, the more encompassing of all reality it proves to be, for "recovery" is not retreat, but expansion, an enhancement of empathy, the positing and discovery of relations in which it has all along, if only tacitly, been enmeshed.

This ambiguous discovery of an alterity both reflexive and intentional constitutes the action of desire, the essence of self-consciousness. As Hyppolite claims, "Concretely, this is the very essence of man, 'who never is what he is,' who always exceeds himself and is always beyond himself, who has a future, and who rejects all permanence except the permanence of his desire aware of itself as desire" (*GS* 166). The experience of desire initiates our education into the Concept; the permanence of desire—the insurpassability of Otherness—is the lived experience of the infinite. Hence, Hyppolite makes phenomenological sense of Hegel's contentions not only that "self-consciousness is *Desire* in general" but that "self-consciousness is the concept of infinity realizing itself in and by consciousness" (*GS* 166).

By interpreting the absolute not as a closure to Hegel's system, but as its inevitable openness, Hyppolite counters the view of Hegel's *Phenomenology* as a movement toward a determinate *telos*. The being that *Geist* achieves is not a plenitude void of negativity, but an infinite movement between positive being and nothingness. In Hegel's original formulation, desire was conceived as that which posited and revealed both self and world as more than externally related opposites. The being that commonly structured self and world was to be understood as an all-inclusive *reflexivity*, a second-order being that contained difference within itself. The effort to find an all-inclusive being that could at once preserve the integrity of its moments and reveal their essential interdependence would not be a Parmenidean mass for which change is simply phenomenal illusion. This being would itself contain the infinite, would have the infinite as a constitutive feature. And yet to speak this way is still to court a substantial model, for if being were a "container" or a substance which either carried predicates within or bore them as so many attachments to its integument, such a being could not serve the purposes of Hegel's vision. In speaking this way, one substitutes a spatial model which assumes substance as a discrete and independent entity to which predicates are only arbitrarily related. To do justice to the dialectical or mutually constitutive relation of substance and predicate in Hegel's view, one must devise a model that accounts for the interchangeability of substance and attribute. The kind of being that "contains" the infinite is also, to extend and, then, undermine the metaphor, *contained by* the infinite. Hence, the relation between substance and predicate is a double relation, one that, in this case, presents the infinite as an aspect of being and also presents being as an aspect of the infinite. The usual hierarchy between substance and predicate is subverted through a constant exchange of roles. Hence, this second-order being is the infinite in this speculative sense of "is." The Concept, that form of knowing and being that structures the being of the self and the being of the world, is *time* itself, infinite displacement, the movement of the world engendered constantly through apparent difference.

If the absolute is infinite, and desire is an "absolute impulse," then desire no longer strives after "satisfaction," but endeavors to sustain itself as desire, "reject(ing) all permanence except the permanence of itself as desire." Only as *dissatisfied desire* is consciousness still alive and united with the being of life, a unity that is the infinite altercation of self and not-self that sets and sustains the organic world in motion. The dissatisfaction of desire must be seen as a determinate dissatisfaction, i.e., a dissatisfaction with an intentionality. It is not a simple craving, the plight of Tantalus infinitely distanced from the object of desire; desire's dissatisfaction is one that is discovered in the midst of life, as a consequence of movement rather than stasis, as a consequence of the impossible project to reconcile determinate identity and time.

This non-coincidence of self-consciousness also implies that the object of desire is always partially undisclosed. The aims of desire are always twofold; there is a determinate object (the intentional aim) and the project to achieve greater autonomy (the reflexive aim). In other words, desire is always after something other than the self, but is also always involved in a project of self-constitution. Because the aims of desire are twofold, any effort to isolate the "real" object of desire necessarily falls into deception. Any effort to subject the object of desire to determinate thinking turns out to be a truncated version of the truth. Thus the problem of desire is the problem of the paradoxical nature of self-consciousness, how to remain oneself in the midst of alterity. If one resolves the aims of desire into the aims of a singular identity to discover and reflect itself, one dispenses with the realm of alterity and thereby loses the self as well. And if one claims that it is in the nature of determinate objects to solicit desire, one neglects the project of identity informing desire. Hence, any effort to determine the true aim of desire is necessarily deceptive. Desire, then, can be said always to operate under the necessity of partial deception; in Hyppolite's words, "desire is in essence other than it immediately appears to be" (GS 160–61).

Because desire is in part a desire for self-reflection, and because desire also seeks to sustain itself as desire, it is necessary to understand self-reflection as a form of desire, and desire as a cognitive effort to thematize identity. Desire and reflection are not mutually exclusive terms, for reflection forms one of the intentional aims of desire, and desire itself may be understood as the ambiguous project of life and reflection. To comprehend the conditions of thought, to become a fully existing being through the reflection on the life that has produced the reflecting posture, is the highest aim of the *Phenomenology*, the all-inclusive aim of desire. Deception emerges as a function of perspective, of the insurpassable fact that human consciousness can never fully grasp the conditions of its own emergence, that even in the act of "grasping" consciousness is also in the process of becoming.

This noncoincidence of life and thought is not, for Hyppolite, cause for despair. The project of attaining capable identity is not to be forfeited simply because there is no guarantee of its success. The project is not necessitated by any natural or teleological principle, nor does it operate with the hope of success; in fact, it is both arbitrary and doomed to failure. The striving to know oneself, to think the conditions of one's own life, is a function of the desire to be free. Only by assimilating Otherness can human consciousness escape the vulnerability of merely positive being. The desire to reflect is thus originally indebted to a desire to establish oneself as a negating being, that which is both ensconced and eluded in finite being.

If there is a *telos* to the movement of desire, an end and motivating force, it can be understood only as death. As a merely positive being, human life would have no capacity to influence its surroundings; it would be merely itself, relationless, brute. As a simple body, this life would appear as a positive being that only exists and perishes and that, insofar as it exists, has a positive existence, and, as dead, is an indeterminate negation. Construed in terms of positive being devoid of negation, human life would itself be negated irrevocably by death. But desire is a negative principle which emerges as constitutive of finite life, as a principle of infinite alteration that strives to overcome positive being through revealing the ever-shifting place of the self within a network of internal relations. Paradoxically, desire enlivens the body with negation; it proclaims the body as more than merely positive being, that is, as an expressive or transcendent project. In these terms, desire is the effort to escape the vulnerability and nihilism of positive being through making the finite body into an expression of negation, i.e., of freedom and the power to create. Desire seeks to escape the verdict of death by preempting its power—the power of the negative.

Although the above sketch is my reading of the implications of Hyppolite's view, it seems clear that Hyppolite does accept the above view of desire and death. In "The Concept of Existence in the Hegelian Phenomenology," he claims that "the negation of every mode of diremption is always revived in the negative principle of desire. It is what moves desire" (CE 27). In a following discussion he claims that it is the principle of death in life that performs this role: "The fundamental role of death in annihilating the particular form of life becomes the principle of self-consciousness that drives it to transcend every diremption and its characteristic being-in-the-world, once this being-in-the-world is its own" (CE 28). We may safely conclude that the negative character of desire draws from a more fundamental principle of negation which governs human life; human life ends in negation, yet this negation operates throughout life as an active and pervasive structure. Desire negates determinate being again and again, and hence, is itself a quieted version of death, the ultimate negation of determinate being. Desire evinces the power human life has over death precisely by participating in the power of death. Human life is not robbed of its meaning through death, for human life, as desire, is always already partially beyond determinate life. Through the gradual appropriation of negation—the cultivation of self-reflection and autonomy—human beings tacitly struggle against their own

[90]

ultimate negation: "Man cannot exist except through the negativity of death which he takes upon himself in order to make of it an act of transcendence or supersession of every limited situation" (CE 28).

Self-consciousness exists partially in rancor against determinate life and views its assimilation of death as the promise of freedom. Hyppolite speculates that "the self-consciousness of life is characterized in some way by the thought of death" (CE 25). This suggestive phrase might be made more specific if we understand desire as "the thought of death," a thought sustained and pursued through the development of autonomy. As desire, the body manifests itself as more than positive being, as escaping the verdict of death's negation. The self is extended beyond the positive locus of the body through successive encounters with domains of alterity. In desire, the self no longer resides within the confines of positive being, internal to the body, enclosed, but *becomes* the relations it pursues, instates itself in the world which conditions and transcends its own finitude.

One might conclude that Hyppolite has engaged Freud's vision in *Beyond the Pleasure Principle* that all desire is in some sense inspired by a fundamental striving toward death, i.e., the desire to die. Although this claim is plausible in the above context, it is important to note that Hegel's (and Hyppolite's) Christianity would seem to imply that the death to which consciousness aspires is itself a fuller notion of life. Hegel is characteristically ambiguous on this point, but his claim in the *Phenomenology* that individuality finds its proper expression in *Geist* would seem to imply that death is not an absolute negation, but a determinate one which establishes the boundaries of a new beginning.

The "trembling" of the bondsman highlights a different aspect of Hegel's thought on death, however, and aligns him more closely with the fear and trembling of Kierkegaard. Following Kojève and Jean Wahl, Hyppolite restricts himself to the interpretation of death offered in the section of lordship and bondage. He takes seriously the facticity of the body, finitude as the condition of a limited perspective, corporeality as a guarantor of death. The vision of a new life, a life beyond death, remains purely conjectural in Hyppolite's view, but it is a conjecture that holds sway in human life. Human desire postulates a life beyond death which the human subject nevertheless cannot inhabit; for Hyppolite, desire affirms *itself as an impossible project,* a project whose fulfillment must remain *imaginary*—a theme that will be elaborated by Sartre throughout his career. That one cannot sustain life after death suggests that death must be sustained *in life:* self-consciousness exists only "through refusing to be." And yet, "this refusal to be must appear in being; it must manifest itself in some way (*GS* 167). Freedom must make itself known in order to be, posit itself in existence and gain reality through the acknowledgment of others. This desire to be a pure freedom, however, is vanquished ultimately by the irreducible facticity of death, a facticity that is anticipated throughout life in the striving of this finite being to supersede its limits:

Consciousness of life is, of course, no longer a naive life. It is the knowledge of the Whole of Life, as the negation of all its particular forms, the knowledge of true life, but it is simultaneously the knowledge of the absence of this "true life." Thus in becoming conscious of life man exists on the margin of naive and determined life. His desire aspires to a liberty that is not open to a particular modality; and all his efforts to conceive himself in liberty result only in failure. ("CE" 24)

From Hegel to Sartre

Both Kojève and Hyppolite accept the formulation that human beings are what they are not and are not what they are. For Kojève, this internal dissonance of the self implies a dualistic ontology that severs human beings into natural and social dimensions; the work of negation is confined to the task of transforming the natural into the social, i.e., a process of the gradual humanization of nature. For Hyppolite, the paradoxical character of human reality suggests that freedom escapes each of the determinate forms to which it gives rise, and that this constant displacement of the self signifies non-coincidence, time itself, the monistic absolute that characterized human and natural ontologies alike. In effect, Hyppolite accepts Hegel's doctrine of negation as including the difference between nature and human reality as a constitutive or internal difference. Kojève's anthropocentric reading of Hegel restricts negation to a creative power that human beings exhibit in the face of external realities; for Kojève, negation is an action of human origin that is applied externally to the realm of the nonhuman. Hyppolite returns to Hegel's original formulation in order to make modern sense of negation, not merely as action, but as constitutive of external reality as well. For Hyppolite negation resides already in the objects that human consciousness encounters; for Kojève, negation is the sole property of an active and transforming human consciousness.

Although Kojève would read desire as a human effort to transform that which appears initially alien and hostile to the human will, Hyppolite views desire as revealing the ontological place of human beings as a temporal movement that embraces the whole of life, which is, in effect, prior to human reality, more fundamental, yet essentially constitutive of human reality as well. While both positions view desire as implicating human beings as paradoxical natures, as determinate freedoms that cannot be simultaneously determinate and free, the one infers from this non-coincidence a dualistic world, and the other establishes duality (inner-negation) as a monistic principle.

Hyppolite wrote of Kojève that "the dualistic ontology that Kojève reclaims is realized by Sartre in *Being and Nothingness*" (F 240). And Sartre's own formulation of human reality as a paradoxical unity of in-itself and for-itself appears to echo almost verbatim Kojève's phrasing: "We have to deal with human reality as a being which is what it is not and which is not what it is" (*BN* 58). It is unclear, however, whether Sartre consistently follows Kojève in adopting a dualistic ontology. Sartre occasionally refers to consciousness as internally related to its world, i.e., as a consciousness "of" the world which is nothing but the world it attends. Other times he suggests consciousness is a "rift" in being, a contingency that can have no necessary relation to that which it refers. Only when Sartre accepts consciousness as *embodied* does he relinquish the vocabulary of dualism for a language of intentionality which returns him in his own fashion to Hegel's recognition that the sensuousness of desire becomes its access to the sensuousness of the world. This becomes clear in Sartre's reflections on sexuality and on writing. I turn to Sartre in order to trace the gradual embodiment of consciousness, the phenomenological fulfillment of Hegel's early contention that desire both constitutes and reveals the relations that bind the self with its world. To make Hegel's doctrine concrete, human desire must be shown not merely to signify abstract ontological bonds, but as the negating activity an embodied and historically situated self.

Sartre's discussions of desire and satisfaction take their bearings within the French reception of Hegel. For both Sartre and his Hegelian predecessors, the ideal of a secular satisfaction becomes increasingly remote. Prefiguring Sartre, Hyppolite disavows the possibility of final satisfaction and understands the relentlessness of desire as a function of human temporality. The project to establish an ontological unity with otherness, to recast apparently external relations as internal ones, is perpetually thwarted by a temporal movement that undercuts any provisional achievement of unity. In every case, satisfaction is tempered by the knowledge of impending time which is grasped phenomenologically as a relentless demand that the self renew its satisfaction in the present. The achievements of desire are consummations which must invariably give way to renewed desire; satisfaction is thus always provisional and never final or definitive. Hyppolite thus transforms Hegel's journeying subject into a Faustian character who, in Goethe's words, is forever "blundering with desire towards fruition, and in fruition pining for desire."[15]

Only through positing an imaginary distinction between history and time can Kojève entertain a true and final satisfaction for desire; history in his view is less subject to time than it is its organizing principle; indeed, for Kojève, time arises as a feature of historical acts or projects, but otherwise exerts no power. One may thus conclude that Kojève's historical acts are historical in a deeply paradoxical sense, for they transcend time in the moment that they consecrate time. History, as the progressive revelation of universal values, is a normative construal of time, a model of unity imposed upon an existential reality of perpetual disunity. In this sense, Kojève's view of history is the denial of existential time, a denial that allows him to imagine a definitive satisfaction to desire.

From both of these formulations, we seem to learn that desire can achieve satisfaction only through the temporary denial of time, i.e., through the *imagined or conjectured state of presence* for which time discriminations are irrelevant. The ideal of self-sufficiency that haunts post-Hegelian thinking is a nostalgia for a life freed of the exigencies of temporality—one that could escape a fate of continual self-estrangement and then death. Kojève essays to recast satisfaction in the secular terms of historical action, while Hyppolite eschews the possibility of self-sufficiency, with the qualification that the "life beyond death" that haunts the project of desire remain a *meaningful* conjecture, an imaginary hope that gives meaning to the actual strivings of finite human beings.

Sartre concurs with Hyppolite on this point: human desire is motivated

[94]

and structured by a projected unity with the world which must remain a pure projection, an imaginary dream. For Sartre, desire labors under imaginary ideals which give meaning to desire even as they elude desire's reach. The effort at anthropogenesis elaborated by Kojève finds existential transcription in the Sartrian contention that all human desire is a function of the desire to become God. But for Sartre, this desire is bound to fail. Kojève, on the other hand, thought that godlike men were possible; he conceived historical agents like Napolean and Hegel as capable of an anthropogenetic creation of history through eliciting the pervasive recognition of Others. For Sartre, however, anthropogenetic desires can only be realized in an *imaginary* mode. In Sartrian terms, then, insofar, as Kojève deems certain individuals to be godlike men, he has transfigured them into imaginary characters. Indeed, whenever we conceive of a satisfaction for desire, we do so only through participating in the domain of the imaginary. Sartre's contention throughout his career is that only in the imaginary can a timeless presence can be entertained, a transfigured temporality that relieves us provisionally from the exigencies of perpetual transience and self-estrangement, and constitutes the ideal of satisfaction. This ideal is thus defined as the privilege of imagination, a position that will have consequences for Sartre's view of the *artistic* world as the exclusive realm of satisfaction, the telos of human strivings.

I will not argue that Sartre's doctrine of desire is derived solely from Hegel and his French commentators, nor will I attempt to prove that Sartre self-consciously sought to extend the tradition we have been following here. However, we can see that Sartre's dualism of in-itself and for-itself is Hegel's logic in modern dissolution,[16] and that his assertion of the internal non-coincidence of human beings reflects both the phraseology and meaning of Hegel's French *explicateurs*. Sartre's contention in *Being and Nothingness* that "man is the desire to be" (*BN 565*) echoes Hyppolite's earlier claim that "the vocation of man (is) to make himself be. . . . We should recall that this being is . . . the being of desire" (*GS* 167). Rather than assert a relation of *influence* between authors—although Sartre apparently attended Kojève's lectures—I restrict myself to a consideration of how the ideal of an absolute synthesis of self and world is taken up by Sartre in his understanding of desire. Accordingly, I will examine once again the role and extent of negation as the principle of desire, and the paradox of determinate freedom which characterized the corporeal pursuit of the absolute. Extending the rift between substance and subject, Sartre can be seen to enhance the powers of the negative—desire comes to be seen as a *choice,* a *judgment,* and a *project of transfiguration.* Desire is always and only resolved in the imaginary, a Sartrian truth which conditions the various projects of desire throughout mundane life, in sexuality, and in the creation of literary works.

Sartre's ontological dualism of for-itself and in-itself can be seen as a reformulation of the paradox of determinate freedom, the perpetual self-estrangement of the subject which makes the ideal of self-sufficiency or final satisfaction into an impossibility. "Desire is the being of human reality" (*BN* 575) for Sartre, but it is desire governed by possibilities rather than actualities. The "desire to be" that characterized the impossible project of the for-itself is the desire to become the foundation of its own being—reflexive and anthropogenetic desire. Yet the factic aspect of existence, particularly the body, cannot be wholly self-created; it is simply given and, in Sartre's view; this givenness or externality is adverse to the project of the for-itself; it is from the start the guarantor of the for-itself's failure. The synthesis of for-itself and in-itself that forms the projected goal of desire is a hypothetical unity of self and world. The synthesis is an impossibility or, rather, a permanent possibility which can never be actualized.

In Sartre's theory of imagination and desire, this permanent possibility is what gives rise to the special character of imaginary works for Sartre: the impossibility of realizing the imaginary in the real world points to a solution that is second best, namely, the imaginative realization of this possibility in the world of the literary text. Imaginary works are so many "noble lies" which allow for the creation of transfigured worlds which remain the elusive dream of desire. Imaginary works, like images, are "essentially nothingness" (*PI* 18), but they are a nothingness with a determinate goal: they manifest the "desire to be" through creating an embodiment—the text—which reflects the self that is its author. The impossibility of realizing the imaginary gives rise, dialectically, to the de-realization of the world in the literary text. The imaginary provides a tentative satisfaction for desire because it effects a momentary denial of the factic; it creates its own temporality, it renders fluid the facticity of matter; it shapes contingency with the authorship of the human will.

In chapter 1, I described the *Phenomenology* as a fictional text, and the

[96]

Hegelian subject as a trope for the hyperbolic impulse itself. *Sa*₁.
*this imaginary dimension of desire explicit, describing human desire a*ₛ ₍.
constant way of authoring imaginary worlds. The pathos of Hegel's
subject remains in Sartre's work, and the inevitable failure of every fictive
journey is underscored as the vanity of all human passions. Reading Sartre
against the *Phenomenology* and the French reception of Hegel, we can
see that he has made explicit the key theme of Hegel's narrative of the
human subject—the metaphysical desire to deny difference through the
construction of false and partial worlds which nevertheless appear as
absolute. In Sartre's appropriation of this insight, desire itself becomes a
fiction-making endeavor, and the author of actual literary fictions becomes the privileged typologist of desire. The subject of desire does not
precede or contain desire, but is manufactured through the labor of desire,
articulated as an imaginary being, gaining reality only through the projection of desire onto the world. Sartre's notion of desire can thus be seen
as the result of a thoroughly dissembled doctrine of internal relations;
consciousness never becomes self-consciousness, but remains ontologically estranged, overcoming this estrangement only through the momentary enchantments of desire's imaginary satisfaction.

The Hegelian framework allowed us to see the ontological significance
of desire as a twofold structure, i.e., as the movement of an identity
comported outside itself in order to be itself. This comportment toward
the (apparently) external domain is analogous to Sartre's view of intentionality. The intentionality of desire characterizes the directionality of
consciousness which seeks to know the world outside itself. For the most
part, Sartre views the world as forever external to consciousness, an
exteriority that can never be assimilated. Because the world cannot be
reclaimed as a constitutive aspect of consciousness, consciousness must
set up another relation to the world; it must interpret the world and
imaginatively transfigure the world. Desire becomes a way in which we
impulsively situate ourselves in the world: it is the primary act, an act
incessantly performed by which we define ourselves in situation. In effect,
desire is the building of ourselves that we perform daily, and only rarely
under the aegis of reflective thought.

The cognitive component of desire—that which constitutes it as a
reflexive and interpretive act of consciousness—is understood by the
Sartre of *Being and Nothingness* as pre-reflective choice. As such, it is

both an epistemological and ontological relation. As non-positional awareness, desire is an epistemological relation which encompasses more than purely reflective kinds of judgments; in effect, desire forms the intentional structure of all emotional judgments—a theme to be addressed later. As an "upsurge" of consciousness, desire reveals human being as a self-determining or choosing being, a contingency that must *give itself* determinate form.

For Sartre, then, desire is both a relation to exteriority and a self-relation; but in post-Hegelian style, these two relations lack mediation in a dialectical unity. Consciousness is in exile from its world, and knows itself only in and through its *exclusion* from the world. Accordingly, the world bends to the human will only in the imaginary mode. Confronted with the impossibility of finding itself as a being, Sartre's existential subject is one who thematizes this very impossibility, who makes it his meditation, and ultimately derives from it a literary form. "The desire to be" is constitutive of human life, and yet the impossibility of ever "being" in a definitive sense appears as an ontological necessity; caught in the paradox of determinate freedom—of being either free or determinate but never both at once—human beings are forced to desire the impossible. And impossibility guarantees the continued life of desire, the paradoxical striving that characterizes human beings essentially.

Desire can relieve human beings of the consciousness of their own negativity—whether that be their temporality or freedom or finitude—only through magically instating a provisional presence. The incantation of presence is an imaginary venture that can only claim plausibility in an imaginary world and hence is still no absolute satisfaction for desire. This incantation can be a reciprocal creation as in the case of sexuality, or it can be a literary transfiguration of the negative, remaining in every instance a struggle against difference which can never wholly be won. Desire thus reveals our ineluctable freedom in the face of ontological exile, a freedom that necessarily attends the world but can never relinquish itself there. We can never wholly lose ourselves, but neither can we achieve that ideal of anthropogenesis that would make us pure freedoms. Sartre's persistent claim seems to be that we interpret the world even as we live it, that all immediacy is tempered by ontological disjunction and some semblance of self-awareness. Even in the experiences in which we appear alien to ourselves, seized or overwhelmed, a pre-reflective strategy of

[98]

choice is at work, a strategy that seeks to establish a determinate reality for the self so that it can be known, and, in being known, created.

For Sartre, desire is the process of creating ourselves, and insofar as we are in that process, we are in desire. Desire is not simply sexual desire, nor is it the kind of focused wanting that usually goes by that name. It is the entirety of our spontaneous selves, the "outburst" that we are, the upsurge that draws us toward the world and makes the world our object, the intentionality of the self. As the world appears as a complex historical and biographical situation, desire becomes a central way in which we seek a social place for ourselves, a way of finding and refinding a tentative identity within the network of the social world.

The theme of desire can only be fully explored for Sartre in the context of a life whose "choice of being" can be reconstructed and explained. For Sartre, biography is precisely such an inquiry. And insofar as Sartre contends that all desire finds an imaginary resolution, it makes sense to see him turn again and again to those lives that have given imaginary forms to desire. Before I examine Sartre's appraisal of two of these lives, Genet and Flaubert, I must first recount the steps of this theory: desire and the imaginary, desire as a choice of being, desire and incantatory creation. In turning to biographical studies, Sartre implicitly asks a question with rhetorical consequences for his own life's work, namely, what is the desire to write? "Why write?" is an extension of "why give desire determinate form?" and, in the case of fiction writers, "why give form to impossible worlds?" I asked at the outset, what makes desire possible? For Sartre, it is precisely the domain of the merely possible that conditions desire; the conditions of desire are the *nonactualities* of our lives, the determinate absences of the past and the merely suggested and unexplored realms of the present.

3

Sartre: The Imaginary Pursuit of Being

A desire is never satisfied to the letter precisely because
of the abyss that separates the imaginary from the real.
Sartre, *The Psychology of the Imagination*

1. Image, Emotion, and Desire

Sartre's early studies of the imagination, *L'imagination* and *L'imaginaire*, differ in style and purpose, but both outline an intentional theory of imaginative consciousness that has far-reaching consequences for a theory of emotion and desire. The first of these, published in 1936, criticizes theories of imagination that fail to distinguish between imagination and perception and that posit the "image" as a self-contained reality posing somewhere between consciousness and its object. In this treatise, Sartre follows the Husserlian program of phenomenology and calls for a reflexive analysis of imagination as a form of consciousness. Sartre here criticizes empiricist and intellectualist theories alike, and calls for an analysis of imagination based on experience, but not on the reduction of experience to sense data. An exercise in the epistemological debates concerning the proper approach to the imagination, this particular work of Sartre's does not address the larger question of the existential origins and meanings of imagining.

The second book, *L'Imaginaire*, published in 1940, restates the thesis of the earlier tract, namely, that images ought to be understood as forms of intentional consciousness, but also makes some forays into the existential ground of imagining. Throughout this book, largely in the context of unsystematic asides, Sartre begins his speculations on the relationship between desire and the imaginary. In this context, intentionality becomes an essential structure not merely of perception and imagination, but also of feeling. Dismissing the claims of representational theories of knowledge, Sartre claims that perception, imagination, and feeling are intentional forms of consciousness, i.e., that they refer to objects in the world and are not to be construed as impoverished perceptions or solipsistic enterprises. Indeed, Husserl's doctrine of intentionality signified for Sartre the end to solipsistic idealism in the tradition of modern epistemology ("I," 4–5).

Sartre's extension and reformulation of Husserl's view of intentionality entails a shift from an epistemological to an existential perspective. Intentionality for the Sartre of the 1930s signifies not merely the various ways in which we stand in knowing relations to things, but also an essential structure of the being of human life. The directionality of consciousness, its comportment toward things outside itself, comes to signify the ontological situation of human beings as a "spontaneity" and "upsurge." As intentional beings, it is not merely our knowledge that is *of* the world, but our essential passion as well; our desire is to be enthralled with the world, to be "of" the world. Intentionality comes to signify human access to the world, the end to theories that close off consciousness and subjectivity from the world, forcing them to reside behind the dense screen of representation.

Sartre discovered the possibility of a non-solipsistic view of consciousness in Husserl's *Ideas*.[1] Against a background of psychologistic theories of perception and knowledge, Husserl appeared to Sartre as the first philosopher successfully to avoid the "illusion of immanence"—the malaise of "digestive philosophy"—which understood objects of perception as so many contents of consciousness, fabricated and entertained within the spatial confines of the mind ("I" 4). In claiming that all consciousness is consciousness *of* an object, Husserl's view of intentional consciousness

[102]

affirmed the capacity of consciousness to reach outside itself and gain knowledge of the world that was not simply an elaboration of the self.

One might suspect that Sartre fashions himself a realist, yet he consistently qualifies the ascription, arguing instead that neither consciousness nor the world is primary, but that both "are given in one stroke: essentially external to consciousness, the world is nevertheless essentially relative to consciousness" ("I" 4). The world does not unilaterally impress itself on consciousness, as if consciousness were a *tabula rasa* to be formed at will by the contingencies of the world; nor does consciousness create the world as a particular representation. Consciousness reveals the world through determinate intentional relations; it presents the world through specific modes without ever denying the essential externality of that world. Although the world never makes itself known outside of an intentional act, this noematic pole of experience—the object pole—is in itself irreducible; every intentional act, by virtue of being directed toward a noematic correlate, affirms the independence and externality of consciousness and its world. In Sartre's early essay on intentionality, he affirms the difference between consciousness and world as an external relation, but insists that this very externality is what binds the two indissolubly. The externality of this relation assures a non-solipsistic encounter with the world: "You see this tree, to be sure. But you see it just where it is: at the side of the road, in the midst of the dust, alone and writhing in the heat, eight miles from the Mediterranean coast. It could not enter into your consciousness for it is not of the same nature as consciousness" ("I" 4).

Consciousness, then, does not apprehend the world in virtue of a common identity with the world, except insofar as consciousness and world represent noetic and noematic poles which are structurally isomorphic.[2] This structural isomorphism, however, does not refute the ontological distinctness of both poles: one intends the world in the mode of fearing, imagining, desiring, yet the world cannot intend consciousness in the mode of fearing or desiring, and neither can consciousness successfully enclose itself in its object without first denying itself as consciousness—the denying of which would, in effect, affirm itself as consciousness, the power to negate. Consciousness eludes the world even as the world—and its own self-elision—remains its proper and necessary theme. Consciousness, for the Sartre of "Intentionality" as well as *The Transcendence of the Ego,* is a translucent revelation of the world, an active presentation,

[103]

which moves toward the world as a nothingness driven to disclose. The ontological difference between consciousness and world is not a difference between *kinds* of objects; indeed, consciousness is not an object at all, but rather the possibility of the presentation of objects. Consciousness confronts the world as a nonactuality actively in pursuit of the actual; the ontological difference between consciousness and world is the difference between nothingness and being; "consciousness (is) an irreducible fact which no physical image can account for except perhaps the quick, obscure image of a burst. . . . I can no more lose myself in the tree than it can dissolve itself in me. I'm beyond it; it's beyond me" ("I" 5).

Sartre viewed the notion of intentionality as a liberation from idealism and as a vindication of the cognitive function of a variety of modes of consciousness apart from representational consciousness: "pure 'representation' is only one of the possible forms of my consciousness 'of' this tree; I can also love it, fear it, hate it . . . hating another is just a way of bursting forth toward him" ("I" 5). Emotions are various forms of presentation, kinds of intentionalities, which, according to Sartre, are "ways of apprehending the world" (*E* 52).

In *The Emotions: Outline of a Theory* and in the cited article on intentionality, desire is referred to as a possible intentional relation, one among many affective presentations of the world; in the *Psychology of the Imagination* desire begins to take on a privileged status as a form of intentionality that informs all other emotional forms of presentation. The discussion of desire in the *Psychology of Imagination*, although unsystematic and largely suggestive, begins to elucidate desire as coextensive with consciousness itself. This text suggests that desire is the fundamental structure of intentionality and that intentional relations—relations of desire—are not merely cognitive in the sense of presentifying acts of consciousness, but signify the ontological status of human beings as "the desire to be."

Before establishing desire as coextensive with intentional consciousness generally, we must turn to the *Psychology of Imagination* and to *The Emotions* to evaluate certain inconsistent, even contradictory, features of Sartre's theory of intentionality. On the one hand, Sartre claims that intentionality guarantees that emotions are actually "about" something outside of the self: "the desirable moves the desiring" (*TE* 56). On the other hand, emotions are considered to be a "degraded" or magical form of consciousness, an apprehension of the world that is essentially imaginary, a flight. Similarly, desire is seen to be a response to the desirable, an "apprehension" and "discovery" of the other, and yet it is also seen to be an imaginary pursuit that must remain a mere "incantation" that can never reach its object but only effect an imaginary construction. An ambiguity, or perhaps a paradox, appears to afflict Sartre's discussion of the intentionality of affective consciousness, for it would seem impossible that desire be at once a revelation *and* an imaginary degradation of the world. My procedure here, however, will be to approach this paradox with generosity. Where paradox characterizes all human activity, one must exercise caution in making charges of contradiction, for contradiction in Sartre's theory may not necessarily indicate the exclusive presence of falsehood, but may indicate that truth never appears unfettered of its opposite.

Sartre's ambiguous relation to Husserl gives us a context for understanding the paradoxical character of his own view. Sartre criticized Husserl's theory of intentionality most notably for the postulation of a transcendental ego that exists prior to its intentional relations. In the *Transcendence of the Ego* Sartre argued that such a postulation deprived the doctrine of intentionality of its most insightful contribution to epistemology, namely, the non-solipsistic character of consciousness. If consciousness is defined by intentionality, then the *object* of consciousness unifies consciousness. According to Sartre, Husserl was mistaken to seek recourse to a Kantian "I" which ostensibly provided for the possibility of synthesizing perceptions prior to any actual synthesis, for if consciousness is directional, and if it is truly "of" the object, consciousness will organize itself in the very process of thinking the object:

> It is possible that those believing "two and two make four" to be a *content* of my representation may be obliged to appeal to a transcendental and subjective principle of unification, which will then be the I. But it is precisely Husserl who has no need of such a principle. The object is transcendent to the consciousnesses which grasp it, and it is in the object that the unity of the consciousnesses is found. (*TE* 138)

In Sartre's view, the "ego is not the owner of consciousness; it is the object of consciousness" (*TE* 97). Moreover, consciousness only discovers itself as an ego when it becomes reflected consciousness. In reflecting upon its own spontaneity, i.e., consciousness as unreflected, the ego is constituted;

agency is discovered and posited only after the act. "Consciousness," Sartre claims, "is aware of itself insofar as it is consciousness of a transcendent object" (*TE* 40). This 'I' which consciousness discovers reflectively is not a ready-made 'I,' but an 'I' that is constituted through the acknowledgment rendered by a reflective consciousness which takes its own spontaneity as its object. For Sartre, "the ego is an object apprehended, but also an object constituted by reflective consciousness" (*TE* 80).

Sartre's rejection of the transcendental ego entailed a radical reinterpretation of the Husserlian "epoché" as well. In Sartre's terms, it was not necessary to leave the natural attitude for a transcendental perspective by which the intentional acts of the empirical ego might be described; for Sartre, the shift between *pre-reflective* consciousness—consciousness that is non-positionally aware of itself as it is aware of an object—and *reflective* consciousness—the consciousness that takes stock of the spontaneous acts of unreflected consciousness as well as the pre-reflective awareness that accompanies those acts—was a shift that occurred within the natural attitude. According to Sartre, we can reflect upon the conditions of the emergence of consciousness from within everyday experience:

If the "natural attitude" appears wholly as an effort made by consciousness to escape from itself by projecting itself into the *me* and becoming absorbed there, and if this effort is never completely rewarded, and if a simple act of reflection suffices in order for conscious spontaneity to tear itself abruptly away from the I and be given as independent, then the ἐποχή is no longer a miracle, an intellectual method, an erudite procedure: it is an anxiety which is imposed on us and which we cannot avoid: it is both a pure event of transcendental origin and an ever possible accident of our daily life. (*TE* 103).

Consciousness, for Sartre, has no need to take distance from itself, precisely because consciousness—as a paradoxical unity of pre-reflective and reflective consciousness—is *already* at a permanent distance from itself. The ego that consciousness creates for itself is a psuedo-self, a construct imposed upon the spontaneity of pre-reflective intentionality, which can never wholly account for it. When we come to understand desire as coextensive with spontaneous consciousness, with pre-reflective intentionality at large, we will see that the consequence of this non-coincidence of pre-reflective and reflective consciousness is that desire always outruns deliberate reflection, even as it is its own mode of pre-reflective consciousness.

The problem of imagination, i.e., imaginative consciousness, became a central problem for Sartre in his effort to expand Husserl's critique of psychologism and representational theories of consciousness. Moreover, the imagination aided in the elucidation of the structure of spontaneous or pre-reflective consciousness. With regard to the critique of psychologism, it was clear that if images were to be construed as intentional, one must account for what an image was "about" or "of." And if an image were nonrepresentational, how could it be construed as referential to something in the world? With regard to the elucidation of pre-reflective consciousness, Sartre sought to show not only that the imagination could be understood as a set of intentional relations, but that the imagination was a necessary constituent of *all* acts of knowing, indeed, that without the imagination the apprehension of objects in their "reality" would be impossible. In this sense, then, the imagination is a kind of spontaneous inquiry into the possible and hidden structures of reality, an epoché of the existing world which consciousness performs *within* mundane experience.

The positive conflation of the real with the existent can be seen fairly clearly in Hume's theory of knowledge, a theory that Husserl's *Experience and Judgement* explicitly criticizes and that Aron Gurwitsch takes as a clear example of what Husserlian intentionality seeks to refute.[3] Hume claims that "our ideas of bodies are nothing but collections formed by the mind of the ideas of the several distinct sensible qualities, of which objects are composed, and which we find to have a constant union with each other."[4] In Hume's view, these sensible qualities are what we directly know; they indicate an object outside of consciousness, but do this only obliquely. As direct impressions, they are actual evidence of what we know; they are, in effect, "real" elements within consciousness. These sensible qualities are both representations and constitutive features of the object itself. Hence, Hume claims, "those very sensations, which enter by the eye or ear, are . . . the true objects . . . there is only a single existence, which I shall call indifferently *object* or *perception* . . . understanding by both of them what any common man means by a hat, or shoe, or stone, or any other impression conveyed to him by his senses."[5] If these sensible qualities are impressions in consciousness, and if sensible qualities are the object itself, it would seem to follow that the object of consciousness is *in* consciousness. "Digestive philosophy" has its feast day.

Hume's identification of the real object of perception with the mass of sensible qualities or impressions presents a clear difficulty with respect to determining the continued identity of the object through time. If every time we confront an object we are in the presence of different sensible qualities—let us assume that the object turns, or we change our perspective—how are we to conclude with confidence that we are in the presence of the same object? How could we, on this view, derive a principle of identity from this theory by which we could adjudge a single object as itself even in its alteration? Hume's answer brings us closer to the problem of imagination that we are to consider in the context of Sartre. Because Hume is committed to the notion that only sensible qualities are real, he must view the organization of successive sense impressions into discrete objects as an act of faith, an imaginary construction that the mind poses for itself in order to make the world more livable. The identity of the object is, in effect, an achievement of the imagination. If only sensible qualities are real, and the criteria used to organize these qualities are not equally real, then the criteria are contingent, and according to Hume, are contributions of the imagination which are to be construed as so many projects of pretense.

Husserl's doctrine of intentionality sought to refute this problem of identity as it emerged from psychologistic theories such as Hume's. For Husserl, the object is "built up" through a series of intentional acts which are directed toward the noematic nucleus that is the object. These intentional acts can include those that simply present that which is immediately given, but can also include those that present dimensions of the object that are spatially or temporally hidden. This is the main concern of Husserl's *Phenomenology of Internal Time Consciousness,* the work that perhaps affected Sartre's appropriation of intentionality more than any other.[6] When we encounter one side of an ashtray, we do not, according to Husserl, take this three-sided entity to be the entirety of the thing; we encounter it as an object that is partially hidden and partially revealed. In other words, in the very perception of the object there is an act of *anticipation* at work which posits the criterion for a completed understanding of the object. This kind of knowledgeable anticipation is possible on the basis of the structural isomorphism that informs the noetic and noematic correlates of experience. Although absent for consciousness, the opaque aspects of the object are nevertheless meaningful to consciousness. The triumph of phenomenology in this regard has been to dignify the realm of the unexpressed and the absent as itself constitutive of meaningful reality. This is also one moment of commonality between Husserlian and Hegelian phenomenology: the essentiality of negation to reality. When we "know" that the hidden side of the object is there, and something about what it must be like, we do not know it through an arbitrary act of imagination that turns out to be an epistemic lie we regularly tell ourselves. The imaginary is structured, and itself structures any determinate act of knowing. The imagination allows us to understand the object in its completeness where perspectival or positivist thinking would fail. It is the move toward omniscience within any determinate act of consciousness.

The imagination is thus crucial for the constitution of objects in Husserl's view. If deprived of the imagination, we would only know truncated objects, the mere surface of things. Hence, Husserl's emphasis on the method of imaginary variation is essential in order to form a complete phenomenological description of any considered object. The imagination is consciousness' mundane effort to surpass perspective; the "presence" of the image is a full reality in itself.[7] The essence of the object, for Husserl, is to be found in its *ideal* reality, and the ideal is indicated through an imaginary inquiry into the object which successively reveals the *Abschattungen* of the object which cannot be simultaneously present to perceptual consciousness.

Sartre's *Psychology of the Imagination* follows upon Husserl's attempt to distinguish between the real and existent and, further, to vindicate the imagination as a bona fide form of consciousness with complex structures that intend objects. While Husserl sought to refute the kind of psychologism indicated in Hume's assessment of consciousness through recourse to the implicit harmony between an intending consciousness and its noematic fulfillment, Sartre clearly thought that a refutation was possible through an elucidation of the positional acts of consciousness. For Sartre, an image is not an object or a content, but a *relation* in which an object is either posited as not present or not existing, or not posited at all but presented in a way that is neutral with regard to the question of existence

(*PI* 16). For both Husserl and Sartre, the imagination is a set of intentional relations directed toward the world; and in the case of Sartre, it is a relation that seeks the de-realization of that world. For Sartre, this imagination is still intentional: it is directed toward the world in the mode of denial or de-realization.

Sartre's critique of Husserl's egological conception of intentionality has specific consequences for his appropriation of Husserl's view of the intentionality of imagination. For Husserl, the noetic pole of imaginary experience is said to intend certain kinds of objects and to contribute to the constitution of those objects. Hence, imaginary objects are to be understood as noematic correlates noetically intended as nonexisting: not as illusions or vague representations, but highly structured objects of consciousness. The imaginary is not a poor representation of the real; it does not aspire after reality at all, but is its own set of objects explicitly intended *as irreal*. Sartre clearly appreciates this achievement of Husserlian phenomenology to circumscribe and dignify the domain of the imaginary as an autonomous and structured domain of consciousness, and yet his refutation of the noetic pole of intentionality—a position that he inconsistently maintains—casts doubt on his ability to sustain this achievement within his own theory. Sartre's claim in the *Transcendence of the Ego* that consciousness is organized by the *object* of experience risks becoming a strongly behaviorist position unless it can offer an account of consciousness's contribution to its object. Sartre clearly wants to maintain that in the case of imaginary objects—images, in his terms—consciousness intends the image through one of four possible positional acts.[8] And yet, if we ask after an account of the structures of consciousness that permit for these four positional relations, we are left with no explanation if we accept the view of consciousness's intentionality as presented in these early works. If consciousness is a pure nothingness, a translucent phenomenon that merely lets the world appear, then we have no way to understand the modes of presentation that let the world appear as hateful, desirable, imaginary, etc. In addition, we have no way of understanding why different consciousnesses present the world differently, i.e., why the world might in one instance appear desirable to one consciousness, and disgusting to another. It cannot simply be the world that acts on consciousness in these various ways, but conciousness must arrange for its own experience, and Sartre's object-oriented version of intentionality cannot account for this apparent fact.

Sartre's interpretation of intentional consciousness as a translucent medium which lets the world appear leads him to the conclusion that emotional and imaginary consciousness, to the extent that they are opaque expressions of consciousness, are degraded forms of consciousness.[9] Image as well as emotion are flights from the world, de-realization that signify a retraction from the world. This aspect of Sartre's theory appears as a direct consequence of his object-oriented view of intentionality in that the denial or transformation of "given reality," i.e., of the world external to consciousness, is at once the congealing of consciousness as a translucent medium. While for Husserl the imaginary constitutes its own domain of objects, and provides a necessary function in the apprehension of given objects, for Sartre the imaginary is a failure of translucent consciousness, rather than a constitutive dimension. By claiming that only that which is *outside* consciousness has reality, Sartre appears to forfeit the claim of Husserlian phenomenology that he cherishes most: "for Husserl and the phenomenologists our consciousness of things is by no means limited to knowledge of them. Knowing of 'pure representation' is only one of the possible forms of my consciousness of this tree: I can also love it, fear it, hate it, and this surpassing of consciousness by itself that is called 'intentionality' finds itself again in fear, hatred and love" ("I" 5).

Sartre is clearly inconsistent on this point. He occasionally claims that images are part of our apprehension of the "real" and yet maintains in other contexts that they are de-realizing phenomena, flights from the real. This ambivalence which runs through *Being and Nothingness* appears to arise not merely as a function of his view of intentional consciousness but also in his contradictory accounts of "being." At times Sartre appears to argue as if the realm of exteriority is the sole locus of reality, and consciousness, a translucent intentionality which can immediately reveal being-in-itelf.[10] According to this view, the objects of consciousness are positive data of experience, and consciousness has no role in the constitution of their existence or meaning. Although an active movement toward objects, consciousness finds its consummate expression as a revelatory presentation, one that dissolves itself in letting the object appear. This belief in direct perception appears to rank Sartre among the positivists whom phenomenology has from its origin sought to refute. Reality is defined as a self-contained domain from which consciousness is excluded, yet consciousness can present or reveal this reality when it is enlightened consciousness, that is, free of imagery and emotion.

This consideration of Sartre's non-egological view of intentionality provides the context for understanding the problematic character of Sartre's view of imagination and, ultimately, of desire. Speaking in Husserlian terms, Sartre claims that images are objects consciousness presents to itself. Referring to positional acts of consciousness, Sartre appears to affirm consciousness as a structured activity that constitutes the objects of imaginary experience. Speaking, however, from what seems to be a positivist perspective, Sartre views images as an escape from the real. The implication of this second perspective is that reality ought to be confined to existing, positive phenomena, the very conflation of reality and existence that Husserl sought to repudiate. Sartre does claim that images are a kind of affective consciousness that is "also knowledge" (*PI* 103); hence, his disloyalty to the Husserlian program is not definitive. The discussion of affective consciousness that comes to inform Sartre's view of desire begins to take on its ambivalent character in the *Psychology of Imagination;* whether affectivity is an "apprehension" of the real or an indicator of solipsism is a question that haunts Sartre's discussion of the imaginary, the emotions, and desire. Insofar as Sarte comes to regard affectivity as a form of knowledge, he is forced to reconstruct his staunch repudiation of the noetic pole of experience. In the course of his theory the noetic is indeed reconstructed, but not along the epistemological lines set down by Husserl. The nonsubstantial being of the self, and of consciousness generally, is reformulated as the presence of choice at the origin of the self. The noetic pole of experience is reasserted, and with it, the cognitive function of affectivity, through the existential conception of the self. Objects are not merely "given" but "constituted" as well. The pursuit of being that characterized intentionality is not a pursuit unilaterally solicited by the world, but is motivated as well by the desire of a self in search of its own emergence. The world is understood in the context of a subjective project, and this project, an expression of the fundamental desire to be, is a *passionate* one; the efforts of knowledge to present the world are,

[112]

thus, always impassioned efforts of the self to find itself in the situation it both discovers and creates.

This shift from an epistemological to an existential model can be discerned within the *Psychology of the Imagination,* although it is not explicitly acknowledged in that text. Although the inquiry fashions itself as a project in descriptive phenomenology, it investigates as well the existential origins of imagining. The image is, for Sartre, strangely self-sufficient, a pure presence that fills its own space completely. Images differ from perceptions in that the latter have "an infinite number of relationships to other things" (*PI* 11). Sartre explains that "to exhaust the wealth of my perception would require infinite time." Images, on the other hand, give themselves in their entirety; they "suffer from an essential poverty" (*PI* 11) insofar as they bear no relationship to the rest of the world of perception, but are a kind of pure presence which the world of perception cannot provide.

The perceptual world is a landscape riddled with negation; the various relationships that hold between discrete phenomena are passively recorded and described by perceptual consciousness, and, *qua* perceptual, consciousness understands itself as inadequate to its world. In the image, the complexity and alterity of the perceptual world is denied, and the sense of limitation attending all perceptual consciousness is overcome. The image presents its object as absent or nonexistent or indifferent to any existential status. This "non-being" of the image is paradoxically the occasion of its fullness and presence. In effect, the absence that occasions the image is filled by the consciousness that attends it; the image is a "presence-within-absence," a way in which consciousness fills absences with itself. Images thus arise in virtue of the lacunae that exists in the perceptual world; they manifest a desire for presence and are a way of interpreting absence: "if the image of a dead loved one appears to me suddenly, I have no need of a 'reduction' to feel the ache in my heart: it is part of the image, it is the direct consequence of the fact that the image presents its object as not existing" (*PI* 17).

The perceptual world forbids the experience of consciousness as author of its world because the facticity and internal complexity of that world outruns perceptual consciousness. Inasmuch as the imagination posits its object as not existing, it is free to create an imaginary world as it sees it.

[113]

In the imagination the factic or perceptual world is put out of play; the imagination is thus a kind of bracketing procedure to be found in the ordinary experience of consciousness, and is a manifestation of that "anxiety" mentioned in *The Transcendence of the Ego* by which consciousness tears itself away from its ordinary involvement with the world. The world gains a kind of temporary presence to consciousness through the imaginary de-realization of the world: "alive, appealing, and strong as an image is, it presents its object as not being" (*PI* 18). The image is nevertheless sustained through a *belief* that the image has some kind of existence. The need to believe in the existence of the image and the inability to sustain this belief forms the ambiguous existential project at the origin of image making: "the false and ambiguous condition we reach thereby only seems to bring out in greater relief what we have just said: that we seek in vain to create in ourselves the belief that the object really exists by means of our *conduct* towards it: we can pretend for a second, but we cannot destroy the immediate awareness of its nothingness" (*PI* 18).

The imagination is thus a form of consciousness that embodies freedom, where freedom is defined as an overcoming of facticity and the transcendence of perspective. In perception the representative element is passive, but in the image, "this element, in what it has of the primary and incommunicable, is the product of a conscious activity, is shot through and through with a flow of creative will" (*PI* 20). Imaginative consciousness thus affords the experience of radical autonomy in Sartrian terms; the de-realization of the world is the advent of consciousness: "it follows necessarily that the object as an image is never anything more than the consciousness one has of it" (*PI* 20). If reality is identified with positive existence, the imagination is a flight from reality, a denial of the real; and yet if, following Husserl, we see absences as constitutive of the real, the imagination is the recourse to significant reality that perceptual life, according to Sartre, cannot attain. In the former case, consciousness falls into solipsism; in the latter, it gains access to hidden dimensions of the real. In either case, consciousness asserts itself at the limits of positive being, not merely constructing the world beyond its positive contours, but constructing itself as a creative activity.

As the existential origins of imagining are considered in greater detail in the section "The Imaginary Life," and in Sartre's references to affectivity throughout the *Psychology of Imagination*, we can see the increasing

[114]

emphasis on a subject-oriented view of intentionality. Sartre's realism which, in identifying the real with the existent, appears as a form of positivism, is increasingly preempted by a view of intentionality for which the project of desire is central. Sartre explains that the image is a subjective project to fancy the self as undaunted will: "the act of imagination is a magical one. It is an incantation destined to produce the object of one's thought, the thing one desires, in a manner that one can take possession of it" (*PI* 177).

Paralleling the view of emotions as magical efforts to overcome adversity, the image is a refusal of the factic world: "In that act there is always something of the imperious and the infantile, a refusal to take distance or difficulty into account" (*PI* 177). Images are not given as adumbrations (unless one purposefully intends the adumbrated version of an image, i.e., Peter in his home yesterday evening, rather than an image inclusive of more perspectives). Unlike perceptual objects, images are given all at once. In this sense, they are objects of desire that do not offer the resistance that objects of the perceptual world do in their external and, for the most part, truncated form. Hence, *an image is a relation to an object fully desired and fully appropriated:* "these objects do not appear, as they do in perception, from a particular angle; they do not occur *from a point of view;* I attempt to bring them to birth as they are in themselves" (*PI* 177). The tentative rise to omniscience afforded by the imagination occasions the momentary satisfaction of desire: "what I want and what I get is just Peter" (*PI* 177). The image thus represents a satisfaction for desire predicated upon the de-realization of the factic world. Desire seeks magically to possess its object through instating itself as the creator of that object. Images accompany most affective states, according to Sartre, because affectivity or emotion has an intentionality that seeks the magical possession of and control over the world; emotions are the magical means by which we imagine alternate worlds. Emotions thus require images in their effort to create the world anew, if only in a possible mode: "To become conscious of Paul as hateful, annoying, sympathetic, disturbing, winning, repulsive, etc., is to confer upon him a new quality, to construct him along a new dimension" (*PI* 99).

Sartre does not provide a formulaic way of understanding the interrelationship of images, emotion, and desire, although his various remarks in *The Psychology of Imagination* do provide a basis for a plausible

[115]

reconstruction of his developing views. Toward the end of that work he ventures the following formulation: "the image is a kind of ideal for feeling, it represents a limited state for the affective consciousness, the state in which desire is also knowledge" (*PI* 103). In his view, most affective states envision reality in a subjunctive mode, and, hence, maintain images as central features of their intentionality: the image is the kind of undifferentiated presence toward which desire strives, and emotions appear to be so many permutations of human desire. On the one hand, the creation of objects appears to be the project that structures affectivity and imagining, for both of these activities are subordinate to a fundamental desire to become the foundation of one's world. In this way, desire, as the desire to ground one's own reality, forms the basis of both emotional and imaginative consciousness. On the other hand, desire is intentional, and not merely reflexive; the objects of desire are "outside" the self, which is the meaning of Sartre's claim that it is the desirable that moves desire. The twofold character of desire as intentional and reflexive requires an explanation that establishes that the idealistic and realistic projects of desire are not simple contradictions but dynamic and constitutive paradoxes.

Sartre's argument that desire seeks to construct its object appears to conflict with his claim that desire is a form of knowledge. We need to ask, what kind of creative knowledge is human desire? Is it conceivable that desire both discovers and creates its object? What sense can we make of this paradoxical view? When Sartre claims that desire is itself a form of knowledge, he appears to differentiate between intentional and representational knowing. Desire does not "know" its object in the sense that the desired object corresponds to the objective object that allegedly stands behind the desired object. "Knowing" for Sartre always takes place through determinate acts of presentation and through determinate modes of appearance. The object is never received immediately apart from a specific manner of presenting the object; indeed, even if the object is to be considered 'objectively', it must be intended as such. Hence, the desired object is not to be differentiated from some "objective" object, for the object must be construed in terms of modes of appearance, and if the object appears as desirable, its desirability is constitutive of its phenomenal being.

The critical problem that attends this explanation is that it seems

[116]

difficult, if not impossible, to differentiate between an illusory and an objective appearance. How would one, on such a view, account for the deceptiveness of desire? How would one account for the experience of displaced wants and illusory objects of desire? Is there a critical difference between image and illusion, between the imaginary world desire seeks to create and self-deception generally? If desire seeks to deceive the self into believing facticity is surpassable, is not all desire a project of self-deception? What sense does it make to refer to desire as a form of knowledge if it is at base a self-deceiving enterprise?

The full answer to these questions requires a turn to *Being and Nothingness* and the discussion of bad faith. At this point, however, we can approach the problem tentatively through our discussion of desire and the image. In Sartre's view, desire is a form of knowledge insofar as it "envisions" its object in a determinate way, i.e., insofar as desiring is always coextensive with imagining. Desire does not attend to what is given in perception, but, rather what is hidden in perception; it is, in a sense, an investigation into the significant dimensions of absence. It thematizes absence and thereby makes it present to itself. In this way desire is fundamentally a desire for plenitude, an effort to fill the vacuums of perceptual life: "the object as an image is a *definite want* (*un manque défini*); it takes shape as a cavity. A white wall *as an image* is a white wall *which is absent from perception*" (*PI* 179). And yet the image of the white wall is not an image of the wall as it appears in perception; the presence which the white wall acquires in imaginary consciousness is unattainable by a consciousness limited by perspective. The knowledge of the world that imagination affords, and that cannot be measured by its correspondence to perceptual objects, is that of the *presence* of things. The consciousness of a pair of smooth, delicate hands, Sartre remarks, "is rather of something fine, graceful, pure, with a nuance of strictly individual fineness and purity." These nuances "appear" to consciousness; they do not "present themselves in their representative aspect." He explains: "this affective mass has a character which lacks clear and complete knowledge: the mass is *present*" (*PI* 101).

Desire discovers an imaginary object that has certain features no perceptual object can possibly have. The *presence* of the object is given to desire, i.e., it is what desire is after, and this presentifying function of desire requires imaginative consciousness to articulate and establish the

[117]

condition of belief in this presence. The object of desire is *unreal* to the extent that it is not perceptual. And yet, perceptual consciousness is unreal to the extent that it is limited by the exigencies of perspective and ad-umbration. Whether one defines "reality" in the terms of perceptual consciousness, or whether one defines it in terms of an hypostasized imagination freed from the constraints of perspective, the definition de-termines whether desire and imaginary consciousness generally is seen to generate illusion or truth. Insofar as Sartre remains within the Husserlian view of intentionality, the second criterion appears to hold: the negative aspect of the object remains constitutive of its objectivity and, correspond-ingly, the negating function of consciousness—its status as desire—gives consciousness access to the absent regions of objects. Insofar as Sartre restricts his definition of reality to positive being, the given objects of perceptual consciousness, desire and the imaginary are, indeed, flights from the real rather than its revelation.

In Sartre's *The Emotions: Outline of a Theory,* published in 1939, a year before *The Psychology of Imagination,* affectivity is presented as both referential and transfigurative. On the one hand, he claims that "the affected subject and the affective object are bound in an indissoluble synthesis" (E 52). And he concludes, "emotion is a certain way of appre-hending the world." On the other hand, he argues that emotions are "flights" and degradations of reality: "the hyper-tension of fear or sadness . . . aims at denying the world or discharging it of its affective potential by denying it" (E 74). And again: "anger appears . . . as an escape: the subject in anger resembles a man who, lacking the power to undo the knots of the ropes that bind him, twists and squirms about in his bonds" (E 37). For Sartre, emotions are ineffective responses to the various difficulties of the world, expressions of a fundamental impotence in which human beings are caught: "[emotions] . . . represent a particular subter-fuge, a special trick, each one of them being a different means of eluding a difficulty" (E 32).

Sartre's interpretation of emotions as imaginary constructs reveals a pessimistic view of the efficacy of emotion. When the angry man is said to be "lacking the power to undo the knots of the ropes that bind him," anger is seen in this context as a manifestation of powerlessness. But it seems we must ask, is not anger also a form of power? When Sartre argues that emotions are fundamentally inefficacious, that they achieve only a magical transformation of the world, we seem compelled to ask, why is it that emotion cannot reach the world? What is the gulf that resides between emotional consciousness and the world toward which it is directed? What makes of emotions the useless passions that Sartre describes?

The difficulty of the world, Sartre argues, is a permanent phenomenological given: "this world is *difficult*. This notion of difficulty is not a reflective notion which would imply a relationship to me. It is there, on the world" (*E* 58–59). The adversity of the world is its inaccessibility to consciousness, its brute givenness, its absolute alterity. And yet this world that resists consciousness cannot be the same world that reveals itself to consciousness in its very structure, in accord with Husserlian noetic-noematic harmonies. Again, "the world" is viewed inconsistently; first as a noematic correlate to a structurally similar consciousness (the Husserlian view), and then, as a brute and impenetrable reality which consciousness can only escape (the positivist view). The validity of this second interpretation seems to be immediately called into question by the apparent fact that emotions *are* occasionally efficacious in transforming the world. If we regard anger not as a sign of definitive impotence but as a possible source of power from which efficacious action might draw, Sartre's view of emotions as *degradations* of the real, as merely *magical* transformations of the world, appears to meet a serious challenge. Robert Solomon suggests that Sartre himself is inconsistent in this regard:

For Sartre, the concept of magic serves to underscore the *ineffectiveness* of emotional behavior, the fact that our emotions merely change the direction of consciousness without really changing *the* world at all. . . . The problem is that Sartre continues, in the fashion of those psychologists whom he castigates, to treat the emotions as "isolated" and the "world of emotions" as a world that is distinct from the "real" world of effective action and commitment. But it is our emotions which motivate our actions and sustain our commitments. The "fundamental project" that dominates so much of Sartre's writings is by its very nature an emotional project, one in which we heavily invest ourselves, even to the extent of reorganizing ("transforming") our entire world around its demands.[11]

An even stronger objection to the view of emotions as exclusively engaged in projects of denial and de-realization can be found by looking at the contribution of emotion to all of consciousness. The "spontaneity" of pre-reflexive consciousness, the "upsurge" of consciousness which constitutes the lived experience of prereflective intentionality, is itself a passion or desire which is the very being of consciousness. Emotions can be understood as various permutations of this fundamental engagement with the world, the fundamental project of human life as "a striving to be." Every act that seeks to make the world present to consciousness, that seeks, in effect, to construct the world as present to consciousness, is an expression of this primary urge toward plenitude which characterizes intentional consciousness and the being of human reality. In effect, no act of consciousness is without this affective structure. *The intentionality of consciousness is lived concretely as the diffuse and insistent experience of human desire.*

I asked at the outset of this discussion whether Sartre's account of affectivity suffered from inconsistency or paradox, assuming that if the former were the case, the theory proves inadequate, and if the latter were true, the theory might be retrieved. Although I have pointed out an inconsistency in Sartre's thought, a conflict over the interpretation of the accessibility of the world and, correlatively, the efficacy of emotional consciousness, I have not exhausted the possible interpretations of Sartre's theory. The either/or that seems to haunt his theory of affective consciousness consists of a battle between solipsism and realism; either desire—and affectivity generally—is structured by a subjective project to achieve an omnipotent presence to the world or desire is "moved by the desirable," elicited and structured by the object of consciousness. *Being and Nothingness* can be seen to take up the problem of this apparent paradox and to devise a philosophical program for making sense of affective consciousness as both referential and magical.

Because the world is "difficult," consciousness can never achieve the projected unity Hegel considered plausible; indeed, we might interpret the succession of theories from Hegel to Sartre as the gradual revelation of the world's inherent difficulty. For Sartre, the ontological disjunction of consciousness and world does not preclude the intentional or referential function of consciousness, but it does suggest that intending the world and identifying with it are very different enterprises. Hegel's contention that consciousness can only come to know that to which it has always already been ontologically bound does not hold true for Sartre. Accordingly, knowledge is not to be understood as a series of acts whereby the identities of consciousness and world are enhanced to include each other, but as a relation of permanent paradox which never gets resolved.

[120]

Sartre's journeying subject does not develop in order to discover, finally, that it has been all along that which it has become; on the contrary, this subject is a novel creation, a being fashioned from nothingness. Accordingly, intentional consciousness comes to know its objects as external to itself, but this externality is never given in unadulterated form; we never know objects or Others outside of the experience of their fundamental difficulty, their exteriority, and, hence, we always bring to those objects our own relations to difficulty—our emotions. I turn to *Being and Nothingness* in order to understand the twofold meaning of exteriority for the project of desire, as that which impassions human beings and as that from which we take flight.

The rift Sartre presents between subject and substance further establishes consciousness as a negativity or, as Kojève claims, "a hole in Being," which can never relinquish its negativity through participation in a more inclusive synthesis. Sartre's notion of consciousness is that of a negating negativity, a negation that turns against itself and thereby produces itself as a determinate being. The desire that motivates human life becomes for Sartre a process of *reflexive negation* which creates a self and a process of *reciprocal negation* between selves through which each creates the Other. I turn first to the labor of negation by which the self creates itself, and then, in the context of Sartre's discussion of sexuality, to the process of intimate recognition through which we constantly bring each other into being.

The Strategies of Pre-reflective Choice: Existential Desire in Being and Nothingness

The point of vision and desire are the same—Wallace Stevens, "An Ordinary Evening in New Haven"

Sartre's discussions of desire in *Being and Nothingness* take place first in the context of intersubjective relations, and then again in the section on existential psychoanalysis. In the former section desire is understood as sexual desire,[12] and in the latter, desire is understood as what might be called existential desire.[13] In the former context, sexual desire is but one permutation of "the desire to be," an existential project that structures the spontaneity of the for-itself. Because existential desire is considered to be more fundamental in Sartre's account, I turn first to the "desire to be" and, in the following section, consider its meaning in the context of a reciprocal sexual exchange.

Sartre's task in "Existential Psychoanalysis" is to show the inadequacies of psychological theories that posit human desire as a substance or natural given, or as a psychic irreducible that serves as a primary cause of human behavior. He argues that the psychological tendency to reduce human behavior to certain primary desires reveals a refusal to radicalize the investigation of desire. For Sartre, one must treat desire not as a cause, but as an expression of a prior and more fundamental choice:

> We are told, for example, that Flaubert had a "grandiose ambition" and all of the previously quoted description depends on this original ambition. So far so good. But this ambition is an irreducible fact which by no means satisfies the mind. The irreducibility here has no justification other than refusal to push the analysis further. There where the psychologist stops, the fact confronted is given as primary. (*BN* 560)

Flaubert's ambition is considered as a positive datum of experience, a contingency that, in Sartre's view, is no different than the qualities that adhere to natural objects. In an ironic portrayal of this kind of psychological empiricism, Sartre remarks, "this rock is covered with moss, the rock next to it is not. Gustave Flaubert had literary ambition, and his brother Achille lacked it. That's the way it is" (*BN* 560).

Sartre rejects a naturalistic view of the relationship of desire to personal identity that is modeled on the relationship of contingent natural properties to their self-identical substance. Although desires might well be understood as "properties" in Sartre's view, they are neither externally nor fixedly related to the substance to which they belong. Following Spinoza, Sartre views such properties as modes through which a substance determines itself:

> In one sense Flaubert's ambition is a fact with all a fact's contingency—and it is true that it is impossible to advance beyond that fact—but in another sense it *makes itself*, and our satisfaction is a guarantee to us that we may be able to grasp beyond this ambition something more, something like a radical decision which, without ceasing to be contingent, would be the veritable psychic irreducible. (*BN* 560)

[122]

For Sartre, then, one does not "have" a desire as one has a possession that one might on another occasion lose by mistake or cast off in a moment of boredom. Desires are not contingent features of otherwise self-subsisting subjects; they are the modes through which the subject comes to subsist; they are, to extend the metaphor, the subject's very subsistence. Desire does not indicate a ready-made self, but reveals instead a self having-to-be-formed; indeed, desire is the mode through which the self comes to be, i.e., its mode of realization.

The investigation that seeks to uncover the ground of Flaubert's ambition would, according to Sartre, have to ask how it was that Flaubert determines himself as ambitious. Ambition is no longer considered as a cause, but as a product of a reflexive relation. The "radical decision" which is, for Sartre, the true psychic irreducible, is a movement of inner negation which establishes Flaubert's ambition as a project and pursuit. And yet Flaubert does not determine himself in a vacuum; he determines himself with respect to a world. Indeed, every desire, like every emotion, indicates obliquely an existential orientation toward the world as such, a decision regarding how to live in the particular world—the *situation*—in which one finds oneself (*BN* 563). Flaubert's desire "to be a great writer" is at once a choice of authorship and a choice of being; authorship is a way of being, a radical decision concerning how to be. Hence for Sartre, the radical decisions expressed in and through desires are always reflexive and intentional; they are projects of self-determination, but always undertaken with reference to the world. Every particular desire indicates an existential choice of how to be:

The most discerning ethicists have shown how a desire reaches beyond itself. Pascal . . . revealed that in an activity which would be absurd if reduced to itself, there was a meaning which transcended it; that is, an indication which referred to the reality of man in general and to his condition. Similarly Stendahl . . . and Proust . . . have shown that love and jealousy cannot be reduced to the strict desire of possessing a *particular* woman, but that these emotions aim at laying hold of the world in its entirety through the woman. (*BN* 562)

Sartre outlines three different but interrelated levels of meaning to desire that elucidate the status of all human desire as indicating the desire to be. Every desire presupposes an "original choice" or a generalized desire to be, an unspecified desire to live and be "of" the world. Second, desires

[123]

indicate a "fundamental choice" which is the mode of being through which a specific individual chooses to live—a way of life or determinate mode of being. And third, there are the myriad particular desires that reflect, through a complex symbolic connection, both the original and fundamental choices (*BN* 562). The first of these choices, the original desire to be, has no separable ontological status, but is expressed essentially through the fundamental choice: "the desire of being is always realized as the desire of a mode of being" (*BN* 567). And neither the original nor the fundamental choice makes itself known directly in experience, but must appear in the "myriads of concrete desires which constitute the web of our conscious life" (*BN* 567). Hence, particular desires express at once the specificity of the self, the radical decision concerning how to be which distinguishes individuals from one another, and the anonymous and universal projects of the self "to be," i.e., to overcome the ontological disjunction of consciousness and its world.

The desire to be is, for Sartre, an effort to gain an absolute presence to the world, to overcome externality and difference, in order that the self might finally coincide with itself and, hence, have a completed self-understanding. This desire to overcome ontological disjunction is, for Sartre, the desire to become God—a striving to overcome the limits of embodiment, perspective, and temporality which maintain the self at an ecstatic distance from itself:

God, value and supreme end of transcendence, represents the permanent limit in terms of which man makes known to himself what he is. To be man means to reach toward being God. Or if you prefer, man fundamentally is the desire to be God. (*BN* 566)

Human beings strive toward this end as a permanent impossibility. As the *desire* to be, this project remains an experience of dissatisfaction; desire reveals the lack in being that consciousness is, a lack that cannot be relinquished save through the death of consciousness. In this sense, desire indicates *freedom* which, in Sartrian terms, can only remain itself through transcending the in-itself. In effect, one is only free to the extent that one desires, for desire is the necessary expression for freedom: "Freedom is precisely the being which makes itself a lack of being. But since desire . . . is identical with lack of being, freedom can arise only as being which makes itself a desire of being" (*BN* 567).

[124]

The project to be God must be realized in and through "the free and fundamental desire which is the unique person" (*BN* 567). Personal identity is a particularized desire to be God, the effort to become the foundation of one's freedom and facticity, the anthropogenetic dream that haunts this post-Hegelian position. Although for Sartre the desire to be God characterizes an essential aspect of all human striving, there is choice with respect to how this project is realized; in effect, one decides what kind of God one wants to be. Sartre's essentialist contention that all human striving is derivative from the desire to be God does not become a determinism of desire; particular choices and situations remain variable features of these strivings. The ends of desire "are pursued in terms of a particular empirical situation, and it is this very pursuit which constitutes the surroundings *as a situation*" (*BN* 567). Like Spinoza's monad who endeavors to "persist in its own being,"[14] human striving is knowable only through its various modalities, and yet this underlying desire eludes determination even as it requires it. Our particular situated desires are our necessary access to the existential project which characterize human identity universally:

The fundamental project, the person, the free realization of human truth is everywhere in all desires. ... *It is never apprehended except through desires* (my emphasis)—as we can apprehend space only through bodies which shape it for us. ... Or, if you like, it is like the *object* of Husserl, which reveals itself only by *"Abschattungen"* and which does not allow itself to be absorbed by any one *Abschattung*. (*BN* 567)

Sartre's argument that the desire to be appears only through the particular desires in which it is expressed raises the problem of whether we can ever know that such a desire does, in fact, exist. If Sartre's postulation that a unifying desire structures the myriad desires of everyday life cannot be supported through direct reference to such a desire, how are we to refrain from dismissing this postulation as an unsupportable speculation? Sartre seems to affirm that a description of these nonempirical desires is possible through a reflexive turn of consciousness:

Fundamentally man is the *desire to be*, and the existence of this desire is not to be established by an empirical induction; it is the result of an *a priori* description of the being of the for-itself, since desire is a lack and since the for-itself is the being which is to itself its own lack of being. (*BN* 565)

Sartre warns against treating the original or fundamental desires as separable from empirical desire, and yet he suggests that there is an opacity to empirical desires that indicates the existential regions by which they are supported:

The desire to be by no means exists *first* in order to cause itself to be expressed subsequently by desires *a posteriori*. There is nothing outside of the symbolic expression which it finds in concrete desires. There is not first a single desire of being, then a thousand particular feelings, but the desire to be exists and manifests itself only in and through jealousy, greed, love or art, cowardice, courage, and a thousand contingent, empirical expressions which always cause human reality to appear to us only as *manifested* by a . . . specific person. (*BN* 565)

The possibility of recovering the existential projects of desire from their particular and determinate manifestations is grounded in the fact that reflective consciousness is itself related to the pre-reflective strategies of spontaneous desires; indeed, this is why Sartre refers to the task of uncovering the opaque projects of desire as a "hermeneutic." Sartre suggests that the catalogue of empirical desires ought to be made the object of appropriate psychological investigations:

Here as elsewhere, truth is not encountered by chance; it does not belong to a domain where one must seek it without ever having any presentiment of its location . . . it belongs *a priori* to human comprehension and the essential task is an hermeneutic; that is, a deciphering, a determination, and a conceptualization. (*BN* 569)

The inquiring subject is able to decipher the hidden projects of desire precisely because he is himself the origin of the object of inquiry. The existential projects of desire are not known through induction; they are discovered through a process more comparable to recollection. The success of the self-interpreter consists of being "able to *know* what he *already understands*" (*BN* 571).

For Sartre, the hiddenness or partial deception that attends desire is not cause to conclude that the aims of desire are in principle irrecoverable. On the contrary, the agent who desires and the agent who reflects upon desire is a unitary agent, although the subjectivity of this agency is capable of paradoxical modes of expression. Because it is the pre-reflective *cogito* that is at the origin of desire—desires arise with consciousness, are coextensive with consciousness, and, in fact, are themselves modes of consciousness—the aims of desire are in principle recoverable through *a*

[126]

reflective thematization of spontaneous consciousness. Sartre's well-traversed criticism of Freud takes its bearing in the context of this problem. Sartre's charge is that Freud effects an ontological disjunction between sign (original desire) and signified (determinate manifestations of this original desire) inasmuch as both the origin and meaning of desires are to be found anterior to consciousness. If desires gain their meaning in the unconscious, and if conscious expressions of desire are reducible to a system that is not recoverable by consciousness, then conscious understandings of desire are by definition always deceptive. Indeed, the conscious effort to understand desire must always remain deceived, and the truth of desire is to be gleaned only from the assumption of a third-person point of view, i.e., the point of view of an unconscious system. That desires are said to exist or originate in the unconscious is, according to Sartre, an absurdity, an hypostatization that can claim no ontological status. The attribution of strategic desire to the unconscious is, according to Sartre, a projection of relations proper to reflective consciousness onto a nonreflective domain. Moreover, such a bifurcation of the human psyche into separate systems appears to preclude the possibility of ever recovering the aims and meanings of desire from within the perspective of subjective consciousness, the domain in which, according to Sartre, any interpretation of desire must receive its final verification (*BN* 568–74; *E* 44–47).

Sartre clearly takes exception to the implicit Freudian view that desire requires an objective or third-person perspective for the disclosure of its significance. Such a view builds alienation into the very structure of the psyche, and makes self-comprehension into a vain illusion. For a recognition of the meaning of desire to be possible, the desire must emanate from the selfsame agency that reflects upon its meaning. According to Sartre, Freud does not provide a unitary account of human agency such that this kind of recognition is possible. In the realm of desire, one can only acknowledge to be true what one has, in a sense, always already known, and Freud, by systematically isolating the unconscious as a nonexperiential cognitive system, undermines on a theoretical level what his practical analysis has achieved. The possibility of knowledge without an origin and final meaning within experience is, for Sartre, an anti-intentional position which definitionally precludes the phenomenological affirmation of its assertions; in other words, Freud's theory is, at best, speculative and, at worst, self-defeating.

[127]

Sartre's response to Freud is analogous to his critique of Husserl's epoché: he seeks in both cases to expand the natural attitude—the point of view of lived experience—to include the kind of radical self-reflection that Husserl thought required a transcendental perspective, and that Freud thought required recourse to the unconscious. Sartre certainly would agree that desire is not a lucid consciousness, and it has opacity and depth which—as with all affectivity—must be interpreted in order to be understood. This is clear from his distinction between the existential and determinate aims of desire. And yet, desire is not opposed to consciousness *per se* as an ontologically distinct phenomenon; indeed, desire *is* itself a mode of pre-reflective consciousness which is opposed on occasion to reflective consciousness. The battle between reason and desire is, according to Sartre, really a battle between a reflective consciousness and the aims of a pre-reflective consciousness. Desire does not oppose a knowledgeable self, but is simply another form of consciousness that challenges the sovereignty of the reflective agency. Pre-reflective consciousness is a non-positional awareness of consciousness in the act of intending a given object. Hence, it is part of an ambiguous experience of consciousness which prevents a lucid apprehension of itself. The existential project of desire is obscured by the object of desire, and yet the determinate project is fulfilled therein. The reflexivity that attends every engagement with the world is one that shows itself obliquely and that can be illuminated only through a reflective thematization of this pre-reflective awareness.

Sartre's discussion of pre-reflective and reflective consciousness in *The Transcendence of the Ego* finds transcription in the terminology of *Being and Nothingness* as the problem of lived experience *(l'expérience vécue)* In the former work, the self is discovered only through the intentional positing of objects. Every intentional movement of consciousness toward a specific transcendent object presupposes consciousness's non-positional awareness of *itself* as the agent of consciousness; and yet this agency only becomes explicit through its actual deeds. The self is not the explicit aim of intentional consciousness, but is given "at the horizon of states" (*TE* 75). It is in this sense that the Sartrian self is said to be permanently *outside* consciousness. Introspection outside the context of intentionality is an impossibility. As in Hegel, we know ourselves only through knowing objects; we *are* the manner in which we know; our identity is the style of our comportment toward the world, the various ways in which we *appear*.

[128]

The self becomes an object for consciousness when it is posited as such, but it can be posited only indirectly, i.e., through the positing of objects; self-revelation is an inadvertent consequence of positing an object that is other to the self. Contrary to Hegel, reflective consciousness does not provide exclusive access to the self, for we are aware of ourselves even in our spontaneity, and this awareness is pre-reflective consciousness.

When we followed the travels of the Hegelian subject, we learned about the naiveté of a consciousness that had not discovered its own reflexivity. Before becoming an explicit object for itself, this subject figured that it did not exist and, moreover, had no ironic awareness of the fact that something, namely itself, must be existing in order to be "figuring" anything at all. Taken strictly, the Hegelian subject only comes to exist for itself through the process of reflexivity and recognition, and even the "striving for" such knowledge is only known in retrospect. The experience of such a subject is difficult to conceptualize, for this subject has no knowledgeable experience of itself prior to the accomplishment of its reflexive task. But what experience of itself *does* this subject have prior to the achievement of reflexive self-knowledge? How can it be described? Sartre's doctrine of pre-reflective consciousness can be seen to address precisely this problem, the quality of immediate self-awareness not yet developed into explicit self-knowledge. If the subject is a negativity in pursuit of a place in being, then how is this negativity experienced prior to its arrival, how does it make itself felt? The pre-reflective can be understood as a peripheral awareness of this negativity, the way in which an emergent self always already haunts the naive consciousness of the world.

Because for Sartre a "unity" with the world is an impossibility, the subject that we ultimately come to confront in the world is always a projection of this negativity, an externalization that differs from that of the Hegelian subject who is lucky enough to discover the world as internal to its own consciousness. Sartre's consciousness instates itself in the world, but never belongs to it; his is a negativity never resolved into a more inclusive being. Hence, the externalization of the subject for Sartre always takes place within the context of the irreducible ontological disparity of self and world, and whatever "unity" appears is always fundamentally a projection and illusion.

We must ask, what is this self that is sensed along the contours of the

[129]

object of desire? It is the project of being, the original choice that structures the spontaneity of the pre-reflective cogito. In effect, it is the discovery of the unitary structure of consciousness, i.e., that it is myself at the origin of my emotional manifestations and myself which, distanced from this spontaneity, reflects upon its meanings. Reflection upon desire is, then, reflection upon myself as a choice of being: *to reflect upon desire is to acknowledge choices one has already made.*

Sartre's argument concerning the unitary structure of reflective, pre-reflective, and non-reflective consciousness is exemplified most cogently in his discussion of bad faith. Let me note the sense of "pre-reflective choice" that is developed in that context, and then apply it to my discussion of the task of deciphering the existential projects of desire.

A common ploy of bad faith is to treat emotions as if they were contingencies rather than determinate expressions of a knowing self. For Sartre, desire and emotion are chosen, although not in any ordinary sense of "to choose." Sartre argues that empirical psychologists tend to treat desires as psychic irreducibles, that is, in determining Flaubert's character, the empirical psychologist traces Flaubert's behavior back to an ostensibly primary desire to succeed, and henceforward considers that desire to be constitutive of Flaubert's identity. In Sartre's view, desire is not a psychic irreducible, except inasmuch as desire is understood as a manifestation of choice. Desire is not given, but, in an important sense, created and recreated; as such, it indicates a free agency prior to its own emergence.

An example from contemporary popular language concretizes this point with respect to pre-reflective choice. In the case of desires that meet with swift or inevitable disappointment, i.e., when one desires another who is, for any number of reasons, inaccessible, one will hear the critical but sympathetic appeal, "but you must have set this up!" The pattern of bad faith that emerges in this context often takes the form of claiming to be victimized by one's desires. In Sartre's view it is impossible to claim that one did not choose one's desires; indeed, in the kind of cases alluded to above, it may well be that a desire for an impossible object is a desire for an object precisely because it is impossible, and because the lack of consummation achieved suits the project of the person in desire. For Sartre, *"desire is consent to desire"* (BN 388). One knows the outcome pre-reflectively in the case above, and one consents to the drama with this knowledge pre-reflectively intact; the surprise, the pain, the keen sense of betrayal, which issue from the drama's denouement are, in actuality, expressions of disappointment that reflective consciousness could not maintain its hegemony. It is oneself who could not be subdued, one's knowledge of the situation that is coincident with the upsurge of desire. When one claims to be victimized by desire, or to be totally enthralled with the object of desire, one temporarily conceals the reflexive dimension of desire, and is aware only of the intentional direction toward the object; and yet, in such a state, reflexivity works its hardest—one arranges for enthrallment, one arranges one's own victimization. In effect, one "sets it up."

The existential project of desire is a phenomenologically discoverable feature of mundane experience. The project is manifest in the quasi-knowledge we have of the hidden aims of desire even as we are in the midst of desire. The pre-reflective is an ambiguous knowledge that lives in the shadows of every act, at once accessible and concealed. As an *awareness* it reveals the bond between engaged (unreflected) and reflective consciousness; it is the possibility of self-recovery. As *non-positional* it is a marginalized consciousness, obscured by the intentional object which it attends.

The postulation of desire as a form of pre-reflective consciousness both affirms and denies the opacity of consciousness. Desire is not, for Sartre, unambiguous immediacy; it is an immediacy that inhabits a middle ground between absorption in the object and self-reflection. For Hegel, opacity is a necessary feature of self-consciousness. Self-consciousness cannot be coincident with itself because it cannot be all of its moments at once. Opposed to externality, self-consciousness is immediately rendered strange to itself; the realm of externality signifies a domain of the self yet to be recovered. The transformation of an external negation into an internal negation—the assimilation of the world to self-consciousness—is the recovery of the self, a recovery that is at once an expansion. The "implicit" dimension of self-consciousness, or its opacity, is considered to be its own identity with the world that is not yet rendered explicit. For Sartre, a similar drama of estrangement and recovery can be seen to characterize the life of desire, and yet the terms of this dialectic are decidedly post-Hegelian. The opacity of the self is a function of pre-reflective consciousness, the consciousness whose reflexivity is obscured by its intentional object. Enthralled with the object, agency is temporarily eclipsed; the opacity of desire is first of all an opacity of the self to the self, an internal alterity between reflective and pre-reflective consciousness. The "implicit" dimension of consciousness is the pre-reflective domain which is less an identity with the world than an interpretive effort to position oneself with respect to the world.

The desire to be a subject identical with the world evidenced in Hegel's *Phenomenology* is, for Sartre, abbreviated as "the desire to be." The hope of becoming coextensive with the world, mutually implicated in the world, never develops beyond the status of a hope. Hence, Sartre's notion of the desire to be God, like Hyppolite's conjecture of a life beyond death, is a vain yet compelling passion. Seeking to overcome the factic limits of perspective, the desiring agent is nevertheless mindful of the futility of this endeavor. For Hegel, the recovery of the self from ecstatic estrangement is the *discovery* of the self as a being already related to other beings. For Sartre, the relation of human beings to each other is not discovered as a prior fact; it is what calls to be established. The implicit dimension of desire is, for Sartre, not the presence of an ontology that explains a pre-established identity, but a certain pre-reflective knowledge that identity is that to be created. Pre-reflective consciousness is awareness of agency in the presence of a world; concretely, it is the determination of the choice of how to be in one's situation.

Sartre's distinct sense of consciousness as a negating activity differs from the Hegelian understanding of negation as a relation that both binds consciousness ontologically to its world and necessitates this encounter as a developmental one. Sartre's understanding of pre-reflective consciousness as a relation of reflexive negation internal to consciousness implicitly refutes the Hegelian contention that all relations of negation are relations of mediation.

The Hegelian theme of mediation is counterposed to Sartre's notion of pre-reflective consciousness in a transcription of a session of the Societé Française de Philosophie in June 1947, four years after the publication in France of Sartre's *L'Être et le néant*.[15] In this session, Hyppolite defends an Hegelian position, arguing that what Sartre terms pre-reflective consciousness is the same as the principle of negativity for Hegel. Hyppolite argues that it makes no sense to talk of a consciousness that is neither immediate nor mediate. If the pre-reflective is a species of knowledge, it must be a principle of mediation, a negating relation which, in the act of distinguishing two disparate realities, reveals their commonality. For Hyppolite, knowledge must always be a synthetic operation of this type. Sartre, however, resists this equation of knowing and synthetic consciousness. The dialogue begins with Hyppolite asking whether a paradoxical consciousness such as Sartre portrays is possible (p. 87). He queries whether there is a passage from pre-reflective to reflective consciousness, and whether the two are dialectically related. Sartre's response eludes the Hegelian categories assumed by Hyppolite's question: "What is pre-reflective consciousness? All the originality and ambiguity of a position which is *not* the immediacy of life and which prepares this act of consciousness which is reflection" (p. 88).

For Sartre, the pre-reflective is an intermediary stage that is not purely dialectical in relating the immediacy of life to the mediation that is reflection. Hyppolite clearly considers such a formulation impossible, resting as he does on an Hegelian epistemology that views knowledge as the exclusive function of reflection. Sartre's argument seeks to show that not all life is transformed into an object of reflection, and, second, that reflection is not the sole locus of cognitive functions. In keeping with Sartre's effort to expand the natural attitude to include a critical reflexivity, he argues that immediacy is not necessarily a source of falsehood and defends valid instantaneous apprehension.

Hyppolite's quarrel with Sartre appears to recapitulate Hegel's criticism of Fichte.[16] Hyppolite appears to reject the introspective capacity attributed to the pre-reflective cogito by Sartre, claiming instead that all knowledge must depend upon the mediation of externality. Sartre's rehabilitation of the Fichtean position is simultaneously a vindication of Cartesianism, that is, the postulation that consciousness can become transparent to itself. Moreover, he claims, Hegelian categories cannot provide an understanding of "discovery pure and simple" (p. 88). Not all knowledge requires a temporal progression, i.e., an altercation between self and otherness which is overcome through a development of that relation. The pre-reflective is the domain of instantaneous knowledge, the vindication of a domain of reflexivity that *attends* rather than succeeds intentional consciousness of objects. The succession of moments within the development of a known object in Hegelian terms are given at once

[133]

through the polyvalent structure of intentional consciousness defended by Sartre. The conceptual understanding of this kind of instantaneous knowledge, according to Sartre, requires a turn from Hegel to Husserl:

I consider Husserl the first philosopher to have spoken of a dimension proper to consciousness which is neither knowledge nor life, nor a kind of indefinite progress of spirit, nor a relation pure and simple to an object, but precisely because it must be, a consciousness of itself. (p. 88)

In the following dialogue Sartre endeavors to explain non-positional awareness to Hyppolite, a notion that can only appear conceptually confused to an Hegelian perspective. Let us consider their dialogue further:

SARTRE: There is an element of mediation in consciousness. You call it negativity, in Hegelian terms. It is a nothingness which touches consciousness, it is an immediacy which is not completely immediate, while nevertheless remaining immediate. That is exactly it.

HYPPOLITE: That is the living dialectical contradiction.

SARTRE: Yes, but given without movement. There is not another movement. In other words, I would like to suggest that there is no innocence; there is neither innocence nor sin. And that is properly to speak of man, precisely because man must become his being. All negativity, all mediation, all guilt, all innocence, all truth, must appear. But this is not to say that he must create all of himself. But, appearing in the world, it is not man who is in himself all of his categories, for that man he will never find in the world.

HYPPOLITE: The only thing which is possible is the *en-soi.* That is what you say.

SARTRE: I add again, that this possibility is only achieved when it realizes itself. (p. 89)

The point of contention between Sartre and Hyppolite is that of the conditions and meaning of self-knowledge. For Hyppolite, freedom is not the instantaneous assertion of self which is designated by the pre-reflective cogito. The self is defined in terms of a progressive unfolding, an opposition to the world which, if never wholly resolved, is nevertheless pursued. For Sartre, this effort to overcome difference is effected, not through mediation, but through the apprehensions of spontaneous consciousness, a spontaneity that is pre-reflectively aware of its own futility. Hyppolite's view of a perpetual altercation between self and world which constitutes

[134]

an "indefinite progress," i.e., one with no credible *telos,* is, like Sartre's, a pursuit that can never find ultimate satisfaction. The difference between their views consists of the fact that Sartre internalizes this "altercation" into the very structure of *spontaneous* consciousness. The project to be which is the structure and meaning of the for-itself knows itself as a vain passion from the start, for it knows itself as an irreducible freedom which cannot be relinquished in the objects it pursues. For Hyppolite, dissatisfaction is revealed; for Sartre, it is assumed.

In the final moments of this exchange, Hyppolite seeks to find an ontological guarantee that there is an immanent progress to freedom. Sartre's response is to reaffirm his primary principle, namely, that existence precedes essence, that there is nothing (!) on an ontological level that can guarantee a progress to freedom or a greater lucidity to self-reflection, but that such a progress can only be achieved by individual choices. Hyppolite asks whether the "power of insurgent life" and a principle of "progress" are not given at once in Sartre's view:

HYPPOLITE: The dialectical progress, as you yourself have pointed out, indicates that freedom is not simply an act of this immediate mediation, but is also the possibility of a perpetual progress, by which man gains ever increasing lucidity over himself.

SARTRE: Whether one moves from one stage of consciousness to another depends on the kind of person one is. But I have never pretended that there was a progress. (pp. 89–90)

Sartre implicitly takes issue with the inexorable development of Hegel's phenomenological *Bildungsroman.* In effect, he is asking the Kierkegaardian question of Hegel that we considered briefly before: what motivates the transitions of the *Phenomenology of Spirit?* What relentless optimism and capacity moves the Hegelian subject to reconstitute its world again and again, and to reconstitute it in such a way that comprehensive self-knowledge is the inevitable outcome of its struggles? For Sartre, the progress of Hegel's pilgrimage cannot be guaranteed through a metaphysical finesse that conflates empirical and normative realities. The only motivation for self-knowledge is choice itself. As radically unconditioned—at least in this stage of Sartre's career—it cannot be predicted as an inevitable development. The person is understood as a fundamental desire which is, in turn, the concretization of a choice; hence, when Sartre

[135]

argues that self-knowledge "depends on the person one is," he means the kind of choice that structures any given person.

But Sartre is not wholly consistent here. Although Sartre states clearly that the pre-reflective does not manifest a normative principle of development, i.e., that it is by itself an amoral structure, beyond "innocence" and "guilt," his own word should not be taken as necessarily true. Intrinsic to Sartre's notion of a unifying pre-reflective project to be is an assumption of a moral force to intentionality. I asked at the outset of this section two interrelated questions: one, how is the project of desire made known to consciousness and, two, how could one support the view of a single, original project of desire that unifies and explains the various determinate desires which appear to belong to a specific individual in the phenomenal world? In response to the first question, it is clear that the pre-reflective cogito is the access to this project of desire. With respect to the second question, we are confronted with a moral dimension implicit in desire. The unifying project to be which for Sartre structures every particular desire appears to fit the criterion posited by Hyppolite that freedom be viewed as a progressive movement. That desire is unified by a single fundamental desire which is constitutive of individuality is, for Sartre, not merely a descriptive truth, but a normative one as well. The unifying of desires under a single project is at once the being of human reality and its highest moral aspiration.[17]

The project to be God is considered desirable precisely because God represents a "complete self-understanding." We can view this aspiration as a moral one insofar as its fulfillment would be identical with perfect freedom. To be God would mean, finally, to achieve a coincidence of for-itself and in-itself such that human freedom would be at the origin of the in-itself. Contingency, facticity—the whole of the perceptual world described in *The Psychology of the Imagination*—would, for such a diety, appear as so many creations of the self; the factic would be subdued, relieved of its alterity and adversity.

This impossible normative ideal for desire reformulates the Hegelian conception of the "reproduction" of the external world as a creation of consciousness. According to such an ideal, the factic would confront consciousness as a product of consciousness rather than its limits. The desire to be can only be satisfied when consciousness manages to convince

[136]

itself that its imaginary creations are real. The satisfaction of existential desire always presupposes the success of bad faith and, conversely, the pursuit of authenticity requires perpetual dissatisfaction.

There seems, then, to be a moral dimension to Sartre's view of existential desire to the extent that a normative view of freedom governs the project to be God. And it seems to occur again in his assumption that the self is a unity, a set of choices that reveal a single, overriding choice (the fundamental choice), that is, a consistent way of being in the world. Insofar as these ideals suggest that human beings desire an escape from facticity, an overcoming of perspective, Sartre seems to be promoting a view of human reality for which the escape from situation is paramount, and this desire to take flight from adversity seems to contrast sharply with his earlier hope that the doctrine of intentionality would establish the self "in the midst of life."

Although Sartre does seem to accept a normative view of human identity as a project to become an omnipotent subjectivity, he recognizes this ideal as an impossibility, and, in other contexts, suggests a view of authenticity as the paradoxical journey of an embodied consciousness. In the discussion of sexual desire, Sartre seems to offer a project for an embodied identity for whom the body is not merely a factic limit to freedom but a material condition for the determination and expression of freedom. In the context of sexual relations, we find that the desire to "be" is not merely a desire for an omnipotent transfiguration of the world, but is also the desire to be known, to come into being through the look of the Other. Moreover, this look is not merely a hostile glance, and the exchange between two selves is not merely a fight in which each seeks to assert himself as God. The situation of reciprocal desire becomes the locus of a progressive movement of freedom, a domain in which the factic is suffused with human will. Although desire does seem to labor under an ideal of disembodiment in the discussion of existential desire, we can see that Sartre has formulated an alternative understanding of the projects of desire in the context of sexual desire. The progression of Sartre's own views on desire in the later works—*Critique of Dialectical Reason, Saint Genet: Actor and Martyr,* and *The Family Idiot: Gustave Flaubert 1821–1857*—attests to his growing awareness that the paradox of an embodied consciousness need not be formulated as an antagonistic

[137]

struggle between body and consciousness. Indeed, in a set of remarks recorded in an interview, "Self-Portrait at Seventy," Sartre suggests that the body can be an expressive medium for consciousness:

SARTRE: For me there is no basic difference between the body and consciousness.

INTERVIEWER: Isn't it true that we only yield our thoughts totally to the people to whom we truly yield our bodies?

SARTRE: We yield our bodies to everyone, even beyond the realm of sexual relations; by looking, by touching. You yield your body to me, I yield mine to you: we exist for the other, as body. But we do not exist in this same way as consciousness, as ideas, even though ideas are modifications of the body.

If we truly wished to exist for the other, to exist as body, as body that can continually be laid bare—even if this never actually happens—our ideas would appear to others as coming from the body. Words are formed by a tongue in the mouth. All ideas would appear in this way, even the most vague, the most fleeting, the least tangible. There would no longer be the hiddenness, the secrecy which in certain centuries was identified with the honor of men and women, and which seems very foolish to me.[18]

Trouble and Longing : *The Circle of Sexual Desire in* Being and Nothingness

In fact everyone will agree that desire is not only longing, *a clear and translucent* longing *which directs itself through our body toward a certain object. Desire is defined as* trouble. . . . *troubled water remains water; it preserves the fluidity and the essential characteristics of water; but its translucency is "troubled" by an inapprehensible presence which makes one with it, which is everywhere and nowhere, and which is given as a clogging of the water by itself.*—Sartre, *Being and Nothingness*

Sartre's view of sexual desire is often interpreted as an existential argument for the inevitability of sadomasochism. Clearly, Sartre does affirm sadism and masochism as permanent possibilities of all sexual encounters,[19] and rejects the category of "dialectic," arguing instead that the sexual drama of master and slave is not *aufgehoben* in a state of universal

[138]

reciprocity. Rather, sexual exchange is a "circle" (*BN* 363) in which the inversion of sadism into masochism, and masochism into sadism, follows according to the ontological necessity that every determinate individual is what he is not, and is not what he is. That no third term or transcending synthesis emerges from the circle of desire does not necessarily imply that sexual roles are fixed and futile. The phenomenon of inversion gives rise to the *consciousness* of inversion, and this consciousness is at once awareness and choice. To take up the role of sadist or masochist as a permanent feature of one's sexual self is to posture as an essentialist, and indulge the bad faith of sexual desire. The constancy of inversion is, for Sartre, a new basis of reciprocity; the impossibility of being both subject and object at once proceeds from the perspectival character of corporeal life. Sado-masochism is the paradox of determinate freedom revealed in sexual life.

For Sartre, consciousness is always an individual consciousness, and as such is distinct from every other consciousness; nothingness persists between the partners of desire as their necessary and ineradicable difference. The interiority of the Other cannot, as Hegel occasionally appeared to think, be revealed through cognition, because the pre-reflective is the private and hidden consciousness of an agency to itself; in this sense, the pre-reflective cogito is a locus of private and inviolable freedom. Sexual desire seeks the interiority of the Other, bids the Other to manifest its freedom in the form of flesh. Knowledge of this freedom requires the mediation of the body. A freedom purified of the body is an impossibility.

The paradox of determinate freedom, the continual problem of existing as an embodied choice, is surpassed in the Hegelian account when the body becomes the generalized body of Christ.[20] In other words, the body is no longer conceived as a limit to freedom where the body is no longer the determinate body of a mortal being whose contours indicate necessary difference. Simply put, Sartre identifies the body with the limit to freedom and the insurpassable condition of individuation. And yet Sartre's view is not wholly negative, for the body mediates and determines freedom in the case of sexual desire. We must, then, turn to Sartre's treatment of sexual desire in order to understand how the body both limits and mediates the various projects of choice.

If freedom is defined as the project to become the foundation of one's own being, and if the body is a contingent facticity—a being that we are but do not choose—it would appear to follow that in every case the body is opposed to freedom as its premature limit. In Sartre's discussion of the circle of desire, the body is not exclusively identified with contingency, and neither is freedom always construed as the freedom to be God. Although claimed as a "factic" dimension of the self, the body is never *purely* factic; it is equally a perspective and a set of intentional relations (*BN* 381-20). Freedom is not always discussed as a project of disembodiment that is doomed to failure. Indeed, freedom is also construed as a project of embodiment, a constant effort to affirm the corporeal ties to the world which compose one's *situation.* In *Being and Nothingness,* and more distinctly in the later biographical studies and *The Critique of Dialectical Reason,* freedom becomes less tied to ontological ideals that transcend history than to the concrete and highly mediated projects of surviving, interpreting, and reproducing a socially complex situation.

The notion of freedom as an *ex nihilo* creation certainly has its moorings in Sartre's thought.[21] Herbert Marcuse's early review of *Being and Nothingness* aptly criticizes this conception of Sartre's, but does not give adequate attention to the notion of *situation* as radically qualifying the *ex nihilo* character of freedom.[22] The same holds true of Merleau-Ponty's critique of Sartre's Cartesianism in *Adventures of the Dialectic* and *Sense and Non-Sense.* Sartre's supposed adherence to an isolated consciousness unrelated to embodiment and sociality has been effectively refuted by Simone de Beauvoir in "Merleau-Ponty et le Pseudo-Sartrisme" and, more recently, by Monika Langer in "Sartre and Merleau-Ponty: A Re-appraisal."[23] We shall see that the alleged opposition between body and consciousness is one that Sartre only tenuously maintains, for the body in its sexual being is not mere contingency, but equally a mode of consciousness and a way of situating oneself in the world: desire is "consciousness *making itself* body" (*BN* 389).

Sadomasochism introduces the paradox of determinate freedom as a drama of consciousness and objectification. Sartre's well-known formulation that one can only come into relations with another through becoming an object for that Other is misleading in its simplicity. Sartre, of course, contributes to the deception by employing the visual metaphor of the "look" for the constituting act by which one consciousness apprehends another as an object. Sartre does not always clarify in what sense the identity of the Other is objectified, nor does he offer a definition of the "look" which distinguishes its literal from its more general formulations.[24]

Occasionally his own prose seems to invite a literal reading so that sexual desire, as an exchange of constitutive "looks," appears to be a circle of voyeurism and exhibitionism: "my being-an-object is the only possible relation between me and the Other, it is this being-as-object which alone can serve me as an instrument to effect my assimilation of the Other's freedom" (*BN* 365).

Only under the Other's gaze does the self acquire being: "the Other's look fashions my body in its nakedness, causes it to be born, sculptures it, produces it as it is, sees it as I shall never see it" (*BN* 364). As a self regarded, the agent of desire can make use of the Other's gaze as the instrument of its own self-objectification. As a self who regards the Other, the agent transcends the limits of bodily perspective and asserts itself as a productive freedom. Primarily the Other appears as the alienation of one's own possibilities. As in Hegel's dialectic of lordship and bondage, the Other appears as an alienated version of myself: "I grasp the Other's look at the very center of my act as the solidification and alienation of my own possibilities" (*BN* 263). As the producer and sculptor of the Other, the sadist tends toward an identity of pure freedom, discovering *the body* as alienated in the Other. As the agent who effects his own objectification, the masochist discovers his *freedom* alienated in the Other.

The Sartrian self can only know itself in its desire insofar as it attends to itself in a pre-reflective mode. This pre-reflective agency is always a non-positional consciousness of choice, the mode in which consciousness determines itself in the world. This awareness is necessarily an awareness of frustration: human reality seeks to know itself as a *being*, and pre-reflective consciousness reveals it as a perpetually elusive agency. The Other appears as an agent who can grasp the self *reflectively*, i.e., as an object or set of realized possibilities. The Other has no access to the pre-reflective cogito, but recognizes the self only through the determinate acts in which freedom is congealed. Hence, the look at once confirms the self as a being—an objectification of possibilities—and threatens to deprive the self of its essential freedom. Although the look confers being, it does so only through becoming an act of deprivation, a violation and an expropriation of freedom. The self so expropriated is, however, only the phenomenal self—the self that appears. Under the gaze of the Other it may appear that there is nothing left of the self being seen and that the Other "has stolen my being" (*BN* 364). And yet, "the nothing left" is not

[141]

an absolute negation, but a determinate posture of freedom, a "nothing" which, in Sartrian terms, is "a non-substantial absolute" (*BN* 561).

The experience of "being seen" gives rise to the experience of "seeing" in Sartre's view. The self regarded is never simply a self appropriated through an Other's glance; indeed, convinced of its own alienation, seeking to recover itself, this objectified self already surpasses the look that defines it. The sense of "being convinced," the striving toward self-recovery, are already postures of freedom—pre-reflective orientations which elude the look of the Other. Failing reflectively to thematize its pre-reflective acts, this self does not see the consciousness of expropriation as proof that expropriation has failed. In this sense, the pre-reflective is the domain of inviolable freedom. The encounter with the Other obscures pre-reflective awareness, and makes the self doubt its own interiority. The self appears outside itself as an ego constituted as a product of another's acts. So constituted, the self experiences itself as grasped, possessed, defined by the Other. The fact that it "experiences itself" in these modes is obscured by the modes themselves; intentional enthrallment conceals pre-reflective choice—the reflexivity of consciousness. As in Hegel, the project developed in response to this enthrallment is that of "the recovery of my being" (*BN* 364). The Other that deprives the self through the look of its freedom is seduced into giving that self a confirmation of its being; this seduction is effected through *looking back*. And this inviting look seeks to effect in turn a vision large enough to take in the self as both body and freedom.

The insurpassability of the "look" is a function of the insurpassability of exteriority between self and Other. The distance is corporeal and, hence, spatial; thus, the "look" signifies the necessity of a spectatorial point of view, a medium of exchange based on physical distance. This exteriority is not, however, a source of indifference because the corporeal distance establishes the Other in a privileged position of sight. The self can be only obliquely conscious of itself; it either senses itself indirectly, or infers from its acts what it might be. The self is burdened by the fact that it must live and reflect upon itself at once; hence, its self-understanding is never complete, for in the moment that it grasps itself reflectively, it escapes itself pre-reflectively. Because the Other does not live the self it sees, it is able to grasp that self purely in reflective terms. The self so regarded seeks to recover itself through an assimilation or absorption of

[142]

the reflective posture of the Other: "thus my project of recovering myself is fundamentally a project of absorbing the Other" (*BN* 364). The effort to absorb the Other's freedom is effected through the appropriation of an objectifying point of view on oneself, and, hence, the surpassing of the perspectival limits of corporeality:

> I want to assimilate the Other as the Other-looking-at-me, and this project of assimilation includes an augmented recognition of my being-looked-at. In short, in order to maintain before me the Other's freedom which is looking at me, I identify myself totally with my being-looked-at. (*BN* 365).

The desiring agent who looks, who monopolizes the power of definition and transcendence, undergoes an inversion into objectification or embodiment in a similar fashion. This Other who "looks," who defines and produces the agent identified with corporeality, is itself a disembodied self, a pure vision ungrounded in the world. Insofar as the "look" signifies a free act of constitution, it is freedom in a limited sense; but the freedom of the pure seer is a rootless freedom which cannot take stock of its own being. The self that is seen has itself reflected as an object and an embodied being; it is seen and affirmed in its corporeal situation. But the self who merely sees does not know itself reflectively, but can only sense itself pre-reflectively as a transcendent flight toward the self it apprehends. Its body is permanently outside, as the Other. Hence, this seer who constantly defines objects and others exterior to itself lacks its own being, and begins paradoxically to seek its own definition. The disembodied flight of the pure seer seeks its own corporeal "definition." As I will show, sadism becomes the concrete expression for the project of disembodiment.

The circle of desire, which comes to be explained in terms of sadomasochism, is the paradox of the body as a determinate freedom played out in the context of reciprocal desire. "The body is a passion by which I am engaged in the world and in danger in the world" (*BN* 388). The body is thus equally a source of productivity and victimization; it is a mode of affecting and being affected by the world; the body "is *a point of departure* which I *am* and which at the same time I surpass toward what I have to be" (*BN* 326). One surpasses the body insofar as one makes of corporeal contingency a project of significance: "we can never apprehend this contingency as such insofar as our body is for us; for we are a choice, and for us, to be is to choose ourselves ... this inapprehensible body is precisely the necessity that *there be a choice,* that I do not exist *all at once"* (*BN* 326). The body is thus insurpassable perspective; it is both our distance from the world and the condition of our access:

The body cannot be made for me transcendant and known; the spontaneous, unreflective consciousness is no longer the consciousness *of the* body. It would be best to say, using "exist" as a transitive verb, that consciousness *exists* its body . . . *my* body is a conscious structure. (*BN* 329)

Sartre concludes that the body belongs to the structures of non-thetic consciousness, and that "consciousness of the body is lateral and retro-spective." We never experience the body as contingency pure and simple, for such a body would be deprived of consciousness and could not be "experienced." Contingency is always given as "that in terms of which consciousness makes itself a choice." Hence, the body, although referred to as facticity, is never experienced outside of an interpretive field. This is clear in Sartre's formulation that "consciousness of the body is com-parable to the consciousness of a sign." And yet the body does not signify a prior or anterior set of meanings; rather, it signifies "the manner in which it affected." This affect that the body expresses is a "constituted affectivity," a mode of being in the world. The affect that the body signifies is "a transcendent 'intention' . . . directed toward the world" (*BN* 330).

Sadomasochistic desire signifies the ambiguous meaning of the body as a limited perspective and as the condition of access to the world, i.e., as both contingency and project. The body is a restricted perspective as well as a perspective that constantly transcends itself toward other perspec-tives. As a sexual experience, the contingent or passive body is never wholly lifeless precisely because it must *maintain itself* in its passivity; moreover, passivity is discovered—or, in principle, can be discovered—as an instrument by which the Other's freedom is assimilated, i.e., the Other's perspective imaginatively and empathetically entertained. In seek-ing his own disembodiment, the sadist endeavors in vain to surpass fac-ticity; he denies his own body without depriving it of existence; in effect, he eliminates his own body from the Other's field of sight. The only way to keep the Other from looking at the sadist and, hence, ruining his project of disembodiment, is to convince the Other to be his body exclusively, that is, to blind the Other to his own capacity for sight.

The sadist constructs distance between his flesh and the flesh of the

[144]

masochist through the transformation of his own body into a pure in-strument of control. As an instrument, it is known only through the effect it causes, and is, thus, left unconsidered as it is in itself: "the sadist refuses his own flesh at the same time that he uses instruments to reveal by force the Other's flesh to him" (*BN* 399). Fashioning the Other as a pure body, the sadist tries to convince this Other to choose this congealment of his possibilities:

> He wishes that the Other's freedom should determine itself to become love—and this not only at the beginning of the affair but at each instant—and at the same time he wants this freedom to be captured *by itself*, to turn back upon itself, as in madness, as in a dream, so as to will its own captivity. This captivity must be a resignation that is both free and yet chained in our hands. In love it is not a determinism of the passions which we desire in the Other nor a freedom beyond reach; it is a freedom which *plays the role* of a determinism of the passions and is caught in its own role. (*BN* 673)

The effort to subdue the Other as pure body fails because of an ambiv-alence intrinsic to both sadistic and masochistic desire. As is clear from Sartre's description above, the sadist does not seek the Other as pure body, but as a freedom that has determined itself as a body. And the masochist could not become this pure contingency even if it were the sadist's true desire, for masochistic desire, like all other desire, is "the consent to desire": "consciousness chooses itself as desire" (*BN* 388). The projects of sadism and masochism necessarily convert into each other, for all flesh gives rise to intentionality and all intentional transcendence requires a ground in corporeal life. Like the lord in Hegel's "Lordship and Bondage," the sadist can only pursue his project of domination insofar as he blinds himself to the futility of the reflexive project simultaneously at work, i.e., the pursuit of disembodiment. The sadist requires of the masochist what the lord requires of the bondsman: *to be the body the sadist endeavors not to be.* And yet, "sadism is a blind alley, for it not only enjoys the possession of the Other's flesh but at the same time in direct connection with this flesh, it enjoys its own non-incarnation" (*BN* 399). Enjoyment or pleasure foils the sexual project of disembodiment, for pleasure reveals consciousness as a body: "if pleasure enables us to get out of the circle, this is because it kills both the desire and the sadistic passion without satisfying them" (*BN* 405).

The project of sadism is subverted through the experience of pleasure

[145]

because pleasure reasserts the body the sadist has tried to deny. As a sexual project that seeks to deny the very ground of sexuality, sadism is a movement of sexuality against itself, an expression of rancor against corporeal life that emerges from within its own midst. Its failure is clear insofar as desire, the medium of this project, cannot be utilized without undercutting the project itself. This is not to say that there are no truly sadistic sexual acts, but that they are not satisfying in the way that they strive to be. Insofar as masochism is a project that also seeks to resolve the ontological situation of having to be a paradoxical unity of corporeality and freedom, it is similarly doomed to fail. The look of the sadist that confers being on the masochist must be sustained; hence, the masochist must keep himself fascinating for the sadist which means, paradoxically, that the masochist must keep his freedom intact so that he can continuously offer it up. The masochist fashions himself an object, not to lose consciousness but to gain an expanded consciousness of himself. By identifying himself with his body, he seeks to elicit a thorough comprehension of himself through the objectifying look of the Other. The masochist wants to be defined by the Other and to participate in the Other's gaze. Hence, his identification with his own body is tacitly an effort to surpass the perspective of that body and take on the perspective of the Other. Masochism is thus an effort to transcend the body through an identification with the body: "I want to assimilate the Other as the Otherlooking-at-me, and this project of assimilation includes an augmented recognition of my being-looked-at. In short, in order to maintain before me the Other's freedom which is looking at me, I identify myself totally with my being-looked-at" (*BN* 365).

Sadism and masochism share a common goal in that they seek to transcend the restrictive character of corporeality; the sadist follows a path of self-denial, whereas the masochist, perhaps more realistically, seeks transcendence by pushing restriction to an extreme. In either case, desire is revealed as fundamentally an ecstatic intentionality in which the body seeks to transcend its situation and fails. Sadism and masochism, as highlighting the two poles of the paradoxical unity of embodied consciousness, are constitutive moments of every sexual expression: "I am at the root of my being the project of assimilating and making an object of the Other" (*BN* 363). This project is rooted in the paradoxical nature of the for-itself: "The for-itself is both a flight and a pursuit of the in-itself; the for-itself is a double relation" (*BN* 362).

[146]

The circle of sadism and masochism might be termed a circle of freedom and embodiment, a circle in which the terms are essentially related although never synthesized into a completed unity. The enactment of sadism and masochism reveal the impossible premises on which these projects are based, and yet the recognition of impossibility does not, as it does in Hegel, give rise to a new, more inclusive framework in which paradox is resolved. The experience of futility gives rise to a consciousness of futility, but this second-order consciousness does not give rise to new possibility. Indeed, there is no resolution of this paradox that is not temporary and imaginary. Desire is an essential paradox for Sartre, and yet it is intrinsic to desire to seek, if only tentatively, a resolution to its own ontological situation. Desire exceeds the world that is given to it, so that any satisfaction to desire requires a turn from a given to a created world. The body can neither be fully denied nor fully sufficient unto itself, so that desire can seek a resolution to this incessant paradox only by arranging for a temporary escape from the exigencies of corporeality. Desire must subject the body to the imaginary; it must create anew its object and itself in order to be satisfied.

In the discussion of *The Emotions* and *Psychology of the Imagination,* affectivity was understood as a response to adversity, a magical effort to transform the facts of the perceptual world, the essential "difficulty" of that world. This distance between the aims of consciousness and the coefficient of adversity which characterizes all facticity can be bridged, in Sartre's view, only through a consciousness that assumes its own facticity and, through that facticity, discovers a "flesh" of objects or, as Merleau-Ponty was to say, an "interworld." As magic is the mode by which emotion transforms the world, so "enchantment" becomes the transformative effect of desire:

The same is true of desire as of emotion. We have pointed out elsewhere that emotion is not the apprehension of an exciting object in an unchanged world; rather since it corresponds to a global modification of consciousness and of its relations to the world, emotion expresses itself by means of a radical alteration of the world. Similarly, sexual desire is a radical modification of the For-itself; since the For-itself makes itself be on another plane of being, it determines itself to exist its body differently, to make itself be clogged by its facticity. (*BN* 391–92)

Sexual desire is not only a transformation of the for-itself, because this transformed for-itself, in turn, *presents* the world in a transformed dimension. The world that sexual desire brings into being is not a magical world counterposed to a "real" or "objective" world. Sartre appears to confirm that sexual desire reveals a magical realm *intrinsic* to the world, a dimension concealed to the perceptual consciousness of mundane life. In *Being and Nothingness* Sartre does not refer to the perceptual world as such, and we can see in his discussion of sexual desire a readiness to admit that the imaginative consciousness is not wholly separate from the everyday perceptual consciousness that attends the factic world. Indeed, in Sartre's discussion of sexual desire, his position comes very close to Merleau-Ponty's in *The Phenomenology of Perception,* where perception itself is seen to contain and depend on imagination in an essential way.[25] Sartre explains that the world of sexuality is not an irrational or deceptive world, but rather, a dimension of reality that requires desire for its disclosure. Desire does not, then, create a solipsistic universe: "Correlatively the world must come into being for the For-itself in a new way. There is a world of desire. If my body . . . is lived as flesh, then it is as a reference to my flesh that I apprehend the objects in the world" (*BN* 392).

In sexual desire, the world loses its primary value as a field of instrumental values and appears instead as *present.* For Sartre, desire is not an instrumental relation toward others and objects, but a twofold effort to incarnate and reveal. The factic is no longer outside, as a difficult and estranged dimension of the world; infused with consciousness, it is the experience of one's own flesh. Facticity is embodied and, as in the case of the image, "shot through and through with creative will" (*PI* 20). As the for-itself, defined primarily as an instrumental orientation toward the world, assumes its own facticity, it discovers a prior relation with the world which its instrumental orientation tends to obscure. Through assuming the body as its necessary expression, consciousness renders itself passive, but this passivity becomes the condition of the revelation of the sensible world:

I make myself passive in relation to [the objects of the world] . . . they are revealed to me from the point of view of this passivity, in it and through it (for passivity is the body, and the body does not cease to be a point of view). Objects then become the transcendent ensemble which reveals my incarnation to me. A contact with them is a caress . . . to perceive an object when I am in the desiring attitude is to caress myself with it. . . . In my desiring perception I discover something like a *flesh* of objects. (*BN* 392)

[148]

For Sartre, the primary relation between the for-itself and its world is that of *distance*, and this distance is breached as consciousness submerges itself in its facticity. The embodiment of consciousness is itself a project in Sartrian terms. Consciousness knows itself primarily as a translucency only dimly aware of its own corporeal dimension. Alienation signifies the initial moment of consciousness's journey toward self-recovery, a movement to recover oneself as flesh, that is, as a body essential to consciousness. Interestingly, this assumption of an initial estrangement between consciousness and body, whereby consciousness exists first and then acquires its own embodiment, contrasts sharply with common intuitive notions concerning child development which assert that the somatic dimension of the self is primary and that consciousness is an emergent phenomenon. In Sartre's account, it is the body that follows upon consciousness. The child for Sartre does not appear to come into the world through flesh, but from an existential void; indeed, this child is not "delivered" but, in the Heideggerian sense, "thrown."

The reasons for the initial estrangement of consciousness from its body in Sartre's philosophy could be approached from a variety of perspectives. Clearly, Sartre often holds to a Cartesian belief that thinking is constitutive of personal identity, and that this constitutive thinking is essentially an abstract activity nonessentially linked to the sensuous. That self and world as sensuous phenomena are known initially at a distance, and are only finally encountered as flesh *after* consciousness molds itself as desire, remains a profoundly counterintuitive notion, and one that appears contrary to Sartre's own emphasis on consciousness as a form of engagement.[26] Indeed, that consciousness in this account must make itself into desire and only then discover the flesh of the world appears to contradict his later claim in *Being and Nothingness* that the for-itself is essentially desire and that "desire is the being of human reality." In the first model, consciousness is a spectator on the world, estranged from the sensuous, a disembodied instrument of knowledge. In the second model, consciousness knows itself as essentially embodied, and primarily engaged.

When Sartre takes the spectatorial view of consciousness, we seem to have an inverse phenomenological description of experience, one that takes the epoché as constitutive of everyday experience and views the entrance into the natural attitude as a philosophical achievement. For this consciousness, the form of an object appears before its matter, and reflection gradually gives way to desire:

In the desiring attitude . . . I am sensitive not so much to the form of the object and its instrumentality, as to its matter (gritty, smooth, tepid, greasy, rough, etc.). In my desiring perception I discover something like a flesh of objects. My shirt rubs against my skin, and I feel it. What is ordinarily for me an object most remote becomes the immediately sensible; the warmth of air, the breath of the wind, the rays of sunshine, etc.; all are present to me in a certain way, as posited upon me without distance and revealing my flesh by means of their flesh. (*BN* 392)

The world of instrumentality is clearly opposed to the world of sexual desire. For Sartre, the usual orientation toward the world is that of an unreflective instrumental engagement which presupposes and reconfirms the distance between agent and object. The rays of sunshine are only felt and made immediately sensible once we lay down our tools, as it were. Instrumental action requires and confirms distance between the agent and his product; desire does not seek to make use of its object, but, rather, to let it appear as it is. Desire is, in this view, a relaxation of the instrumental mode; it is the emergence of the world not as a field of purposes and ends, but, rather, in its *presence*.

According to Sartre, the Other is the occasion of the appearance of the world as present. The world as flesh only appears to the body that has been transformed into flesh, and this latter transformation is only possible through the look of the Other. We will recall that "the Other's look fashions my body in its nakedness, causes it to be born." The body is no longer an instrument once it is desired; it becomes a creation, a presence which, in turn, makes present the flesh of Others and the world.

Here we can see most clearly the significant relationship between desire and imagination, as it is considered in *The Psychology of the Imagination*; emotions as magical transformations, as outlined in *The Emotions*; and sexual desire in *Being and Nothingness* as "an attitude aiming at enchantment" (*BN* 394). Sexual desire is, for Sartre, a way of imagining the Other, but this imagining is not a source of delusion or solipsistic creation. The self is not a ready-made identity which desire endeavors to apprehend; the self is a gradual embodiment of freedom, the body become flesh, a process of becoming that the desire of the Other facilitates and confirms. The problem of solipsism considered in the *Psychology of the Imagination* no longer applies, for the Other is not a positive datum, a self-identical being, but a process of choosing itself; as such, it is an identity that requires its own social constitution in order to be. The self only comes to be through the look of the Other that affirms and creates this self. Clearly, the self is not wholly created by the Other; before the look of the Other, the self is a body and sustains instrumental relations with the world, but remains at a distance from its own flesh and from the sensible presence of Others and the world. Before the constitutive exchange of desire, the self is mute and, perhaps, functional, closed in on itself, bearing within itself an implicit history and a thwarted set of possibilities. The desire of the Other brings that self into being; it does not cause that self to exist, but rather, to assume its being, that is, to begin its process of creating itself through determinate acts which are affirmed through the recognition of the Other.

The constitutive exchange of desire takes place against a background of negation; the ineradicable differences among selves, the irreversible distance between consciousness and the sensible world gives rise to a need for presence, a yearning for unity which we saw in Hegel as the fundamental project of desire. That difference is an ontological given does not imply that it is given in static form. Although desire cannot, for Sartre, overcome difference, it can formulate it in various ways. The effort to formulate difference, to thematize negation, such that the negative is circumscribed and subdued through a perpetual creation of presence is the tacit project of sexual desire. As in our considerations of Kojève and Hyppolite, desire reveals human beings as able to endure the negative, i.e., loss, death, distance, absence, precisely because they appropriate the power of the negative and express it in the form of freedom. In the case of sexual desire this freedom takes the form of incarnating the self and the Other, the experience of consciousness and the sensible world which, while sustaining difference in the form of tension, nevertheless creates a tentative configuration of presence.

Sartre describes the effort of sexual desire as a pursuit of the Other's facticity and "the pure existence of things" (*BN* 394). The "world of desire" is a "destructured world which has lost its meaning, a world in which things jut out like fragments of pure matter" (*BN* 395). Absorption in the flesh of the Other is an impossible effort to merge with matter or facticity itself, a purposeful "clogging" of consciousness which seeks to forget situation and environment and the whole of the perceptual world

[151]

riddled with negation. In this sense, then, desire is an effort to congeal the world, to reduce it to the flesh of the Other, to recreate the world as flesh. The pursuit of being that forms the tacit project of desire establishes desire as "an absolute impulse."[27]

This movement toward absolute presence necessarily meets with frustration because the incarnation of the Other requires the incarnation of the self. Sartre appears to understand the initial project of desire as absorption in the Other: "desire is not only the desire of the Other's body; it is—within the unity of a single act—the non-thetically linked project of being swallowed up in the body" (*BN* 389). Desire is always haunted by "disturbance" or "trouble" which intimates "the presence of an invisible something which is not itself distinguished and which is manifested as pure factual resistance." The presence of facticity is an essentially ambiguous presence: it promises a resolution for negation at the same time that it reaffirms its necessity. Pleasure, for Sartre, is the "death and failure of desire" (*BN* 397) precisely because it returns each partner of desire back to his separate corporeality; indeed, it reminds both partners that the creation of a presence that could effectively subdue difference was a *magical* creation, an enchanted creation that could not be maintained.

We ought not to construe the life and death of desire as a movement to a magical world that is doomed to return to a rational world. It is not as if desire creates a momentary fantasy of overcoming ontological differences and then forfeits that fantasy upon the reminder of inevitable separateness. Rather, the movement toward magical creation is necessitated by this ontology of difference; the inevitability of the negative conditions and necessitates desire as a magical project, a phenomenon of belief. In "The 'Faith' of Bad Faith" Sartre writes, "we take belief as meaning the adherence of being to its object when the object is not given or is given indistinctly" (*BN* 67). Desire is, in effect, always "troubled" by the absence of the Other, i.e. that "invisible something" that signifies the interiority of the Other who is in principle inaccessible. Belief is, according to Sartre, a mode of attributing being to something not given or given indistinctly; hence, it undergirds the imaginary which, as we noted, posits nonexistent or absent objects. Insofar as the world remains hidden from consciousness, appearing in partial and adumbrated form, we are forced to believe. Belief arises in the confrontation with non-being,

[152]

and asserts itself as the way in which consciousness survives this everpresent absence. Because human reality is fundamentally the desire to be, an absolute urge toward presence, it encounters non-being primarily in the mode of suffering. It undergoes absence as an annihilation of itself. And yet this passivity that corresponds to non-being—and that is itself a kind of deterioration of the self's being, a disappointment of its constitutive desire—is not a static mode of being; passivity turns to passion which becomes the essential way in which human beings exist in the face of the negative.

Sexual desire is predicated on belief insofar as it is a way of attributing being to an unattainable reality, and is a mode of passionately encountering the ineradicable differences between selves. In *The Emotions* Sartre maintains that "the body is belief" (*E* 86). In the sense that the body, lived as flesh or the contingency of pure presence, reveals a world of flesh, the body effects a magical transformation of the perceptual world. The flesh of the world is not a unilateral creation of the body lived as flesh, but it is a dimension of the already given world elucidated and made present. The body as flesh is a passive mode of presenting the world, but it is a passivity turned passionate: "the objects of the world . . . are revealed to me from the point of view of this passivity, in it and through it (for passivity is the body, and the body does not cease to be a point of view)" (*BN* 382). Desire thus indicates a tenacity of belief as its own necessary precondition. This primary act of "making present" that constitutes belief also makes possible the image and, consequently, the creative or constitutive activity of desire. We might understand the essential "desire to be" as a kind of pre-reflective enthrallment, a readiness to believe, to attribute being to the nonexistent, absent, or lost. Similarly, we can understand ambivalent desires as indicating a prior crisis of belief. And the inability to desire at all might be understood as a radical disbelief in the possibility of overcoming any differences at all.

Although sexual desire nears the experience of presence that would satisfy the ontological aims of desire in general, Sartre also clearly states that desire is doomed to failure. The experience of pleasure, he argues, gives rise to "attention to pleasure" (*BN* 397) and we may conclude that pre-reflective enthrallment of desire is thereby extinguished through the reflective posture that disengages itself from belief. In the *Transcendence of the Ego* Sartre claims that "reflection poisons desire" (*TE* 59). Referring to Sartre's discussion of belief in *Being and Nothingness,* we can conclude that reflection poisons desire insofar as it undermines the magical belief that sustains desire. And insofar as human reality is a paradoxical unity of reflective and prereflective consciousness, the perpetual emergence and decline of desire is inevitable. Desire thus never escapes the doubt reflective consciousness introduces. Unabashed desire reveals simple faith, an abandon to the life of the body that signifies belief. Sartre follows Hegel in claiming that simple faith cannot endure as such:

> This which I define as good faith is what Hegel would call the *immediate.* It is simple faith. Hegel would demonstrate at once that the immediate calls for mediation, and that belief by becoming *belief for itself,* passes to the state of non-belief. . . . if I know that I believe, the belief appears to me as pure subjective determination without external correlative. . . . To believe is to know that one believes, and to know that one believes is no longer to believe. (*BN* 69)

Sartre's contrast between reflection and belief should not lead us to conclude that disbelief is rational, and belief is irrational. Instead, it seems crucial to consider that rationality appears in dual form. If an object crosses my path and then is gone, is it rational to conclude that the object no longer exists? Clearly, the domain of pre-reflective belief and, coincidentally, of desire, is necessary if we are to have a rational understanding of a world suffused with negation. The pre-reflective allows us to navigate the realm of negation in that it disbelieves the final word of positive reality. In this sense, the pre-reflective is its own kind of disbelief, an unwillingness to accept the hegemony of reflective consciousness. If the world is both presence and absence, then a rational comprehension of the world requires a consciousness which is both belief and disbelief.

Sexual desire has thus appeared in Sartre's discussion as an effort to enact with an Other the original desire to be that is constitutive of human reality. And yet a reference back to my discussion of existential desire immediately raises a set of questions. In that treatment, Sartre claimed that desire must be approached at three different levels; first, as an original choice, the anonymous desire to be that characterizes all human reality; second, as a fundamental choice, a determinate mode of being that characterizes a specific life; and third, as the myriad particular desires that indirectly express the prior two choices. Sartre's discussion of sexual desire remains almost exclusively on the level of the first choice. Sexual desire is considered in its universal dimension, as an activity that emerges

[154]

through an ontological necessity. As Sartre indicated as early as *Being and Nothingness* and made clear in *Search for a Method*, the concrete analysis of desire must take place through an existential psychoanalysis of an individual in situation.[28] Considering the universal or anonymous features of desire, Sartre can claim that it is the flesh of the Other that we desire. And yet certainly he must answer the question he posed to Freud: why is it *this* Other rather than someone else whom we desire? And if he is to claim that every life is structured by a fundamental choice that distinguishes it from other individual lives, then we need to understand in the context of a life what this desire is, and how it can be known.

I return to my original question, namely, who is the subject of desire? We can conclude on the basis of *Being and Nothingness* and the earlier works that desire makes the subject present as flesh, and, in the context of reciprocal desire, reveals this embodied self as that which it has implicitly always been, but never known itself to be. We have seen *that* the self is created through the reciprocity of desire, and we have seen *that* this self emerges from nothingness, but we have not seen *how*. As it stands, Sartre's theory is an interesting ontological inquiry, but the question remains whether it is a satisfactory phenomenological account of experience.

What narrative can Sartre tell to convince us of this theory? I turn to the biographical studies of Genet and Flaubert with precise questions in mind. Because a thorough account of either work is impossible and unwarranted in this context, I consider them here only in relation to the question I pose of desire: what can desire tell us about a given life? How does desire signify the project of a life, and how does it constitute that life? Genet and Flaubert were of special interest to Sartre because they, like himself, chose to determine their lives in words.[29] Their works not only explicitly trace the life of desire through their various characters, but are themselves the products of desire. As in Hegel's *Phenomenology*, the labor of desire makes itself known through narrative structures. For Sartre, the narratives of desire are of necessity imaginary works; as such, they do not merely tell about desire, but the "telling" itself is desire's essential transformation from nothingness to a linguistic and imaginary presence. In asking after the structure of desire, we ask after the origin and meaning of fictional articulation, and, for Sartre, the philosophical narrative about desire cannot escape these fictional constraints. In tracing the evolution of desire into literary words and works, the philosopher-biographer thus becomes a literary artist as well. For Sartre, then, the analysis of desire must take place within the reconstruction of the life of the literary writer, for only then can we see the transitions from negation to desire to the imaginary and its literary secularization. Sartre is himself implicated in the ontological situation of desire, and his own narrative must enact the rhetorical structure that he seeks to understand in Genet and Flaubert. As we shall see, this hermeneutical quandary of the biographer returns him to the central question of desire and recognition posed in *Being and Nothingness:* to what degree can we know another human being, and to what extent, in knowing him, are we destined to create him?

Desire and Recognition in Saint Genet and The Family Idiot

Each torpid turn of the world has such disinherited children, to whom no longer what's been, and not yet what's coming, belongs.—Rainer Maria Rilke, *Duino Elegies*

Biography appeared a promising form of philosophical inquiry for Sartre as early as *Being and Nothingness* (1943), for it seemed to be the only way to establish the truth of his claims about the structure of human reality in concrete and demonstrable terms. As Hazel Barnes has pointed out, the biographical studies of Genet and Flaubert fulfill the expectation that *Being and Nothingness* aroused—the performance of a concrete existential psychoanalysis of individual lives.[30] In the chapter "Existential Psychoanalysis," Sartre maintains: "this psychoanalysis has not yet found its Freud. At most we can find the foreshadowing of it in certain particularly successful biographies. We hope to be able to attempt elsewhere two examples in relation to Flaubert and Dostoevsky" (*BN 575*). In a related passage Sartre makes clear why the reconstruction of an individuual life is crucial for the fulfillment of his own philosophical project: "to *be,* for Flaubert, as for every subject of 'biography,' means to be unified in the world. The irreducible unification which we ought to find, which is Flaubert, and which we require biographers to reveal to us—this is the unification of an *original project,* a unification which should reveal itself to us as a *non-substantial absolute"* (*BN 561*).

Human beings are indistinguishable in this "original project" to achieve and become a substantive presence in the world. They begin to exhibit individuality in the various ways they contend with the everpresent problem of elusive substance. Hence, the self is a style of responding to inevitable dissatisfaction, a particular configuration of longing which, over time, becomes distinctively one's own. Desire is, then, the hermeneutical occasion for the disclosure of an individual's fundamental project, the unified legacy of choices over how to be in a world where substantial and final being is an experiential impossibility.

The hermeneutical task of discovering a fundamental project in and through desire proves problematic in *Being and Nothingness,* and the turn to biographical inquiry seems a necessary supplement to the schematic character of the earlier text. In *Being and Nothingness* desire was considered as a unity of three interrelated projects: the original project (the anonymous and universal desire to be), the fundamental project (the individual desire to be a determinate way), and the myriad projects of everyday life (the particular desires directly manifest in lived experience) (*BN* 567). Sartre argues that these three desires are only analytically separable, and that in experience they are given in one stroke as a symbolic unity. As early as *Baudelaire* (1947), the biographical studies sought to clarify the interrelationship of these various dimensions to desire in the context of a concrete individual.

In Hegelian terms, Sartre attempts in the biographical inquiries of Genet and Flaubert to exemplify these two individuals in their "concrete universality," elucidating affective life as a symbolic unity of particular and universal elements. In terms that recall the Kierkegaardian filter through which Sartre appropriates Hegel's view of the subject, Sartre claims to illuminate Flaubert's life as a "universal singular."[31] The mediation of particular and universal desires is less an assumption of ontology—an inexorable development—than a task or demand to which every individual effects an original response. Although Sartre's study of Flaubert is written after Sartre's Marxist turn, the existential framework still serves his theory of the self. Sartre's acknowledgment of the profound effects of infantile development and social and political structures on the life of desire does not culminate in a renunciation of the doctrine of choice; rather, choice is recast as a subtle process of appropriation and reinterpretation, a daily task of reproducing a complex historical situation in one's own terms, reworking this history, fashioning it anew. Flaubert's struggle with substantial being takes on historically specific terms: "summed up and for this reason universalized by his epoch, he in turn resumes it by reproducing himself in it as singularity" (*FI* ix).

Both Genet and Flaubert singularly reproduce their personal and historical circumstances in their literary works, and these works, in turn, become for Sartre the unified symbolic expression of their fundamental desires. Because desire always and fundamentally intends an object beyond its reach, satisfaction resides in a merely possible, or imaginary, world. Desire manifests the pre-reflective choices at its origin through the imaginary—the symbolic expression of desire. Sartre's selection of Genet and Flaubert as the intentional objects of his biographical desires seems hardly accidental; both authors sought resolution for desire in the imaginary realm, and both concretized or "realized" the imaginary in actual literary works. Sartre remarks, "The reason I produced *Les Mots* is the reason I have studied Genet or Flaubert: how does a man become someone who writes, who wants to speak of the imaginary?"[32] Questioned on why he chose Flaubert, Sartre answers in words that might well explain his choice of Genet as well; "Because [Flaubert] is the imaginary. With him, I am at the border, the barrier of dreams."[32]

Sartre is interested in how these individuals come to dream and how their dreams are *realized*, how they take form as literary works, and how these works reflect the fundamental passions that constitute these lives. Desire's goal finds satisfaction only in the realm of impossibility; the imaginary, as a postulated presence, relieves consciousness temporarily of its estrangement from plenitude. The particular ways in which Genet and Flaubert author the imaginary universe reflect their fundamental attitudes toward being; thus, the literary transcription of the imaginary becomes the hermeneutical situation in which to read back the tacit intentionality of desire, the cultivated style of responding to impossibility and conjuring presence, the singular choice implicit in that response.

The literary "realization" of the imaginary provides a tentative satisfaction of the desire to overcome the ontological disjunction between consciousness and substantial being. Literary works foster the illusion that consciousness can transfigure substance itself. Genet takes issue with a social world that seems intractable; through the production of literary works, he achieves a sense of personal efficacy otherwise denied him. The "difference" he overcomes is between himself and others; through the performance of his plays, "he forces others to dream his dream" (*SG* 546). In his earlier vocation as thief, Genet imagines that his crimes will disrupt the complacency of bourgeois life, but he cannot sustain this dream of disruption precisely because he is caught. Genet's desire to create a dream that effectively transforms the social world is realized only through art. He cannot escape this defining—and degrading—look of the Other, so he endeavors in his plays and poetry to direct the Other's look, to captivate his audience and thereby gain mastery over their perspective on him. Sartre writes, "The fact is that if he prefers the work of art to theft, it is because theft is a criminal act which is derealized into a dream, whereas a work of art is a dream of murder which is realized by an act. ... Murderers achieve glory by forcing good citizens to dream about crime" (*SG* 485).

Genet seeks to escape the look of the Other, to become an invisible power, noncorporeal, who inconspicuously determines the experience of others as they watch or read his plays. But Genet also *solicits* recognition through writing; as Sartre points out, "with words, the Other reappears" (*SG* 455). The transformation from thief to poet is predicated on the recognition of the Other's inevitability. And yet for Genet, the Other cannot simply be accepted; from childhood on the Other has signified a social reality that has excluded and illegitimated Genet. Banished from the world of the Other, Genet attempts through art to assimilate the Other to *his* world, the inverted world of the bourgeoisie in which crime, vulgarity, and sexual license are prevailing norms. As Sartre remarks, "incapable of carving out a place for himself in the universe, he *imagines* in order to convince himself that he has created the world which excludes him" (*SG* 468).

Sartre's biography of Genet traces a career that begins with victimization and culminates in radical invention. Genet inverts his relationship to the social world through an original reproduction of language. As a young orphan alienated in his adopted home, Genet decides to steal silverware from his adopted family. Genet is caught and called a "thief," whereby he becomes in others' eyes the social outcast he already sensed himself to be. According to Sartre, Genet's theft is his first act, the moment in which he determines himself as the kind of individual others fear and loathe. Illegitimate by birth, Genet takes up this illegitimacy and transforms it into a personal mission. He will become the illegitimate child who robs others of their tokens of legitimacy. His tools are wrought from the weapons originally turned against him; he becomes a master of inversion, sensing and exposing the dialectical possibilities of the social opposition between himself and others.

The possibility of a dialectical inversion of the power relations characterizing his original relations with others is to be found in language: " 'I'm a thief,' he cries. He listens to his voice whereupon the relationship to language is inverted: the word ceases to be an indicator, it becomes a being"(*SG* 42). "Thief" is, in effect, Genet's initiation into poetic words. The word does not refer, but creates; through being so named, Genet has become the name itself. The name clings to him as an essential moment of his being. Sartre argues in *Saint Genet* that "poetry uses vocables to constitute an apparent world instead of designating real objects" (*SG* 512). Hence, poetic words are those that constitute imaginary realities, just as the vehement appelation, "thief," transforms the child Genet, invests him with an identity, a destiny, and restricts his possibilities. The transformative power of language will become Genet's weapon in forcing others to "dream his dream." Upon the discovery of this power, Sartre maintains, "Genet wanted to name, not only to designate, but to transform" (*SG* 280). And the object of his transformative acts will be the social world of "the just," the instrumental world of the bourgeoisie, and the rigid and hypocritical moralities that sustain those orders.

Sartre's biographical narratives of Genet and Flaubert trace the resolution of desire into the imaginary, and the imaginary into a set of literary works in which a long-standing struggle for recognition is taken up and pursued. For both Genet and Flaubert—indeed, also, for Sartre—*words* become the vehicle through which childhood is renewed and revised. The primary desire to be implies the primary desire *to be affirmed,* and this lifelong struggle for recognition is thematized and reenacted in the linguistic construction of imaginary worlds. Moreover, in both cases the literary appropriation of this struggle effects an inversion of the power dynamics constituted by the original situation. Sartre's biographical study of Genet has been called his most Hegelian work,[35] but we can also see in *The Family Idiot* the constituting role of recognition in Flaubert's struggle to create a self. For both Genet and Flaubert early childhood is a scene of deprivation; Genet is excluded from the legitimate social community, while Flaubert is *mal aimé*. These original situations of victimization are reinterpreted—although not entirely overcome—through the imaginary transcription of the scene. In Sartre's view, the literary works transform the meaning of early childhood suffering through the active process of its imaginary representation. Imaginative writing makes use of the passive and receptive sensibilities of early childhood, effecting enough critical distance from these sensibilities to embody them in literary form. Writing does not transcend or resolve victimization, but is condemned, as it were, to reformulate this original situation again and again. As active reformulation, writing becomes an assertive response to a passive past, but that is not to rewrite the past, nor to escape it as a necessary and relentless theme. As Sartre says of Genet, "to write is to explore systematically the situation into which one is thrown" (*SG* 558).

Sartre understands the struggle for recognition intrinsic to early childhood as the self's dramatic evolution into existence. The desire to be at its earliest stages is the urge to exist for another—in other words, the need to be loved; this primary relation to the Other forms the pathic structure of every individual life. Rejecting the tendency in *Being and Nothingness* to treat fundamental projects as choices emerging *ex nihilo* from the for-itself, Sartre claims in *The Family Idiot* that "what is important here is to reject idealism—fundamental attitudes are not *adopted* unless they first exist. What is taken is what is at hand" (*FI* 43). The original and constituting project of the self is thus primarily a relation to others, and the development of the self over time is the reenactment of these earlier relations. Incorporating this Freudian insight into his own terms, Sartre realizes that the ontological sketch of desire in *Being and Nothingness* must give way to an analysis rich with biographical detail. In *The Family Idiot* Sartre writes, "without early childhood, it is obvious that the biographer is building on sand" (*FI* 44).

Sartre shows in *Saint Genet* and *The Family Idiot* how these dissatisfied children come to assume adult careers as authors of the imaginary. Genet and Flaubert seem to exemplify truths that characterize the human situation universally for Sartre. Their dissatisfactions are so many appearances of a primary human dissatisfaction. As desire is a "useless passion," so the constituting desires of Genet and Flaubert persist without a final destination in being. Although Sartre refers to the abused child Genet as a "crack in the plenitude of being," he refers to human beings generally in such terms; indeed, consciousness is said to be a "rift" in being. The loneliness of the unloved child reflects the existential loneliness of every consciousness, its differentiation from substance, its exile from the realm of being.

The turn to the imaginary as a possible satisfaction for desires is precipitated by the belief that worldly fulfillment is impossible. The absence of a primary Other who might attend and recognize the child culminates in an adult belief that the world as such is hostile to human desire. For Genet, this constitutive absence in his life prompts his turn to imaginary worlds as a temporary and compensatory filling for the impoverished social landscape. Inferring his illegitimacy, Genet reacts to this lack of recognition through the linguistic invention of a universe, effecting his own transubstantiation into words. Without a body, Genet tacitly figures that he will be exempt from the need for recognition. Genet writes, "this wonderful language reduces the body, wears it down until it is transparent, until it is a speck of light." Genet's self-denial becomes the precondition of his illuminary life. Sartre concludes: "Genet evaporates; he believed seriously, profoundly, in a transubstantiation that would wrest him from his actual life and embody him in words, those glorious bodies" (SG 20). Flaubert suffers a somewhat altered fate at the hands of his mother: "Gustave is immediately conditioned by his mother's indifference; she desires *alone*" (FI 133). As a child Gustave suffers from intense lethargy, and Sartre describes him as living in a state of "passive emotion." Lacking recognition, i.e., lacking parental love, Gustave becomes convinced of his own inevitable inefficacy and resolves, paradoxically, to use his characteristic receptivity to absorb the world:

Without *value*, Gustave feels need as a gap, as a discomfort or—at best and most frequently—as a prelude to an agreeable and immanent surfeit. But this discomfort does not break away from subjectivity to become a demand in the world of others, it remains inside him, as inert and noisy emotion; he suffers it, pleasant or unpleasant, and when the time comes he will suffer satiety. . . . He has neither the means nor the occasion to externalize his emotions through outbursts of any kind; he savors them, someone relieves them or else they pass, nothing more. With no sovereignty or rebellion, he has no experience of human relations; handled like a delicate instrument, he absorbs action like a sustained force and never returns it, not even with a cry—sensibility will be his domain. (FI 130–31)[36]

Sartre argues in *The Family Idiot* that the constitution of the self follows from the internalization of parental attitudes. The parental "look" becomes the manner of the child's self-regard, and the "self" that one sees is always the self first seen and, hence, constituted, by Others. To make a demand for oneself, to translate desire into speech and action, presupposes the existence or possibility of an Other who might respond. Where there is no Other, desire turns back on itself and becomes rigid and mute. Unconvinced of the possibility of such an affirming response, Gustave the child remains mute and inexpressive, unable to discover or know himself. Of Flaubert, Sartre writes: "He was . . . frustrated well before weaning, but it was a frustration without tears and rebellion" (*FI* 129). Similarly, Genet's early abandonment leaves a mark of essential poverty on his character; Genet does not grieve or despair over his loneliness because "grief and despair are only possible if there is a way out, whether visible or secret" (*SG* 191). Both Genet and Flaubert lack the means to recognize their own substantiality, and because they cannot see themselves reflected in their parents' gaze, they are forced to *invent* themselves. Imaginary characters become the key ways in which these unmirrored selves find objective reflection in the social world. Remarking on the youthful Flaubert, Sartre writes, "Gustave is certainly tormented by the need to know himself, to unravel his tumultuous passions and find their cause. But he is put together in such a way that he can understand himself only through invention" (*FI* 211). Genet is denied the benefits of early recognition, and although he senses his exclusion as a determinate, though negative, relation to others, he still lacks the means to see himself as the exiled being that he is. After he commits his crime, the young Genet "is ready to hate himself if he can only manage to see himself" (*SG* 47).

Although the early childhood struggle for recognition is surely definitive of adult life, it does not *determine* the texture of adult experience in a strict sense. The earliest dramas of desire establish the reigning motifs of a given life and circumscribe the domain of possible choices. Early childhood does not unilaterally produce adult life; its causality is less mechanical than dialectical. Childhood maintains its power in adult experience to the extent that its themes are appropriated and reinterpreted in contemporary terms. Gustave remains passive only because he continuously believes that this is his only option. Sartre explains: "passivity does not simply exist; it must continually create itself or little by little lose its force. The role of new experience is to maintain or destroy it" (*FI* 42).

Sartre understands subjectivity not only as the culmination of a history of circumstances but, more importantly, as the singular realization or determination of this history. The individual appropriates historical and biographical circumstances and concretizes—or realizes—them in his own personality: this is the concept of the universal singular. In *The Family Idiot*, Sartre refers to the individual as both sign and signifier, and suggests that the effects of history and circumstance ought to be understood as constituting the person as sign. He concludes that "if every person in the singular contains in himself the structure of the sign, and if the totaled whole of his possibilities and his projects is assigned to him as its meaning, the hard, dark core of this meaning is early childhood" (*FI* 44). Sartre's fundamental project of *Being and Nothingness,* now filtered through the medium of early childhood, calls for reformulation: choice becomes the incessant process of taking up a childhood drama that has already asserted itself as the guiding motif of one's life. One is not free to take this motif up again—one must: subjectivity is bound to thematize the conditions of its own existence; this is the necessity of its reflexive structure, and the inherent logic of its desire.

Sartre makes use of Hegel's formulation of self-consciousness in claiming that the particular historical situations of Genet and Flaubert gain their significance only through their *realization*. Midway through the first volume of *The Family Idiot*, Sartre warns his readers that a comprehensive understanding of Flaubert's life cannot be content with a causal history of his internal life, for no "cause" can take "effect" save through the moment of its appropriation or realization in the person of Flaubert. Hence, Sartre argues that we must seek an explanation in terms of Flaubert's intentional aims, his fundamental project. In language that recalls Hegel's doctrine of self-consciousness, Sartre writes:

Intimate experience is characterized ontologically by doubling, or self-consciousness. It is therefore not sufficient to have shown the original structure of this life and its particular kind of alienation, not even to have reconstituted its immediate savour; starting with the facts at our disposal we must determine the way in which this experience is made living. If he is condemned, how does Gustave *realize* his condemnation?(*FI* 382)

[164]

As in his earlier works, Sartre questions in *The Family Idiot* the origin of the fundamental projects of human beings. In contrast to the analysis offered in *Being and Nothingness,* Sartre's ontological categories in *Saint Genet* and, particularly, in *The Family Idiot* reveal the concrete mediations through which fundamental projects appear. In *Saint Genet* and *The Family Idiot,* the earlier categories still prevail: the fundamental projects of Genet and Flaubert are formulations of a "lack," responses to a "look," incorporated in desire. But the biographical studies also historicize these categories: the "lack" from which human projects emerge is understood as the concrete deprivations of childhood; the "look" of the Other that constitutes identity is understood as the earliest forms of affirmation that a child receives. Desire itself is seen as a nexus of agency and cultural life, a complex mediating act by which the past is taken up and reproduced, a way of concretizing one's history and determining its course.

Paradoxically, Flaubert must seek to realize a past that never was, that is, to give form to a history that is the history of absence. Without value, he has no right to exist, so he must borrow the rights of his father. He gains a sense of legitimacy by darkening himself in his father's shadow. Sartre explains, "[Gustave] derives his right to be born only from his relationship to his progenitor, he bases it equally on the material whole that represents him: feudal property" (*FI* 330). The symbolic fusion of father and feudal lord becomes, in Sartre's view, a primary interpretation of the Other for Flaubert. As the young bondsman, Flaubert struggles for recognition always within the terms of this dynamic:

Their connection, *experienced,* becomes a subjective structure within him. Not that it is ever felt or suffered; it is a matrix, an infinity of *practices*—actions, emotions, ideas—evoked by the most diverse situations and unwittingly, invisibly marked; without ever assuming its role, these practices reveal or reproduce the original connection in the objects they pursue. Thus the subjective moment is the moment of mediation; the first relation is internalized so as to be externalized once again in all other areas of objectivity. (*FI* 330)

In his adult life, Genet carries his early experience of rejection with him as "a melodious child dead in me" (*SG* 1). Starved of recognition, the young Genet does not "exist," in effect, he is a stillborn condemned to live: "to the child who steals and masturbates, to exist is *to be seen by adults,* and since these secret activities take place in solitude, they (and he) do not exist" (my addition). Genet's criminal acts are ways of realizing what he takes to be his fate—his exile. In Sartre's words, "we do not see that he lives on two levels at the same time. Of course Genet condemns theft! But in the furtive acts he commits when he is all alone *he does not recognize* the offense which he condemns. He, steal?" (*SG* 15). Genet does not understand himself as an offensive being prior to the offensive act that reveal this identity, but his awareness of this identity—this internalization of the Other's disapproving glance—persists tacitly or prereflectively. This sense of his own social undesirability precipitates the desire to steal and is, in turn, confirmed through the realization of that desire. The pre-reflective sense of his identity surfaces in experience as anguish, urgent and ill-defined. Sartre writes, "The truth is that he is impelled by anxiety. At times he feels obscurely within himself a kind of budding anguish, he feels that he is about to see clearly, that a veil is about to be torn and that he will know his destitution, his abandonment, his original offense. So he steals. He steals in order to ease the anguish that is coming on. When he has stolen the cakes and the fruit, when he has eaten them in secret, his anxiety will disappear, he will once again find himself in the lawful and sunlit world of honesty" (*SG* 15).

Neither Genet nor Flaubert ever comes to believe in his own social substantiality; neither ever gains what Sartre understands as the right to desire and to receive an affirming recognition. Both individuals retreat into imaginary worlds, attesting to their abiding belief in the impossibility of a real fulfillment. This exclusion from reality, however, is itself realized in the making of literary works, and for both individuals literary production subverts the projects of self-defeat. Both Genet and Flaubert create fictive Others, embody them, struggle with them, and give them the material form of a written text. Through the public delivery of their productions, both Genet and Flaubert create and receive the affirming looks of Others, indeed, come to be held in high "regard."

The recognition that both authors procure from their audiences is less a reparation of the past than a paradoxical affirmation of the past as it was and continues to be. In other words, both Genet and Flaubert remain *absent* in their works, escaping the direct looks of Others, and yet their characters and linguistic creations are ways in which their absence from reality becomes very present. As a writer, Genet is described by Sartre as "a perpetual absence," a disembodied vision which escapes another's

[166]

stare even while creating the spectacle that entrances him. Flaubert as well is lost to his objectifications, claiming that he *is* Madame Bovary, then appearing in the figure of Satan, recapitulating the themes of infinite dissatisfaction that have structured his identity from the start.

In the case of Flaubert, literary works thematize the infinite dissatisfaction of desire, thereby giving present and recognizable form to an abiding absence. Sartre argues that the success of Flaubert's literary works depends upon the failure of Flaubert's desire. In becoming a writer, Sartre maintains, Flaubert does not alter his desire's inefficacy—he merely uses this inefficacy to his advantage. It becomes the lack from which his novels emerge. In Sartre's words, "praxis becomes the efficacy of the passive" (*FI* 139). Literary praxis does not resolve passivity, but gives it a form that lets it persist and produce.

The intimate link of desire and defeat in Flaubert's consciousness contains within itself the seeds of subversion. Flaubert desists from desire, convinced of the inevitability of dissatisfaction. And yet this refusal to desire implicitly avows the infinite life of desire. Flaubert's characters time and again evidence the boundless passion of passivity. Sartre remarks that "in all [Flaubert's] early works there is an identical motif, that of alien *intentionality* or *stolen freedom;* in every life a great computer has worked out the *Umwelt* beforehand, as well as its tools and circumstances, so that each desire should be evoked at the very moment when the organization of the surroundings makes it most inopportune" (*FI* 379). For Sartre, this literary characterization of defeat thematizes Flaubert's fundamental dilemma. In a sense, defeat is the necessary precondition of Flaubert's desire, for only as a *defeated being* can Flaubert recognize himself. Flaubert is not quite without a self—he has internalized an impoverished self, a self devoid of rights. As all desire tacitly seeks to make explicit the fundamental projects that form identity, Flaubert's desire seeks to realize and confirm his essential poverty. In effect, he can only realize himself as a de-realized being; hence, he requires the imaginary to exist. Flaubert thus lives a life of pure desire, dwelling only among the possibles of a literary universe, much like the disembodied souls of Dante's Hell or the figure of Satan in Flaubert's own "Rêve d'enfer" whose lack of organs precludes the satisfaction of desire.

As much as Sartre's earlier ontological schematism is historicized through his biographical inquiries, his search for the concrete details of these individual lives returns him to the broader ontological concerns of *Being and Nothingness*. Flaubert's lack of rights makes him into a suitable existential hero for Sartre, because Flaubert, like Genet, is born "illegitimately" into this world. This absence of a "birthright" characterizes every human birth for Sartre; one comes into existence without necessary reasons or purposes, unjustifiably, without ontological legitimation or "place." The figure of the unloved child exemplifies the existential abandonment of every individual. Note in the following how Sartre's ontology seems to find literary transcription in Flaubert's symbolism:

"Sovereignty . . . seems to be *desired* rather than truly possessed. At this point in the investigation we discover the depth of Flaubert's descriptions and the convergence of his symbols; the *nothingness* that touches being, the negativity that can engulf all positive plenitude, the *suctioning void* that sucks up reality is quite simply pure subjectivity, inchoate and *conscious* insofar as it has become pathos, meaning the desire for valorisation. The basis of the non-existent rights which the envious person maintains are his against all odds and which cause him suffering is *desire in itself*, which knows its impotence and is preserved in spite of everything as a gaping demand, all the stronger because unheeded. (*FI* 418–19)

Flaubert's life of dissatisfaction confirms Sartre's view of desire as a lack in search of an impossible plenitude. Presumably, all human desire would have this character, including the desire of those who claim to have found satisfaction and set up permanent lodgings there. Flaubert suits Sartre, however, precisely because he renounces the bad faith of the satiated. That human reality is "fundamentally desire" means, for Sartre, that human beings generally labor under impossible goals. Imaginary writers thus undertake this definitively human task in explicit ways, and thus provide the rest of us with an illuminating view of ourselves. That desire always fails does not imply that human life is necessarily failure; indeed, desire's permanent dissatisfaction underscores our ontological status as *striving* beings. And the human response to inevitable dissatisfaction may become the stuff of true success. Flaubert reveals Sartre's ontology by responding to his exile from substantial satisfaction with the desire to invent insubstantial worlds. This reminder of human limitation becomes the occasion for unexpected hubris:

From the beginning, Flaubert experienced his desire as a need since he recognized the impossibility of satisfying it and managed to internalize that impossibility through experienced *death* . . . this desire stands on good grounds, posing its own impossibility, tearing itself apart; its wounds embitter but inflame it. Better, it would be quickly soothed, suppressed, if the thing desired were within reach; because that is impossible, it swells. Impossibility conscious of itself awakens desire and provokes it, adding rigor and violence; but desire finds this impossibility outside itself, and the object, as the fundamental category of the desirable . . . man defines himself as a *right to the impossible. (FI* 420)

Sartre seems to say that human beings are less interested in satisfaction than in desire itself. The fundamental desire unifying particular desires is the desire to sustain desire. Sartre claims, "Desire *comes afterward.* If dissatisfaction characterizes desire, it is because [desire] is never awakened except by the acknowledged impossibility of being satisfied"*(FI* 426).

In the wake of desire's dissatisfaction emerges the ineradicable alterity and specificity of the substantial world. In effect, desire's failure returns consciousness to an appreciation of the world's texture. No longer interested in a fusion with substance that would eradicate difference, consciousness dissatisfied becomes alert to *qualities.* In this sense, the experiences of dissatisfaction occasion the successive revelation of the world in its alterity and variegation. This Sartre seems to find confirmed in Flaubert:

When Gustave claims that the essence of desire is contained in the lack of gratification, he is far from wrong. Still, this claim must be properly understood. Desire, aside from all the prohibitions that mutilate and curb it, cannot be gratified to the extent that its *demand* is not amenable to a correct statement or has no rapport with articulated language; whatever its current objective, it seeks a certain relation of interiority to the world which cannot be conceived or consequently realized. With the exception that in the present, pleasure exists, even if it is seen as corresponding imperfectly to what was demanded; in order to perceive that by the sexual act one is asking for *something other* that vanishes, one must still "possess" the body of the other and take pleasure from it. In this sense it would be more valuable to say that desire is revealed as ungratifiable the more it is gratified. *(FI* 421)

Desire seems also to be an assertion of freedom in the face of factic limitations. In discussing "Rêve d'enfer," Sartre suggest that Flaubert is like Satan, reveling in the expansive world of pure desire. "Satan professes to be prey to infinite and insatiable desires; only the lack of organs, he tells us, makes him deficient. He is boasting. In actuality, he effects imaginary desires because he desires to desire" *(FI* 263–64). Flaubert prefers his disembodiment as well, for without his body Flaubert belongs to no place and no time—free of his history, he becomes a pure freedom. Sartre argues that infinite desire is Flaubert's strategy to "wrench himself away from the ponderings that tear him apart, from the grip of the past, from that retrospective passion which makes him advance backward, his eyes fixed on a childhood lost forever . . . to negate the deep, narrow circle in which his passions revolve." Denying his own body, Flaubert projects that body outward in literary characters who desire audaciously and ceaselessly. On the one hand, Sartre observes, "this driven, morose, fierce, and wretched adolescent wants to take, and refuses to give himself, the freedom to desire, to love, in a word to live." Yet Flaubert's abstention becomes the condition of authorial omniscience. In Sartre's words, Flaubert has "set against the iron collar of his finitude . . . the immense abyss of his unreal desire for everything, that is, for the infinite" (*FI* 264).

Because both Genet and Flaubert had childhoods marked by deprivation, and because each took to the imaginary world of literature to thematize this primary void, they illustrate in clear terms the doubling of a consciousness exiled from substantial identity. Sartre writes in a post-Hegelian framework that no longer assumes that all negativity will be harnessed within the wider circumference of being. The thematization of the negative is not its resolution into substance for Sartre—it is its imaginary life. Sartre heeds the negations that structure these lives. He sees these children as ill-loved, unattended, undervalued. The question he poses to these lives echoes the Hegelian drama that all subjectivity must undergo: how can a negation, through self-negation, posit itself as positive being? Hegel's answer seems to be this: a negation that inverts itself and becomes a positive being must have been all along a positive being, but in implicit form. Every negation is revealed to belong to a prior unity that required the labor of the negative for its disclosure. Sartre challenged Hegel's "ontological optimism" in *Being and Nothingness,* and his revival of certain Hegelian themes in the biographies does nothing to diminish the force of that earlier challenge. Denying the postulation of prior unities, Sartre argues that a negation that resolves itself into positive being is an impossibility. The doubling of consciousness does not restore us to a hidden substance, but becomes a meditation on the ontological disjunction between consciousness and substance. In other words, human beings can thematize and reformulate the constitutive negativities of their lives, but that reflection or repetition is not reparation.

[170]

The lack characterizing human existence remains an indisputable premise in Sartre's works, but in *Genet* and again in *Flaubert* we begin to understand the historical fluidity of this category. Every life begins as a negativity, but also as a determinate relation—this is the meaning of an infant's need to be loved by another. The specificity of that relation gives a peculiar form and style to negativity—it helps to form a distinctive desire. Although this lack is never overcome, human beings remain preoccupied with its thematization, the discovery and recapitulation of the determinate absences, deprivations, separations, and losses which make human personalities what they are. These negations are repeated (doubled or given positive expression), often with the hope that this time satisfaction will be at hand; negation's repetition, however, succeeds only in reaffirming its inevitability.

For Sartre, then, desire does not articulate a substantial self that has been there all along, but neither does it invent an identity *ex nihilo;* it labors within the terms of historically entrenched relations. Consonant with Freud's theory of ego formation,[37] Sartre's biographical works, especially *Flaubert,* view personal identity as a derivation from early experiences of separation or dissatisfaction. In Freudian terms, the ego arises as a defense against loss, as a self-protective agency which infers its exclusion from parental presence. If desire is a double-negation that creates the being of the self, then we might in Sartrian spirit understand desire as a vain striving to heal this wound at the inception of life, the wound of original separation, through a repetition that seeks to be reparation but never can. Human beings can negate the negations that constitute them only by creating a fantasy of pure presence. For Sartre, the imaginary poses as such a seamless presence, but is truly a "nothingness." Hence, the imagination reenacts negativity only to instate it once again. For Sartre, the enactment or thematization of negation is the limit to what human beings can do with respect to the losses of the past, but this re-presentation can also be the occasion of singular achievement. Indeed, the meaning of Genet and Flaubert for Sartre seems to reside in the extreme fertility of these authors of the imaginary who transformed their losses into occasions of unparalleled literary creation.

The biographical narratives of Genet and Flaubert trace the careers of these two lives, but also establish the contours of a developed theory of desire and personal identity. The self appears as a paradoxical task of

representing a constitutive lack. In the case of Flaubert, his passive constitution becomes a source of pathos and, in turn, a singular literary
presentation of passion. Like every consciousness, Flaubert must objectify
himself to know himself. Paradoxically, the self he comes to know cannot
be said to exist prior to its objectification. And yet there is experience
prior to this self-objectification, if only in the mode of the desire to become
objectified. This inchoate "self" prior to its objectifying acts is, for Sartre,
the lived experience of internalized early relations with others. Surfacing
as anxiety, this tacit self, this unarticulated history, is taken up and given
form, thereby coming into "existence." Flaubert writes from his passivity,
and yet in writing pathically, he subverts the passivity at the source of his
writing. The realization of a lack always entails a process of inversion;
the act of representing asserts itself as a constitutive of the self it seeks to
represent. In effect, there is no knowable self prior to its representation.
The representation draws upon a latent history and reworks that history
in the moment of its representing. The act of representation thus itself
becomes integral to the fundamental project of the self. Representation
becomes the mode of projecting an implicit past, and instating it as part
of the present.

   Writing becomes for Sartre the paradigmatic act of self-negation that
effects this transition from a latent history to an invented self. In Hegelian
terms, the literary work emerges as the necessary mediation between the
mute and inchoate dimensions of the self and the recognition that confers
value and objective existence on that self. This double-negation forms the
activity of writing, although writing is less a solution than a continuous
reflection on a life that can have no solution. Writing also becomes a way
in which Flaubert and Genet sustain desire, for both write imaginatively—
they desire impossible worlds. Words become the realization of desire,
and its perpetual reinvention. In Sartre's terms, "the love which is lived
cannot be named without being reinvented. One will be changed by the
Other, discourse and lived experience. Or rather, the claims of feeling and
of expression are mutually heightened . . . since both issue from the same
source and interpenetrate from the beginning. (*FI* 28)"

   Sartre's reflections on writing, desire, the invention of the self and the
invention of the Other bear rhetorical consequences for his own biographical writing. In one interview Sartre maintained that *The Family Idiot* was
less empirical research than a novel in its own right. He termed this work

a "true novel"[38] and proceeded to question whether biographical narrative was not the only novel possible today. Similarly, when Genet disputed the accuracy of Sartre's portrayal of his life, Sartre found the criticism inconsequential. It remains purposefully ambiguous whether these biographies as novelistic enterprises, *report* or *invent* the lives they consider. Sartre's developed view of interpersonal relations seems to indicate that "to know" and "to invent" an Other are indissolubly linked. When Sartre predicts, "one will be changed by the Other," he means, too, that Flaubert, dead though he is, will be transformed by Sartre. Biography is less an empirical study whose truth consists in correspondence to the facts than it is an original effort to take up one's own cultural history through its embodiment in another person. Sartre is not a neutral observer of Flaubert; Flaubert is Sartre's cultural past, the champion of French Letters, and Sartre's participation in the tradition so greatly influenced by Flaubert makes clear that his writing about Flaubert is an effort both to recover and invent Sartre's own cultural past.

Sartre maintained that *empathy* is the biographer's proper attitude.[39] We might well speculate that this attitude was one Sartre cultivated over time with regard to Flaubert, who, Sartre confessed, always evoked antipathy in him.[40] Sartre's project in writing *Flaubert* might partially have been to transform this antipathy into empathy. And we might well ask whether this emotional transformation required that Sartre find common ground with Flaubert. The subject of biography is almost always a subject of the past, and we can see that Flaubert is to a certain degree Sartre's cultural past as well as his past vocation as a writer. That Sartre no longer writes literature by the time he writes *The Family Idiot*, indeed, that he concludes that novels must now become biographical narratives, suggests that there is no standpoint of pure inventiveness that does not sustain a relation to the cultural and personal past. Biography is the kind of invention that enters into an ongoing story to tell it again slightly altered. The dream of a leap into the imaginary that releases one from the weighty facticity of history is no longer a tenable pursuit for Sartre; invention, choice, desire must mediate the present through the past that produces it, and through that mediation, produce the past anew.

Sartre's project to "overcome" the "difference" of Genet and Flaubert is pursued in Hegelian terms inasmuch as both Genet and Flaubert become, as subjects of biography, immanent features of Sartre the biographer. As in the *Phenomenology*, the words that pursue difference become an inadvertent means of overcoming difference. Words are thus subjected to the project of desire and facilitate its satisfaction; they give presence to negativity, constructing both the subject and its tentative satisfaction.

Two questions emerge about Sartre's literary project of existential psychoanalysis. The first has to do with the limits of what can be articulated, and the second, internally related to the first, with the accessibility of the personal past. Sartre assumes that language brings forth the history of negation that constitutes an individual, but is it fair to assume that infantile development, understood in terms of primary repression, is wholly accessible to consciousness and to words? What happens to words when what cannot be spoken makes itself felt in speech? As we shall see, the answer to this question poses a severe challenge to Sartre's entire theory of the subject, its autonomy, and the nature of its linguistic power.

4

The Life and Death Struggles of Desire: Hegel and Contemporary French Theory

> *"It is the subject who introduces*
> *division into the individual."*
> Lacan, *Écrits*

The twentieth-century history of Hegelianism in France can be understood in terms of two constitutive moments: (1) the specification of the
subject in terms of finitude, corporeal boundaries, and temporality and
(2) the "splitting" (Lacan), "displacement" (Derrida), and eventual death
(Foucault, Deleuze) of the Hegelian subject.[1] In the course of this history,
the Hegelian traveler in pursuit of a global place which he always already
occupies loses his sense of time and location, his directionality and, hence,
self-identity. Indeed, this subject is revealed as the trope it always was,
and one comes to see the hyperbolic aspirations of philosophy now clearly
inscribed in the very logos of desire. But Hegel is not so easily dismissed,
even by those who claim to be beyond him. The contemporary opposition
to Hegel rarely evidences signs of indifference. The difference from Hegel
is a vital and absorbing one, and the act of repudiation more often than
not requires the continued life of that which is to be repudiated, thus

[175]

paradoxically sustaining the "rejected Hegel" in order to reconstitute contemporary identity in and through the act of repudiation again and again. It is as if Hegel becomes a convenient rubric for a variety of positions that defend the self-sufficient subject, even those positions that defend a Cartesian view of consciousness which Hegel himself clearly rejects. Hegel's popularity among the early twentieth-century French interpreters was followed by a rebellion of the second generation, the students of both Hyppolite and Kojève, who were also simultaneously reading Nietzsche, Freud, Marx, structuralist linguistics and anthropology, and developing postphenomenological positions from the late works of both Husserl and Heidegger. Hegel was never approached purely scholastically in France, and in some respects we might understand the French reception of Hegel as a movement *against* scholasticism. Even Jean Wahl's 1929 work, *Le Malheur de la conscience dans la philosophie de Hegel,* attempted to show that Hegel was not primarily a "systematic" philosopher, but one who anticipated both his religious and existential critics. And yet this early reading of Hegel which found resonances in the lectures and writings of Kojève, Hyppolite, Henri Noël, and Mikel Dufrenne, was already an effort to move away from a metaphysics of closure and a theory of the autonomous subject with a firm metaphysical place in history. Already in those early works, the Hegelian subject is paradoxical, and metaphysics itself is understood as a terrain of dislocation. Hence, it is curious to watch the generation that follows Hyppolite, a generation largely spawned from his own seminar, which repudiates Hegel for being all the things that both Kojève and Hyppolite argued he never really was. In other words, the immanent critique of the self-identical subject is in many ways overlooked by Derrida, Deleuze, and others who proceed to view Hegel as championing the "subject," a metaphysics of closure or presence, that excludes difference and is, according to his Nietzschean critics, also anti-life.

And yet, the critique of Hegelianism retains its ambivalence. It is unclear whether the break with Hegel is as severe as it is sometimes said to be. What constitutes the latest stage of post-Hegelianism as a stage definitively beyond the dialectic? Are these positions still haunted by the dialectic, even as they claim to be in utter opposition to it? What is the nature of this "opposition," and is it perchance a form that Hegel himself has prefigured?

[176]

A Questionable Patrilineage: (Post-)Hegelian Themes in Derrida and Foucault

Although Foucault's work is usually traced to Nietzsche, Marx, and Merleau-Ponty as its intellectual predecessors, his reflections on history, power, and sexuality take their bearings within a radically revised dialectical framework. Included first in an anthology in honor of Hyppolite, Foucault's "Nietzsche, Genealogy, and History" is at once a critique of a dialectical philosophy of history and a reworking of the Hegelian relation of lordship and bondage.[2] Similarly, Derrida is usually considered to be indebted to Husserl, structuralism, and semiology, but his significant relationship to Hegel is evident in *Writing and Difference, Glas* and, for our purpose, an essay originally presented in Hyppolite's seminar, "The Pit and the Pyramid: An Introduction to Hegel's Semiology."[3]

Both Foucault's and Derrida's essays take up Hegelian themes in order to suggest radically different philosophical points of departure. Derrida's essay considers Hegel's comments on language, and effects a rhetorical analysis to show that Hegel's theory of the sign implicates him in a metaphysics of presence, the very opposite of the theory of negativity and dynamism Hegel explicitly defends. Foucault's essay summarizes a few central tendencies of historical explanation and challenges what he takes to be the prevailing assumption that historical change and development can be adequately described in unilinear terms; Foucault asks whether historical experience ought to be understood in terms of rupture, discontinuity, arbitrary shifts and confluences, and further questions the implicit cosmogonic assumption in historiography that the origin of an historical state of affairs can be found and, if found, could shed any light on the *meaning* of that state of affairs. The implicit philosophy of history that he criticizes can be understood as obliquely Hegelian inasmuch as the dialectical explanation of historical experience assumes that history manifests an implicit and progressive rationality. Foucault argues that the presumption of immanent rationality is a theoretical fiction historians and philosophers of history employ to defend against the arbitrary and multiplicitous (non)foundations of historical experience which resist conceptual categorization. Given that both Derrida's and Foucault's essays are rather strong criticisms of certain aspects of Hegelianism, the question arises, how are we to understand these essays as intended for Hyppolite?

It seems fair to assume that these essays are efforts to pay homage to Hyppolite, and that the critical tenor of both pieces of work might be understood to be a continuation and revitalization of a critical attitude embodied by Hyppolite himself. And yet these criticisms can no longer be understood to be revisionist in their purposes or to constitute an "immanent" critique of Hegelianism in the sense that Kojève's "reading" and Hyppolite's "commentary" remain within Hegel's essential framework. In effect, it appears that Derrida accepts the Hegelian project to think difference itself, but wants to argue that Hegel's own method for achieving that goal effectively precludes its realization. Hegel argues that philosophical thinking must turn away from the Understanding, that mode of cognition that tends to fix and master its object, and that philosophy must now engage the Concept, the mode that Hyppolite understands to be "thinking of the being of life." According to Derrida, however, it appears that Hegel has simply instituted the project of mastery at the conceptual level, and that "difference" and "the negative" are always finally thought *within* the confines of a philosophical language that pretends to be that to which it refers, a pretense that seeks to instate plenitude, the principle of identity, a metaphysics of closure and presence. This makes itself clear, according to Derrida, in Hegel's theory of the sign— or, rather, the rhetoric that formulates that theory—which tends to preempt the signified, to be an act of symbolic enclosure and constitution, and so to forbid reference to anything that is not always already itself. Against the symbolic relation of sign to signified, Derrida suggests that reference to the signified is always displaced, indeed, that such "reference" is internally paradoxical. Hence, Derrida concludes that the limits of signification, i.e., the "difference" of the sign from what it signifies, emerges time and again wherever language purports to cross the ontological rift between itself and a pure referent. The impossibility of referring to the pure referent makes such linguistic acts into paradoxical enterprises, whereby referring becomes a kind of display of linguistic inadequacy.

The rupture between sign and signified becomes the occasion for Derrida's own form of Hegelian irony, and might well be understood as the domain in which he reformulates Hyppolite's ironic project in terms of his own theory of signification. Just as Hyppolite everywhere revealed the ironic consequences of the non-self-identical subject who presumes his own adequacy to self, so Derrida exposes the hubris of the philosophical sign's presumption to refer. In both cases, the critique of the principle of identity exposes the limits of human instrumentality, and constitutes a challenge to Hegel's anthropocentric presumptions. For Derrida, the failure of the sign reveals the absolute subject as full of metaphysical ambition and utterly helpless to achieve that ambition through language and that the "subject" is itself the fiction of a linguistic practice that seeks to deny the absolute difference between sign and signified. Hence, the theory of the efficacious sign, one that is allegedly defended by Hegel in his own theory of language, creates the conditions of necessary self-deception. For Derrida, then, this Hegelian practice requires a more radical commentary, indeed, a kind of commentary that exposes the linguistic ruse that produces and sustains the subject in its fictive efficacy.

Derrida and Hyppolite both pursue the moment of ironic reversal, and yet Derrida wants to show that the true pursuit of this moment necessitates playing a final joke on Hegel. Although both Hyppolite and Derrida reveal the limits of the autonomous subject, Hyppolite wants to retain the subject as an *internally* contradictory being, while Derrida argues that the subject no longer makes conceptual sense if referentiality is impossible. Indeed, the ironic reversal that the autonomous subject suffers, according to Derrida, reveals the necessity for a critique of the subject itself and of the conceit of referentiality: the subject only exists as a user of the referential sign, and the critique of referentiality implies that the subject, as a figure of autonomy, is itself no longer possible. In effect, the subject becomes that conceit of referentiality which language bears, but which is dissolved or, rather, deconstructed through a rhetorical analysis that reveals the ironic reversals intrinsic to any pursuit of referentiality. The subject is a subject to the extent that it effects a relationship to exteriority, but once that nonrelationship becomes recognized as the constitutive "difference" of all signification, then the subject is revealed as a fiction language gives itself in an effort to conceal its own ineradicable structure: it is the myth of reference itself.

The turn from Hegel to semiology thus casts the discourse on difference permanently outside the framework of internal relations; the exteriority of the signified can never be reappropriated, and language itself becomes the negative proof of this finally inaccessible exteriority.

Foucault's essay, "Nietzsche, Genealogy, and History," takes up Hegelian themes in a much more oblique fashion, and yet it is clear that an

[179]

implicit critique of Hegel's postulation of reason in history is underway, that Foucault is reformulating the master-slave relationship in a framework that at once preserves the relationship of inversion but displaces this relationship from its dialectical framework. Hence, like Derrida, Foucault is paying homage to Hyppolite, but in such a way that a proper elucidation of Hegelian themes requires a turn *away* from Hegel. In the case of Foucault, as for Deleuze, that turn is at once a turn toward Nietzsche. Foucault's essay takes issue with narratives of historical experience that presume that the multiplicity of present historical phenomena can be derived from a single origin, and that the complexity of modern historical experience can be traced back through a single cause. Reversing this historiographical trope of the Fall, Foucault suggests that in the beginning was multiplicity, a radical heteronomy of events, forces, and relations which historiographers have concealed and rationalized through the imposition of orderly theoretical fictions.[4] Clearly, we can understand the narrative development of the *Phenomenology of Spirit* as precisely such an orderly theoretical fiction, an account of an increasingly complex historical experience through a metaphysics of dialectical unities which is ever-accommodating. Like Derrida's suggestion that the contradictions of the subject cannot be contained, Foucault's point regarding the multiplicitous character of historical experience is that it cannot be appropriated and tamed through a unifying dialectic. Indeed, Foucault's analysis of modernity attempts to show how the terms of dialectical opposition do not resolve into more synthetic and inclusive terms but tend instead to splinter off into a multiplicity of terms which expose the dialectic itself as a limited methodological tool for historians.

Foucault's references to domination in this essay underscore both his appropriation and refusal of dialectical strategies. Clearly, the references to master and slave are based on Nietzsche's analysis in *On the Genealogy of Morals,* but it is illuminating to read Foucault's comments as a Nietzschean reworking of the Hegelian scene. Foucault tends in this essay, as elsewhere, to understand historical experience as a struggle of "forces" that results not in an ultimate reconciliation, but in a proliferation and variegation of force itself. Force is to be understood as the directional impulse of life, a movement, as it were, that is constantly embroiled in conflict and scenes of domination; force is thus the nexus of life and power, the movement of their intersection. These forces, what Nietzsche would have referred to as "instincts," constitute value in and through the conflictual scenes in which stronger forces dominate weaker ones. Value emerges as the "show" of strength or superior force and also comes to conceal the force relations that constitute it; hence, value is constituted through the success of a strategy of domination; it is also that which tends to conceal the genesis of its constitution. In Foucault's terms, "what Nietzsche calls the *Entstehungsherd* of the concept of goodness is not specifically the energy of the strong or the reaction of the weak, but precisely this scene where they are displayed superimposed or face-to-face. It is nothing but the space that divides them, the void through which they exchange their threatening gestures and speeches" (p. 150). Significantly, the strong and the weak, the master and slave, do not share a common ground; they are not to be understood as part of a common "humanity" or system of cultural norms. Indeed, the radical difference between them, conceived by Foucault as a qualitative difference in onto-logical modes, is the generative moment of history itself, the invariant conflictual scene in which power is produced, diverted, redeployed, and in which values come into being. The moment of "emergence" in which the conflict of forces produces some new historical configuration of forces can be variously understood in terms of proliferation, multiplica-tion, reversal, substitution. For Foucault, "emergence designates a place of confrontation, but not as a closed field offering the spectacle of a struggle among equals ... it is a 'non-place,' a pure distance, which indicates that the adversaries do not belong to a common space. Conse-quently, no one is responsible for an emergence; no one can glory in it, since it always occurs in the interstice" (p. 150).

For Hegel, and for most readers of Hegel in France, the confrontation between an agency of domination and a subordinate agency always takes place on the presumption of a shared social reality. Indeed, it is the recognition of this common social ground that constitutes each agency as a social agency and so becomes the basis of the constitution of historical experience. Kojève is perhaps most clear about the role of mutual recog-nition in the constitution of historical experience, and claims that without this insight into consciousness as an agent of recognition, it would be impossible to conceive of historical experience as shared. Foucault ap-pears, then, to be reversing the Hegelian claim altogether, arguing that historical experience "emerges" precisely at that point where common

[181]

ground *cannot* be ascertained, i.e., in a confrontation between differentially empowered agencies whose difference is not mediated by some more fundamental commonality. Indeed, for Foucault, domination is not a single stage in an historical narrative whose ultimate destination is decidedly beyond domination. Domination is, rather, the ultimate scene of history, the repeated scene, one that does not engender a dialectical inversion but continues to impose itself in various ways. It is not a self-identical scene, but one that is elaborated with great detail and historical variation. In effect, domination becomes for Foucault the scene that engenders history itself, the moment in which values are created and new configurations of force relations produced. Domination becomes the curious *modus vivendi* of historical innovation. In Foucault's words:

Only a single drama is ever staged in this "non-place," the endlessly repeated play of dominations. The domination of certain men over others leads to the differentiation of values; class domination generates the idea of liberty and the forceful appropriation of things necessary to survival and the imposition of a duration not intrinsic to them account for the origin of logic. This relationship of domination is no more a "relationship" than the place where it occurs is a place; and, precisely for this reason, it is fixed, throughout its history, in rituals, in meticulous procedures that impose rights and obligations. . . . Following traditional beliefs, it would be false to think that total war exhausts itself in its own contradictions and ends by renouncing violence and submitting to civil laws. On the contrary, the law is a calculated and relentless pleasure, delight in the promised blood, which permits the instigation of new dominations and the staging of meticulously repeated scenes of violence. (p. 150)

For Foucault, domination is not, as it is for Hegel, an impossible or self-contradictory enterprise. On the contrary, the prohibitive or regulative law must find ways to implement itself, and the various strategies of that law's self-implementation become the occasions for new historical configurations of force. Regulative or prohibitive laws, what Foucault will come to call "juridical" laws, are curiously generative. They create the phenomena they are meant to control; they delimit some range of phenomena as subordinate and thereby give potential identity and mobility to what they intend to subdue. They create inadvertent consequences, unintended results, a proliferation of repercussions precisely because there is no prior dialectical prefiguration of what form historical experience must take. *Without the assumption of prior ontological harmony, conflict can be seen to produce effects that exceed the bounds of*

[182]

dialectical unity and result in a multiplication of consequences. From this perspective, conflict does not result in the restoration of metaphysical order, but becomes the condition for a complication and proliferation of historical experience, a creation of new historical forms.

This "non-place" of emergence, this conflictual moment which produces historical innovation, must be understood as *a nondialectical version of difference,* not unlike the "difference" which, for Derrida, permanently ruptures the relation between sign and signified. For both Derrida and Foucault, the Hegelian theme of relational opposition is radically challenged through a formulation of difference as a primary and irrefutable linguistic/historical constant. This inversion of Hegel's prioritization of identity over difference is achieved through the postulation of certain kinds of "difference" as historically invariant and insuperable. In effect, the differences whereof Foucault and Derrida speak are differences that cannot be *aufgehoben* into more inclusive identities. Any effort to posit an identity, whether the identity of the linguistic signified or the identity of some historical epoch, is necessarily undermined by the difference that conditions any such positing. Indeed, where identity is posited, difference is not *aufgehoben,* but concealed. In fact, it appears safe to conclude that for both Derrida and Foucault, *Aufhebung* is nothing other than a strategy of concealment, not the incorporation of difference into identity, but the denial of difference for the sake of positing a fictive identity. We shall see that for Lacan the role of difference functions similarly. For both Derrida and Foucault, difference displaces the metaphysical impulse from its totalizing goal. The Derridean moment of linguistic misfire where the conceit of referentiality debunks itself, undermines the Hegelian effort to establish sign and signified as internally related features of a unified reality. Similarly, the Foucaultian moment of conflict seems capable of producing only ever greater complexity in its wake, proliferating opposition beyond its binary configurations into multiple and diffuse forms, thus undermining the possibility of an Hegelian synthesis of binary opposites.

It is clear that both Derrida and Foucault theorize from within the tradition of a dialectic deprived of the power of synthesis. The question that emerges in a consideration of these post-Hegelians is whether the "post-" is a relationship that differentiates or binds or possibly does both at once. On the one hand, references to a "break" with Hegel are almost always impossible, if only because Hegel has made the very notion of "breaking with" into the central tenet of his dialectic. To break with Hegel and yet to escape being cast into his all-encompassing net of inter-relations requires finding a way to be *different from* Hegel that he himself cannot account for. On the other hand, it becomes necessary to distinguish between *kinds* of difference, some of which are dialectical and always reinstate identity subsequent to any appearance of ontological difference, and others of which are nondialectical and resist assimilation into any kind of synthetic unity. To find the latter sort of difference is to change the very meaning of the "labor of the negative," for this "labor" consists of building relations where there seemed to be none, in the "magic power that converts the negative into being." Nondialectical difference would convert the negative only and always into further negativity or reveal difference itself, not as the negative, but as a qualitative permutation of Being; in effect, nondialectical difference, despite its various forms, is the labor of the negative which has lost its "magic," a labor that does not construct a higher-order being but either deconstructs the illusions of a restorative ontological immanence and posits nondialectical difference as irreducible, or rejects the primacy of difference of any kind and offers a theory of primary metaphysical plenitude which eludes Hegelian categories and entails a defense of affirmation on nondialectical grounds.

It would, of course, be ill-advised to speak of "post-Hegelian thought" or "contemporary French philosophy" as if it were a univocal signifier and true universal. Clearly, the philosophers of difference have differences among them, and for some, the very notion of difference is a matter of indifference. And yet my narrative continues with Lacan, Deleuze, and Foucault in that they all concern themselves with a theme that, however indirectly, connects them with the Hegelian tradition: the subject of desire. The problem of ontological difference and the notion of the human subject, their interrelatedness in the Hegelian tradition, are given a radical reformulation, especially when desire is no longer understood to denote the metaphysical projects of a self-identical subject. Although Derrida is clearly influenced by Hegel, he nevertheless excludes himself from the discourse on desire. Indeed, in *Glas*, he argues that desire is a theme that is restricted to an anthropocentric discourse on presence, although he does not elaborate on this suggestion.[5] The "anthropocentrism" of the discourse on desire, however, will be taken up in my final considerations of Foucault.

In the above discussion of Kojève, Hyppolite, and Sartre, we saw the growing instability of the subject, its placelessness, its imaginary solutions, its various strategies for escaping its own inevitable insubstantiality. The desire to create a metaphysically pleasurable fictive world, fully present and devoid of negativity, reveals the human subject in its metaphysical aspirations as a maker of false presences, constructed unities, merely imagined satisfactions. Sartre's biographical studies in particular construe the subject itself as a fictive unity projected in words. While the subject in Hegel is projected and then recovered, in Sartre it is projected endlessly without recovery, but nevertheless *knows itself* in its estrangement and so remains a unitary consciousness, reflexively self-identical. In the psychoanalytic structuralism of Lacan and in the Nietzschean writings of Deleuze and Foucault, the subject is once again understood as a projected unity, but this projection *disguises* and falsifies the multiplicitous disunity constitutive of experience, whether conceived as libidinal forces, the will-to-power, or the various strategies of power/discourse.

The difference between Sartre's Hegelianism and the post-Hegelianism of structuralism and post-structuralism becomes clear in the reformulation of desire and "projection." For the Sartre of *The Family Idiot*, human desire always implicitly serves the project of self-knowledge; it dramatizes the self, the specific history of negativity that characterizes any individual, and this projection provides the condition for self-recognition. Hence, the fictive projection of the self is always an informative or transparent fiction, an occasion for recuperative knowledge, a fiction immanently philosophical. For Sartre, the Hegelian project of desire is evident in the rhetorical dramatization of desire in which a fiction (unreality) is articulated (realized), the negative magically transformed into being. Hence, for Sartre, the externalization of desire is always potentially the dramatic revelation of identity, the unitary agency of choice which serves as the unifying principle of any given life. In very different ways for Lacan, Deleuze, and Foucault, the projected self is a false construct imposed upon an experience that eludes the category of identity altogether. At its most general level, the subject is postulated in an effort to impose a fabricated unity on desire, where desire is now understood as the multiplicity and discontinuity of affective experience which challenges the integrity of the subject itself.

In the considerations that follow, I will trace the effect of the broken dialectic on the fate of the subject, the reconceptualization of desire, pleasure, and the body outside of dialectical terms, and, lastly, I will consider the status of this "outside." Why, it seems we must ask, do these post-Hegelians return to the scenes of the *Phenomenology* in order to make their anti-Hegelian points? What peculiar form of philosophical fidelity implicitly structures these rebellions against Hegel? Or is rebellion successful, and what kinds of analyses does this deposing of Hegel permit?

Lacan: The Opacity of Desire

Psychoanalysis alone recognizes this knot of imaginary servitude that love must always undo again, or sever.—Lacan, *Écrits*

The work of Jacques Lacan not only appropriates the Hegelian discourse on desire, but radically limits the scope and meaning of desire through the transposition of certain themes from the *Phenomenology* onto a psychoanalytic and structuralist framework. For Lacan, desire can no longer be equated with the fundamental structure of human rationality; Eros and Logos resist an Hegelian conflation. Desire can no longer be said to reveal, express, or thematize the reflexive structure of consciousness, but is, rather, the precise moment of consciousness' opacity. Desire is that which consciousness in its reflexivity seeks to *conceal*. Indeed, desire is the moment of longing that consciousness may be said to suffer, but which is only "revealed" through the displacements, ruptures, and fissures of consciousness itself. Hence, desire is only indicated by the discontinuities in consciousness, and so is to be understood as the internal incoherence of consciousness itself.

For Lacan, then, desire comes to signify the impossibility of a coherent subject, where the "subject" is understood to be a conscious and self-determining agency. This agency is always already signified by a prior and more efficacious signifier, the unconscious. The subject is thus split off from an original libidinal unity with the maternal body; in psychoanalytic terms, this split is the primary repression that effects individuation.

[186]

Desire is, then, the expression of a longing for the return to the origin that, if recoverable, would necessitate the dissolution of the subject itself. Hence, desire is destined for an imaginary life in which it remains haunted and governed by a libidinal memory it cannot possibly recollect. For Lacan, this impossible longing affirms the subject as the limit to satisfaction. And the ideal of satisfaction necessitates the imagined dissolution of the subject itself. The subject can no longer be understood as the agency of its desire, or as the very structure of desire itself; the subject of desire has emerged as an internal contradiction. Founded as a necessary defense against the libidinal fusion with the maternal body, the subject is understood as the product of a prohibition. Desire is the residue of that early union, the affective memory of a pleasure prior to individuation. Desire is thus both an effort to dissolve the subject that bars the way to that pleasure and the contemporary evidence of that pleasure's irrecoverability.

The internal contradiction of the subject cannot be resolved through the creation of a dialectical synthesis, and neither can it be understood in terms of an insoluble paradox. The bar or prohibition that separates the subject from the unconscious is a negative relation which fails to mediate what it separates. In other words, the negativity of repression cannot be understood on the model of Hegelian *Aufhebung,* and the difference that is posited between the unconscious and the subject is not an "internal" difference characterizing a more inclusive unity. Indeed, the splitting of the subject that occurs must be conceptualized as the positing of a difference between unity (the founding pretense of the subject) and disunity (the irrecoverability of the unconscious). This difference, then, is constitutive of the subject as a necessarily split phenomenon.

Lacan's quarrel with the Hegelian notion of *Aufhebung* becomes clear in a dialogue with Hyppolite, recorded in the French edition of *Écrits,* in which the meaning of *Verneinung* or denial is disputed.[6] For Hyppolite, the negation that characterizes the action of denial is a double-negation and, hence, productive of a synthetic structure. The denial of any given event or desire is simultaneously a way of giving existence to that which is being denied. In other words, denial is a positive act which seeks to negate a given thing, but culminates in an inversion of intention whereby that which is denied gains a new significance. Denial is thus understood as a determinate negation, a peculiar modality in which a given thing is posited. Moreover, that which is denied (negated) is itself some form of negativity, some form of longing or desire, some event or scene that is already forgotten, some content of the unconscious, so that denial itself becomes a double-negation, a paradoxical way in which a negativity is brought into language. Hyppolite understands this action of double-negation as the very structure of Eros,[7] the constructive or creative movement of rendering negativity positive. The positing of the negation is understood to be its thematization, the way in which it becomes designated in and through the modality of negation.

Lacan takes issue with the dialectical grace of Hyppolite's explanation. For Lacan, the "lack" characteristic of an unconscious content can never be properly thematized, and the denial in which it is embodied does not act as a positive relation internally related to that which is denied. Indeed, denial operates through the mechanism of displacement and substitution with the consequence that what is posited through the act of denial has no necessary relation to what is being denied, but is only *associatively* related to what is being denied. For Hyppolite, what is negated is taken up by that which is posited and remains an intrinsic feature of that position; as a result, the negative is always indicated and revealed through what is posited; indeed, the negative is subordinated to the position and necessarily becomes positive through any act of positive representation. The Hegelian conceit which structures Hyppolite's position requires that language is able to represent the negative, transforming negativity into positive being, and that language itself is medium of positivity which allows for that wholesale transformation.

Lacan, however, argues that signifying the negative only happens through a displacement of the signified, and that the language that is intended to represent or indicate the negative can only succeed in a further deflection and concealment of the negative. In other words, *the positivity of language is part of the strategem of denial itself,* and representation generally is understood to be founded in a necessary repression of the unconscious. What is posited, the sign, is only arbitrarily related to what is negated, the signified, and there is no logical way to discover the signified through an examination of the sign. Indeed, for Lacan, denial is not a double-negation that obliquely reveals what it is designed to conceal, but, rather, a negation that gives rise to a set of substitutions, a proliferation of positives, a chain of metonymic associations. The associative links

[188]

between these substitute representations reiterate the negation at their origin, revealing the rupture between language and the unconscious again and again without that revelation effecting a reparation of any kind. Language is no longer understood to be internally related to the negative, but is conceived as that which not only rests upon the splitting off of the subject from the unconscious, but continuously effects this splitting off through the mechanism of displacement and substitution. This is a "difference" that cannot be superseded, but only reiterated—endlessly. Indeed, it is fundamental to signification itself as the constitutive difference between sign and signified.

Lacan explicitly criticizes Hegel for restricting his analysis of desire to an analysis of self-consciousness or, in psychoanalytic terms, to consciousness. As a result, the unconscious is disregarded as the signifier of conscious activity, and conscious agency is privileged as the false locus of the signifier. The split between consciousness and the unconscious has consequences for the fundamental opacity of desire. Thus, Lacan criticizes Hegel for disregarding the opacity of the unconscious and for extending the Cartesian presumption of transparent consciousness:

The promotion of consciousness as being essential to the subject in the historical after-effects of the Cartesian *cogito* is for me the deceptive accentuation of the transparency of the "I" in action at the expense of the opacity of the signifier that determines the "I"; and the sliding movement [*glissement*] by which the *Bewusstsein* serves to cover up the confusion of the *Selbst* eventually reveals, with all Hegel's own rigour, the reason for his error in *The Phenomenology of Spirit*. (*Écrits* 307)

For Lacan, the "opacity of the signifier that determines the 'I' " is not Sartre's pre-reflective dimension of the "I", nor Hegel's unrealized but immanently realizable experience of self-consciousness as mediated reflexivity, but *the unconscious* as a chain of signifiers that interferes repeatedly with the coherent, seamless self-presentation of the conscious subject. The unconscious is not conceived topographically by Lacan, but as the various negativities—gaps, holes, fissures—that mark the speech of the "I." Structured as a series of metonymic significations, the unconscious is manifest in speech "at that point, where, between cause and that which it affects, there is always something wrong" (*FFCP* 22). This opacity which emerges in the midst of a broken causal chain designates a prohibition, that which has been precluded from realization. The con-

[189]

scious subject cannot account for this discontinuity through recourse to itself, because it is *subjected to* this discontinuity, signified by the unconscious which is the absent signifier.

The unconscious first appears as a phenomenon in the form of discontinuity and vacillation (*Écrits* 299). It is a metonymic system of signification to the extent that it makes itself known through substitute representations internally unrelated to the unconscious itself. The unconscious as signifier is only arbitrarily related to consciousness, or the subject, as signified, and the ontological discrepancy between them indicates the irrecoverable opacity of the unconscious. And yet the subject can be understood both as a product of the signifier, and as a defense against its recovery.

The unconscious is the *unrealized* (*FFCP* 30) which only becomes present in speech as a "vacillation" in displacement, condensation, negation *(Verneinung)* and other metonymic significations. In Lacan's words, "the gap of the unconscious may be said to be pre-ontological" in the sense that it precedes the ontology of the subject, and constitutes a universal beyond dispute. In effect, the unconscious delimits the context in which any discourse on ontology can take place. The function of the unconscious in any individual indicates this universal function, although in no case does the breach between signifier and signified become resolved in an overarching Hegelian synthesis (*Écrits* 29).

As Lacan explains;

If there still remains something prophetic in Hegel's insistence on the fundamental identity of the particular and the universal, an insistence that reveals the measure of his genius, it is certainly psychoanalysis that provides it with its paradigm by revealing the structure in which that identity is realized as disjunctive of the subject, and without any appeal to tomorrow. (*Écrits* 80)

The disjointed individual, better described as the signifier and the subject, maintains a kind of split or alienation which cannot be overcome through a progressive journey of any kind. There is "no appeal to tomorrow" precisely because this disjunction is constitutive of human experience and human culture universally. An appeal to "tomorrow" would be an appeal beyond culture itself; hence, an impossibility. The unconscious is a kind of negativity which achieves being through a substitute conscious representation, but this expression is arbitrary, and the difference between signifier and signified irretraversible. The positing of the

[190]

Lacanian unconscious thus implicitly raises a philosophical question of how we are to know the unconscious if the only means of its representation are in consciousness, and consciousness has no mimetic or structurally isomorphic relationship to the unconscious.

When the analysand speaks in a psychoanalytic session, Lacan suggests that it is necessary to bracket the subject who seems to speak and to ask, " 'Who is speaking?' when it is the voice of the unconscious that is at issue. For this reply cannot come from the subject if he does not know what he is saying, or even if he is speaking, as the entire experience of analysis has taught us" (*Écrits* 299). The speech of the analysand is said to reverberate with the significations of the unconscious: "The relation of the subject to the signifier—a relation that is embodied in the enunciation (enonciation) whose being trembles with the vacillation that comes back to it from its own statement (*énoncé*)" (*Écrits* 300). Hence, the unconscious can be heard in the meanings a statement creates that are unintended by the speaker. The associations that a given statement evokes in the language in which it is spoken are metonymic significations which structure the unconscious itself. The unconscious *is* the Other, for Lacan, and the chain of signifiers, the link of metonymic associations in language is itself the unconscious. Hence, to be in language is to be presented with an ineradicable Other, the otherness of signification itself, its constant escape from subjective intentions. Hence, it is not the subject that is estranged from itself, in which case a principle of identity would still tacitly hold, but the subject from the signifier itself.

Lacan accounts for this split in terms of the repression of oedipal desires, a founding prohibition, which survives in desire as the Law of the Signifier and conditions the individuation of the subject. This primary repression also constitutes desire as a *lack*, a response to an originary separation which is less the separation of birth than the result of prohibited incestuous union. For Lacan, desire is a "want-to-be," a *manque-à-être* (*FFCP* 29), which is perpetually frustrated because of its subjection to the Law of the Signifier, i.e., because it is in language but, therefore, only obliquely present; hence, desire appears together with its prohibition, and so takes the form of a necessary ambivalence.

Elaborating upon Freud's distinction between the object and the aim of the drive,[8] Lacan understands the tacit project of desire to be the recovery of the past through a future which, of necessity, prohibits it;

desire is the pathos of the cultural being, the postoedipal subject: "Desire . . . is a lack engendered from the previous time that serves to reply to the lack raised by the following time" (*FFCP* 215). The prohibition that constitutes desire is precisely what precludes its final satisfaction; hence, desire is constantly running up against a limit which, paradoxically, is what sustains it as desire. Desire is the restless activity of human beings, that which maintains its disquiet in relation to a necessary limit: "Desire, more than any other point in the range of human possibility, meets its limit somewhere" (*Écrits* 31).

Like Kojève, Lacan accepts a distinction between animal and human desire, although "animal desire" is now termed "need," while desire is exclusively human. Also like Kojève, desire for Lacan is distinguished in and through its manifestation in speech. For Kojève, the speaking of desire precipitates the "I" as an inadvertent consequence; the first-person singular retrospectively emerges as a necessary precondition of the articulation of desire. Lacan accepts the verbalization of desire as its necessary precondition, but maintains that the metonymic chain of associations which desire be-speaks is the locus of its intractable opacity. Following Hyppolite, Lacan agrees that desire is always desire for the Other, but he maintains that this desire can never be satisfied inasmuch as the Other, the unconscious, remains at least partially opaque. Moreover, desire is not to be identified with the rational project of the subject, something Hegel and Kojève seem readily to accept, but exists as the discrepancy between need (biological drive) and demand (*which is always the demand for love, for thorough recognition* through the recovery of preoedipal union). "Thus desire is neither appetite for satisfaction, nor the demand for love, but the difference which arises from the subtraction of the first from the second, the phenomenon of their splitting (*Spaltung*)" (*Écrits* 287).

Here we begin to see the very different relation between desire and language that Lacan maintains over and against his Hegelian precursors. Clearly, for Kojève, the speaking of desire is internally related to desire itself; speaking is desire's rhetorical enactment, its necessary complement and expression. Indeed, for Sartre as well, expression is always an inadvertent affirmation of desire; and rhetoric generally, from Hegel through Sartre, effects a unification of phenomena even when a negation or distinction is being spoken. The implicit view of language as a set of internal relations, a web that binds discrepancies together, is maintained by all of the Hegelian thinkers considered here. Lacan differs dramatically in accepting Saussure's position that the signifier determines the signified but is not directly manifest in it; hence, it is the *breakage* between signifier and signified that generates significance, not the revelation of their previously hidden *unity*. Lacan is clear about the transposition: "If linguistics enables us to see the signifier as the determinant of the signified, analysis reveals the truth of this relation by making 'holes' in the meaning of the determinants of [the subject's] discourse" (*Écrits* 299). Desire, then, appears as a gap, a discrepancy, an absent signifier and thus only appears *as that which cannot appear*. The speaking of desire does not resolve this negation. Hence, desire is never materialized or concretized through language, but is indicated through the *interstices of language,* that is, what language *cannot* represent: "In the interval intersecting the signifiers, which forms part of the very structure of the signifier, is the locus of what . . . I have called metonymy. It is there that what we call desire crawls, slips, escapes, like the ferret" (*FFCP* 214).

For Lacan, then, desire is always linked with a project of impossible recovery, where what is to be recovered is both the repressed libidinal field constitutive of the unconscious, and the "lost object," the preoedipal mother. This project of recovery is impossible precisely because the subject desires to be identical with the signifier, and yet such an identification is precluded by language itself. Indeed, the subject is what replaces the lost object and can be understood to be the incorporation of that loss. Hence, the subject is, according to Lacan, "the introduction of a loss into reality"[9] and the speech of such a loss-ridden subject is itself riddled with absences. Moreover, that speech at once indicates the "loss" it represents, and also bespeaks the desire to overcome that loss; hence, that speech is governed by the pursuit of the phantasm of the Other that is lost.

For Lacan, then, the speech of the subject is of necessity a speech of displaced desire, one that constantly analogizes the lost object with the present object, and constructs false certainties on the basis of partial similarities. The subject who speaks is a "fading" subject, one who is constantly fading into the unconscious that the subject represents, i.e., the *loss* that the subject represents, that which the subject *desires;* the subject is constantly vacillating between its own particularity and the lost Other who, in effect, is also represented by it.

Lacan thus understands desire to be a principle of linguistic displacement, and to be present in the metonymic function of all signification. In "Of Structure as an Inmixing of an Otherness Prerequisite to Any Subject Whatever," Lacan explains:

The question of desire is that the fading subject yearns to find itself again by means of some sort of encounter with this miraculous thing defined by the phantasm. In its endeavour it is sustained by that which I call the lost object . . . which is such a terrible thing for the imagination. That which is produced and maintained here, and which in my vocabulary I call the object, lower-case, *a*, is well known by all psychoanalysts as all psychoanalysis is founded on the existence of this peculiar object. But the relation between this barred subject with this object (*a*) is the structure which is always found in the phantasm which supports desire, in as much as desire is only that which I have called the metonymy of all signification. (p. 194)

The effect of desire's articulation is the perpetual displacement of the signified. Inasmuch as the demand for love present in desire is a demand for the proof or evidence of love, desire is coordinated not with the object that would satisfy it, but with an originally lost object. This object, conceived psychoanalytically as the preoedipal mother, is, of course, prohibited through the Law of the Father, in Lacan's terms, which is consonant with the Law of the Signifier. When Lacan states that "Man's desire is the desire of the Other," this is his version of the Absolute, for the desire of the Other is both the origin and final aim of the demand for love. This Absolute, this "being" that is lacked, is also termed *jouissance*, the fullness of pleasure which, in Lacanian terms, is always frustrated by the oedipally conditioned pain of individuation. Because it is "castration which governs desire" (*Écrits* p. 323), "desire is a defence (*défense*) and a prohibition (*défense*) against going beyond a certain limit in jouissance" (*Écrits* p. 322). It is the world of desire before the subject becomes discrete that is the nostalgic ideal of desire:

What am "I"? "I" am in the place from which a voice is heard clamouring, "the universe is a defect in the purity of Non-Being." And not without reason, for by protecting itself this place makes Being itself languish. This place is called *jouissance*, and it is the absence of this that makes the universe vain. (*Écrits*. p. 317)

Inasmuch as desire implicitly seeks an impossible recovery of jouissance through an Other who is not the original object of desire, the process of desire becomes a necessary series of *méconnaissances* which are never wholly illuminated. Insofar as repression founds desire, deception is desire's necessary counterpart. The desire of the Other's desire is thus only possible through listening to what is not said, what is denied, omitted, displaced: "The desire of the Other is apprehended by the subject in that which does not work, in the lacks of the discourse of the Other" (*FFCP* p. 214). This is not a kind of listening that belongs to the rarefied domain of the psychoanalytic listener, but is evidenced in and through the child's desire: "A lack is encountered by the subject in the Other, in the very intimation that the Other makes to him by his discourse. In the intervals of the discourse of the Other, there emerges in the experience of the child something that is radically mappable, namely, *He is saying this to me, but what does he mean?*" (*FFCP* p. 214).

The "meaning" that the child asks after is more than the subject's intention, but is something akin to the metonymic interminability of the Other. Lacan asks,

is there not, reproduced here, the element of alienation that I designated for you in the foundation of the subject as such? If it is merely at the level of desire of the Other that man can recognize his desire, as desire of the Other, is there not something here that must appear as an obstacle to his fading, which is a point at which his desire can never be recognized? This obstacle is never lifted, nor ever to be lifted, for analytic experience shows us that it is in seeing a whole chain come into play at the level of the Other that the subject's desire is constituted. (*FFCP* p. 235)

This chain of metonymic significations, associations, and substitutions, which re-present the desire of the Other, is simultaneously a displacement of that desire, so that the effort to know desire is always deflected from its course.

Lacan takes issue with Hegel precisely on this point. According to Lacan, Hegel conflates eros and logos, linking all desire to the desire for self-knowledge. In this sense, desire is subjected to the overriding project of knowledge, evidenced by the early supersession of desire in the *Phenomenology*.[10] Assuming that the Hegelian subject is self-transparent, Lacan credits psychoanalysis with introducing the notion of opacity into the Hegelian doctrine of desire:

For in Hegel it is desire *(Begierde)* that is given the responsibility for that minimum connection with ancient knowledge *(connaissance)* that the subject must retain if truth is to be immanent in the realization of knowledge *(savoir)*. Hegel's

[195]

"cunning of reason" means that, from beginning to end, the subject knows what it wants. It is here that Freud reopens the juncture between truth and knowledge to the mobility out of which revolutions come. In this respect: that desire becomes bound up with the desire of the Other, but that in this loop lies the desire to know. (*Écrits* 301)

Lacan's criticism assumes that Hegel's subject, in fact, "knows what it wants," when we have seen that this subject systematically misidentifies the object of desire; indeed, Lacan's own term, *méconnaissance,* might well serve to describe the misadventures of Hegel's traveling subject. And yet it is clear that the "cunning of reason" can operate as a metaphysical finesse in effecting the transitions between chapters in the *Phenomenology,* and it makes sense to ask whether some relentless *logos* does not direct the Hegelian show from the start. The subject itself, however, does not know what it wants from the start, although it may implicitly *be* all that it does come to know about itself in the course of the *Phenomenology.* Hence, this subject constantly misidentifies the Absolute in much the same way that the Lacanian subject of desire remains lured by an ever-elusive jouissance. In disregarding the comedy of errors that mark the Hegelian subject's travels, Lacan unjustifiably attributes Cartesian self-transparency to the Hegelian subject. The fact remains that the very meaning of the Absolute *changes* for the subject of the *Phenomenology,* and as that notion of the Absolute changes, so, too, does the scope and structure of the subject.

Lacan's argument that the philosophical impulse, the desire to know (the love of wisdom), emerges from within the circle of the desire of the desire of the Other, is, indeed, a striking departure from the Hegelian program. Lacan's position seems to be that knowledge only becomes a relevant pursuit for human beings inasmuch as they desire the desire of the Other. In seeking to know what is meant behind what is said, in listening to the negativities of the speaker in order to hear his desire, human beings become pursuers of knowledge, but this pursuit is always conditioned and contextualized by the chain of signifiers, the interminable metonymy of the Other. Hence, Lacan offers here a sketch of what a psychoanalytic understanding of the philosophical impulse might be like. Desire would be less the consummation of philosophical truths than its disavowed condition, the truth it defends *against.* Inasmuch as philosophy savors the postulation of a self-adequate subject, philosophical discourse purports to say all that it means, and never to mean more than it actually says. The psychoanalytic deconstruction of philosophy would, then, consist in listening to the lacks and gaps in philosophical discourse, and theorizing on that basis what kind of defense against desire the philosophical project seems to be.

And yet, for Lacan, Hegel's formulation is not wholly wrong, for as *demand*, desire is a project of knowledge. Although desire cannot be assimilated to demand, existing as the differential between demand and need, it nevertheless maintains something of the transcendental pursuit of presence which we have seen in the Hegelian thinkers. Lacan explains, "Demand in itself bears on something other than the satisfactions it calls for. It is demand of a presence or of an absence—which is manifested in the primordial relationship to the mother. . . . Demand constitutes the Other as already possessing the 'privilege' of satisfying needs, that is to say, the power of depriving them of that alone by which they are satisfied" (*Écrits* 286). Demand seeks proof of love rather than satisfaction, and thus wants *to know* that the Other can offer an unconditional love. Thus, the offerings of this Other are not measured by the satisfaction they accord, the pleasure or the fulfillment of needs, but only as *signs* of unconditional love, Lacan's psychoanalytic reformulation of Hegelian recognition. The transcendental feature of demand manifests its utter disregard for particular shows of affection, or, rather, it reads each and every particular show for the unconditional proof of love it may represent. In fact, demand can result in the utter renunciation of needs, for the satisfaction of needs appears as the presence of so many false particulars, random and insignificant shows of attention of no use to the unconditional demand for love. In this context, *desire* emerges as a sacrificial mediator, one for which the accomplishment of mediation is impossible. Desire enacts the paradox of need and demand and, like Kierkegaardian passion, can never effect a harmonious unity between particular needs and universal demands, but can only elaborate the contradiction, pursuing the impossible in the mundane without promise.

Lacan can be seen to reformulate his Hegelian precursors. Desire emerges for Lacan as a necessarily paradoxical activity, and in this regard we can see his version of desire as a psychoanalytic transposition of Hyppolite's notion of paradoxical desire. In showing how need continues to reside in the exercise of desire, Lacan reveals Kojève's strict distinction between desire and need as phenomenologically naive. Moreover, the articulation of desire in speech reveals the problem with the essentially romantic symbolism that governs the theories of language and expression in Hegel, Kojève, Hyppolite, and Sartre. In these cases, language is always understood as an object's further life, its necessary externalization, its most explicit form, the dialectical conclusion of its development. For Lacan, language always signifies a rupture between signifier and signified, an irretraversible externality, with the further consequence that linguistic signification is a series of substitutions that can never reclaim an original meaning. In effect, to be in language means to be infinitely displaced from original meaning. And because desire is constituted within this linguistic field, it is constantly after what it does not really want, and is always wanting what it cannot finally have. Desire thus signifies a domain of irreparable contradiction.

Although Lacan further breaks down Hegel's doctrine of internal re-lations, he nevertheless remains within Hegelian discourse to the extent that demand retains the Hegelian ideal, and desire remains the bearer of this ontological bad news. In fact, Lacan finds in Hegel's dialectic of desire a preferable discourse to the physiological discourse on "instinct" that predominates in some psychoanalytic circles. Fully aware of the false promises of progression and unity that Hegel's phenomenological expla-nations offer, Lacan nevertheless remains convinced that Hegel's dialectic contains features of universal value, features that are indirectly confirmed by the findings of both structural linguistics and psychoanalysis. Lacan objects to the standard English translation of *Trieb* as instinct, and argues that the Hegelian notion of desire contains the ambiguity that Freud originally intended the drive (*Trieb:* literally, *push* or *drive*) to have.[11] Countering the naturalistic reading of drives as physiologically based and constituted, Lacan argues that, for Freud, the natural is always tempered by the unnatural, indeed, that naturalness is a paradoxical signification inasmuch as it is always expressed in a linguistic discourse which intrin-sically denies the "natural" as an isolable domain:

What psychoanalysis shows us about desire in what might be called its most natural function, since on it depends the propagation of the species, is not only that it is subjected, in its agency, its appropriation, its normality, in short, to the accidents of the subject's history (the notion of trauma as contingency), but also that all this requires the co-operation of structural elements, which, in order to intervene, can do very well without these accidents, whose effects, so unharmonious, so unexpected, so difficult to reduce, certainly seem to leave to experience a remainder that drove Freud to admit that sexuality must bear the mark of some unnatural slip (*fêlure*). (*Écrits* 310)

The demand for love under which desire labors, that is, in the shadow of which it always exists, is not itself reducible to physiological need. The specifically human desire for unconditional recognition cannot be further reduced to a crude materialism of affective life. Lacan views Hegel as a crucial corrective to the reductive materialism of a physiologically based psychoanalytic theory:

Need I now say that if one understands what sort of support we have sought in Hegel to criticize a degradation of psychoanalysis so inept that it can find no other claim to interest than being the psychoanalysis of today, it is inadmissible that I should be thought of as having been lured by a dialectical exhaustion of being. (*Écrits* 302)

Because desire is the differential between demand and need, it exists, as it were, midway between silence and speech. Need is always evident as a subjective opacity, but it is always diversified and reduced (*Écrits* 309) through language, although never adequately expressed therein. Between the intractable silence of need and the logocentric clamor of demand, desire is the moment in which the limits to language are incessantly problematized. Lacan's firm conviction that no logical or linguistic form could reconcile this difference marks his break with Hegel's ontological optimism: "Far from ceding to a logicizing reduction where it is a question of desire, I find in its irreducibility to demand the very source of that which also prevents it from being reduced to need. To put it elliptically: it is precisely because desire is articulated that it is not articulate" (*Écrits* 302).

Lacan thus defends Hegel when he opposes the naturalization of psychoanalytic theory, and criticizes Hegel—and Sartre—when he argues against the postulation of an autonomous subject. In effect, both the physiological and philosophical positions misunderstand desire as the differential between demand and need. In Hegelian terms, they are false solutions to a paradox; in anti-Hegelian terms, the paradox is intrinsically insoluble. In criticizing the psychoanalytic appropriation of "instinct," Lacan makes use of both Hegel and Sartre, but insists upon a psychoanalytic criticism of the self-grounding of consciousness. The notion of

[199]

negativity appears as that which must be superseded from its Hegelian and Sartrian context; the negative must be transposed from the domain of the subject to that of the signifier, and only then will Hegelianism be able to survive on psychoanalytic grounds. This becomes clear in Lacan's assessment of "the death instinct," that source of aggression in the face of an Other which parallels the opening paragraphs of Hegel's rendition of lordship and bondage. In trying to explain "the evident connection between the narcissistic libido and the alienating function of the 'I' [and] the aggression it releases in any relation to the other," Lacan notes that "the first analysts . . . invoked destructive and, indeed, death instincts" (*Écrits* 6). Lacan suggests that these analysts might have benefited from a psychoanalytic appropriation of the philosophical notion of negativity:

In fact, they were encountering the existential negativity whose reality is so vigorously proclaimed by the contemporary philosophy of being and nothingness. But unfortunately that philosophy grasps negativity only within the limits of a self-sufficiency of consciousness, which, as one of its premises, links to the *mé-connaissances* that constitute the ego, the illusion of autonomy to which it entrusts itself. This flight of fancy, for all that it draws, to an unusual extent, on borrowings from psychoanalytic experience, culminates in the pretension of providing an existential psychoanalysis. (*Écrits* 6)

The task of the psychoanalyst is thus to grasp negativity within the relation of signifier and subject. Lacan suggests that such a transposition is to be found in the notion of *Verneinung*[12] or denial that we considered earlier: "if the *Verneinung* represents the patent form of that function, its effects will, for the most part, remain latent, so long as they are not illuminated by some light reflected onto the level of fatality, which is where the id manifests itself" (*Écrits* 6–7). This "level of fatality" is understood as the repressed oedipal conflict which, for Lacan, is described as a life and death struggle. Repression occurs under the imaginary threat of "murder," the punishment for incestuous desires, which leads Lacan to question "whether murder is the absolute Master" (*Écrits* 308). The repression of incestuous impulses punishable by death eventually gives rise to a speech riddled with *Verneinung*, disavowal, denial. Similarly, the desire for the death of the prohibitive father constitutes another sphere of primary repression, which in turn is manifest as a pronounced negativity in speech. The psychoanalytic appropriation of negativity is thus to be understood within the double-negation of repression and disavowal (*Ver-*

[200]

neinung), an escape from an imaginary death which itself must be denied. The prohibitive law enacted through repression creates the double-negation of neurosis, and the "aggression" discerned in relation to Others gains its significance in the context of the oedipally conditioned life and death struggle. The aggression against the Other is the aggression against the prohibitive law, the *nom du père*, the limit to desire. This aggression can be understood as existential negativity, a negativity that, through its own negation, constructs a subject, in the sense that repression grounds the ego itself. In effect, the fear of death grounds individuation, and this is as true of the oedipally conditioned ego as it is for the trembling bondsman of the *Phenomenology of Spirit*. For Lacan, this is made clear by Lévi-Strauss' argument that the incest taboo conditions all acculturation. Hence, for Lacan, the threat of death emerges as a consequence of the law, and because the law is itself an intractable and universal feature of culture, all identity finds itself grounded in the fear, not simply of death, but of murder.

But it becomes necessary to ask, who is afraid in this scene and of whom? In psychoanalytic terms, it is the young boy who suffers the murderous injunctions of the incest taboo, and the paternal law that is understood to be that which is capable of inflicting punishment. Although Lacan's writings on sexual difference are highly indebted to Freud's *Three Essays on the Theory of Sexuality*, he explains the effect of the oedipal complex in radically different terms. For Lacan, the oedipal complex does not designate an event or primary scene that could be empirically verified, but indicates instead a set of linguistic laws that are foundational to gender and individuation.[13] The incest taboo is not a law pronounced at a crucial moment of early sexual confusion and thereafter retained as a burning memory; rather, this taboo makes itself known in a variety of gradual and subtle ways. Indeed, the paternally enforced prohibition against union with the mother is coextensive with language itself, and makes itself understood in the elementary structures of reference and differentiation, particularly in the structures of pronominal reference. Just as Lévi-Strauss was to claim that the incest taboo is foundational to all kinship, so Lacan argues that the paternally enforced taboo against incest is foundational to language itself. It is operative in the primary forms of differentiation that separate the child from the mother, and that locate the child within a network of kinship relations. The prohibition against incest not only regulates and forbids certain kinds of behavior, but also generates and sanctions other kinds of behavior, and thus becomes instrumental in giving a socially sanctioned form to desire. This system of linguistic differentiation is understood to be based upon the differentiated relations of kinship, and differentiation itself is said to characterize language in its inception. Indeed, the process of differentiation itself is a consequence of the prohibition against incest. This language based on principle of differentiation is understood as the Symbolic and is considered by Lacan to be a language governed by the Phallus or, more appropriately, governed by the fear of the Phallus, the effects of paternal law.[14] The Phallus is thus understood to be the organizing principle of all kinship and all language. We never confront this law in an immediate or direct way, but the law makes itself known in the mundane operations of signification. The Phallus is not one symbolic order among others, but designates *the* symbolic order that conditions all signification and, hence, all meaning (as Foucault says of the Lacanian position, "we are always-already trapped" (*HS* 54)). Hence, the infant's entrance into language is coincident with the emergence of the Law of the Father, the phallocentric system of meaning. In yet other words, the human subject only becomes a discrete "I" within the matrix of gender rules. Hence, to exist as a subject is to exist as a gendered being, "subjected" to the Law of the Father which requires that sexual desire remain within the rules of gender; in fact, the subject's sexual desire is dictated, sanctioned, and punished by the rules of gender.

The constitution of the subject is initiated by the paternal law and is itself based on the splitting off of the male subject from its maternal attachment and identification. The male subject not only renounces its pre-linguistic libidinal attachment to the mother, but posits the feminine itself as the locus of a "lack."[15] Because the male subject retains its longing for the pre-linguistic fusion with the maternal body, he constructs the feminine as the imaginary site of satisfaction. Defined in terms of this gender-specific scenario, desire appears to be sanctioned as a male prerogative. Female desire follows the course of a "double-alienation"—a renunciation of the mother and a shift of libidinal attachment to the father that is then prohibited and displaced. Although the mother is renounced as an object of desire for the girl, she nevertheless remains an object of identification. As a result, the task of female sexual development is to

[202]

signify the mother both for herself (the appropriation of the object through incorporation and identification) and for the male subject (who requires a substitute representation of the prohibited mother). For Lacan, then, female desire is resolved through the full appropriation of femininity, that is, in becoming a pure reflector for male desire, the imaginary site of an absolute satisfaction. The "double-alienation" of the woman is thus a double-alienation from desire itself; the woman learns to embody the promise of a return to a preoedipal pleasure, and to limit her own desire to those gestures that effectively mirror his desire as absolute. For Lacan, the differentiation of genders must be understood as a difference between those with the privilege to desire, and those who are without it. Hence, it is not possible to refer to a female desire inasmuch as this desire consists in a double-renunciation of desire itself. To desire at all means to participate in the right to desire, a right that the male still retains; although he cannot desire the original object, he can nevertheless still desire, if only a substitute object. The particular fate of the female, however, is to deflect from satisfaction twice, and in the course of the second deflection (becoming that which is desired for a man who is deflecting from his mother), she is obliged to become a sign or a token of the forbidden maternal, an ideal or fantasy which can never be fully appropriated, by only "believed in."[16]

For Lacan, it seems, desire is still in search of the Absolute, but this desire has become specified as a male desire, and this Absolute is understood to be the fantasy of maternal fulfillment that women are obliged to represent. Lacan's position poses the question of the psychoanalytic constitution of the Absolute, that is, the constitution of a belief in an ultimate satisfaction which is at once a memory of lost infantile *jouissance* and a fantasy of its recovery. Indeed, it is unclear that this primary, undifferentiated pleasure can really be said to have existed, considering that our only access to this pleasure is through a language that is predicated on its denial. The Absolute, then, might just as well be a *fantasy* of lost and forbidden pleasure rather than a memory or actual stage of infantile development. It makes sense, then, to ask whether Lacan has not rediscovered a religious dream of plentitude in a fantasy of lost pleasure that he himself has constructed. Although Lacan understands himself to have refuted the possibility of a dialectical pursuit of plentitude, a seamless web of internal relations, the belief in such a state is evident in the nostalgia that, according to Lacan, characterizes all human desire.

There are a number of reasons to reject Lacan's psychoanalytic account of desire, of sexual difference, his assumptions regarding the cross-cultural prevalence and function of the incest taboo, but such a discussion would take us into a wholly different inquiry. And yet, there is one kind of objection that appears to concern Lacan's feminist critics as well as his philosophical successors: the prohibitive law, the Law of the Father, appears to act in a universal fashion and is considered to be foundational to all language and culture. An original experience of pleasure is understood to be prohibited and repressed, and desire emerges as a "lack," an ambivalent longing that embodies that prohibition even as it seeks to transgress it. Is it necessarily the case that desire is not only founded by prohibition, but structured in terms of it? Is the law so rigid? And is satisfaction always so phantasmatic?

The postulation of an *Urverdrängung*, or primary repression, which constitutes the subject, and the consequent formulation of desire as a lack, requires that we accept this juridical model of the law as the fundamental political and cultural relation informing the structure of desire. In the works of Deleuze and Foucault, it is precisely this structuralist assumption of the primacy of juridical law and the formulation of desire in terms of the binary opposites of lack and plentitude that come into question. Both Deleuze and Foucault accept Lacan's decentering of the Hegelian subject, and his postulation of the cultural construction of desire, but they view his psychoanalytic program as exemplifying the illness it is meant to cure; they argue that the reification of the prohibitive law is an ideological means of confirming that law's hegemony. In different but related ways, Deleuze and Foucault challenged the formulation of desire in terms of negativity, arguing that not negation, but *affirmation* characterizes primary human longings, and that recognition of this fact will depose the Hegelian subject once and for all. Indeed, in their respective views, the negativity of desire is its cultural illness, one that is sustained by *both* dialectics and psychoanalysis. Thus it remains to be seen whether desire can be disjoined from negation, and whether the theory of affirmative desire that follows is really as free of Hegelianism as it purports to be.

[204]

Deleuze: From Slave Morality to Productive Desire

The true visionary is Spinoza in the garb of a Neapolitan Revolutionary.—
Deleuze/Guatarri, *Anti-Oedipus*

In a variety of works, Gilles Deleuze has attempted to reconstruct the genealogy of desires that turn against themselves, and to provide an alternative conception of desire as a productive and generative activity. In his view, the discourse that conceptualizes desire as a lack has failed to account for the genealogy of this lack, treating the negativity of desire as a universal and necessary ontological truth. In fact, according to Deleuze, desire has *become* a lack in virtue of a contingent set of sociohistorical conditions which require and reinforce the self-negation of desire. In *Nietzsche and Philosophy* (1962), "slave morality" characterizes the Judeo-Christian cultural ideology responsible for the turning of desire against itself, and in *Anti-Oedipus* (1972), that cultural ideology is specified in contemporary terms in the joint effects of psychoanalysis and the self-justificatory practices of advanced capitalism. In this last work, Deleuze maintains: "Lack *(manque)* is created, planned and organized through social production."[17] The ontological condition of a "lack" is revealed as the reification of the economic concept of scarcity, appearing as a necessary condition of material life, impervious to social transformation. Deleuze thus subjects the entire discourse on desire and negativity to an ideology-critique which exposes the ostensibly privative character of desire as the effects of concrete material deprivation. Whether rationalized in terms of "slave morality," psychoanalytic necessity, or the iron laws of capitalism, Deleuze considers this ideology reactive and anti-life. In asserting as much, Deleuze lets us know that emancipated desire is of another order, beyond "lack" and "negativity," a function of a productive and generative affirmation of life. Hence, his theory proceeds in two complementary ways: (1) as a critique of desire as negativity and (2) as the promotion of a normative ideal for desire as affirmation. The former project involves ideology-critique, and the latter entails a reconstruction of Nietzsche's will-to-power and Spinoza's *conatus* in the service of a theory of affective emancipation.

Like his Hegelian precursors, Deleuze is more than willing to understand desire as the privileged locus of human ontology: *"there is only
desire and the social, and nothing else."*[18] Such a statement is not qualified
through reference to given social or historical conditions, but serves as an
invariant feature of Deleuze's own ontology. Indeed, the life-affirming
desire which he comes to oppose to Hegelian negativity also emerges as
a universal ontological truth, long suppressed, essential to human emancipation. Only in Foucault's *The History of Sexuality* does the historical
question of why desire has become so central to speculations on human
ontology get asked, but we can see the groundwork for such a question
already established in Deleuze's selective genealogy of desire.

To the degree that Deleuze historicizes the negative formulation of
desire, he effects a break with Hegel that cannot be accounted for within
Hegel's own system. If there were a genealogy to negativity within Hegel's
philosophy, it would be a developmental account which would retrospectively confirm that negativity was "always already" there. On the
other hand, Deleuze argues that negativity, the lack characteristic of
desire, is instituted through ideological means in order to rationalize a
social situation of hierarchy or domination. Like Lacan, Deleuze traces
the repression of an original desire characterized by plenitude and excess
which culminates in the derivative form of desire as lacking and deprived.
The negativity of desire is, thus, symptomatic of a forgotten history of
repression, and the deconstruction of that negativity (at least in the case
of Deleuze) promises a liberation of that more original, bounteous desire.
For Lacan, the prohibitive law that institutes lack is the law of the symbolic
father, the grounding prohibition against incest which universally initiates
the process of acculturation. Deleuze rejects the universal relevance of the
oedipal construction, and turns instead to Nietzsche where the prohibitive
law is specified as the Judeo-Christian "slave morality," that turning of
desire against itself which, for Deleuze, finds contemporary expression in
the psychoanalytic law of primary repression and the capitalist assumption of necessary scarcity. Deleuze's notion of slave morality has no
historical necessity, and so can be overthrown by the forces of the will-
to-power, the life-affirming desire free of the constraints of the prohibitive
law. In other words, Deleuze claims that the will-to-power has access to

[206]

that jouissance or Being which Lacan viewed as beyond the limits of desire, i.e., the limits of the constituting law of culture. For Deleuze, no matter the hegemony of that law, it not only *can* be broken, but *ought* to be.

   Nietzsche and Philosophy sustains a critique of Hegelianism as a slave morality, exposing both lord and bondsman as culminating in the selfsame denial of life. In the *Genealogy of Morals,* Nietzsche characterizes slave morality as *ressentiment* and envy, resulting from the turning of the will against itself. For Deleuze, the Hegelian subject is precisely such a negative power which has, in effect, *become* negative through a crippling of its own powers. The Hegelian "subject," like the Lacanian "ego," is not an autonomous self-generating agency, but a manufactured construct generated through the slave's self-denial. Hegel's notion of a subject potentially adequate to its world is criticized for disguising a truer and deeper resource of generative power—the play of forces of the will-to-power. Hence, the ostensibly autonomous Hegelian subject is enslaved by his own refusal of the non-dialectical multiplicity of impulses that undergird his apparent negativity. As in Lacan, the subject is once again understood as a defense against a primary configuration of desire, and the "labor of the negative" which characterizes Hegelian desire is understood as a deprived desire which disguises the genealogy of its deprivation.

   For Deleuze as for Nietzsche, the Hegelian subject is the false appearance of autonomy; as a manifestation of slave morality, this subject is *reactive* rather than self-generating. Nietzsche finds the ideal of autonomy better satisfied in the will-to-power or what, in the *Genealogy of Morals,* is understood as aristocratic values of life-affirming physical strength, the moral position beyond envy. Nietzsche appears to target Hegel as the philosophical exemplar of reaction. In section ten of the first essay of the *Genealogy of Morals,* Nietzsche argues that "the slave revolt in morality begins when *ressentiment* itself becomes creative and gives birth to values: the *ressentiment* of natures that are denied the true reaction, that of deeds, and compensate themselves with an imaginary revenge."[19] The "true deed" is a source of self-affirmation from which the slave is precluded. Like Sartre's Genet, this agency unable to act becomes powerful only through its dreams of revenge. Nietzsche continues the exposition by

[207]

suggesting that Hegel's subject is precisely such an impotent slave filled with *ressentiment,* incapable of self-generated action and restricted to reactive self-subversion:

While every noble morality develops from a triumphant affirmation of itself, slave morality from the outset says No to what is "outside," what is "different," what is "not itself;" and this No is its creative deed. The inversion of the value-positing eye—this *need* to direct one's view outward instead of back to oneself—is of the essence of *ressentiment:* in order to exist, slave morality always first needs a hostile external world; it needs, physiologically speaking, external stimuli in order to act at all—its action is fundamentally reaction.[20]

According to Deleuze, Nietzsche's noble morality consists in an affirmation of difference which resists the dialectical tendency to assimilate difference into a more encompassing identity. What is different from the self-affirming agent does not threaten his project of identity, but works instead to enhance that agent's power and efficacy. This is made clear for Deleuze in Nietzsche's theory of forces, which Deleuze interprets as "the cutting edge" of Nietzsche's anti-Hegelianism. In Deleuze's view:

In Nietzsche the essential relation of one force to another is never conceived of as a negative element in the essence. In its relation with the other the force which makes itself obeyed does not deny the other or that which it is not, it affirms its own difference and enjoys this difference.[21]

The Nietzschean will is itself a multiplicitous play of forces which consequently cannot be contained by a dialectical unity; these forces represent currents of life, interests, desires, pleasures, and thoughts, which co-exist without the necessity of a repressive and/or unifying law. Hence, identity is a misnomer in Deleuze's terms, one which misapprehends the essential multiplicity of this subject. Because the Deleuzian subject is not defined by a single law or unifying concept, it can be said to maintain opposition without unity, unlike the Hegelian subject which requires that opposition be assimilated to identity. Indeed, this requirement is understood by both Nietzsche and Deleuze as a sign of weakness and decadence; if the subject only exists through the assimilation of an external opposition, it therefore is dependent upon this negative relation for its own identity; hence, it lacks the power of self-assertion and self-affirmation characteristic of the 'strong' person, the *übermensch,* whose relations with Others transcend radical dependency. The Nietzschean will, on the other hand, does not affirm itself apart from a context of alterity, but differs from Hegelian

[208]

desire in its fundamental approach to alterity. Because distinction is no longer understood as a prerequisite for identity, otherness no longer presents itself as that to be "labored upon," superseded or conceptualized; rather, difference is the condition for enjoyment, an enhanced sense of pleasure, the acceleration and intensification of the play of forces which constitute what we might well call Nietzsche's version of jouissance. Once the requirement of discrete identity no longer governs the subject, difference is less a source of danger than it is a condition of self-enhancement and pleasure. Deleuze describes this difference between Nietzsche and Hegel: "Nietzsche's 'yes' is opposed to the dialectical 'no'; affirmation to dialectical negation; difference to dialectical contradiction; joy, enjoyment, to dialectical labor; lightness, dance, to dialectical responsibilities" (p. 9).

Although Deleuze views the Hegelian dialectic as weighed down by the "spirit of gravity," we might justifiably wonder how the bachanallian revel Hegel mentions in the preface to the *Phenomenology* could get under way if it were, in fact, governed by such a spirit. The bachanallian revel is intended to characterize the speculative thought of the Absolute as an incessant and all-encompassing dialectic, the achievement of the "labor of the negative," the "lightness" at the end of Hegel's admittedly arduous journey. Deleuze does not take into account this celebratory conclusion to the *Phenomenology*, and we can surmise that he does not think it possible within Hegel's own terms. If the *Phenomenology* is a *Bildungsroman* which narrates a journey that turns out to lead to where the journeyer has always been, then the *Phenomenology* is like Dorothy's dream in the *Wizard of Oz* which not only takes her back home, but which is exclusively composed of the transvaluated elements of her home. If immanence is the final truth of the *Phenomenology*, then it would seem that Hegel's revelers are dancing in place, fixed within a single frame, like the frozen joy on Keats' Grecian urn.

The *Phenomenology* treats the theme of enjoyment explicitly in the context of the lord who enjoys the fruits of the bondsman's labor *(im Genusse sich zu befriedigen)*. Enjoyment is here achieved without labor or, more precisely, is made possible through the labor of others. Enjoyment is modeled on consumption, and the lord turns out to be dissatisfied by his life of satisfaction; his dependency on the bondsman ruins his sense of self-sufficiency, his experience of his own negativity is restricted to consumption, and he misses a sense of his own efficacy. Enjoyment becomes intolerable precisely because it undermines the project of autonomy that the lord wants to pursue. The hierarchical relation between lord and bondsman also becomes intolerable because it thwarts the realization of autonomy or, in the case of the bondsman, because the unexpected realization of autonomy provides a greater satisfaction. Clearly, satisfaction *(Befriedigung)* is not the same as enjoyment *(Genuss)* for Hegel; the former signifies that the law of identity has been reasserted and thus provides a conceptual kind of gratification, while the latter is a decidedly more sensuous affair, more immediate and, hence, less philosophical.

Deleuze takes issue with at least two of the central Hegelian postulates mentioned above: the formulation of enjoyment as an ultimately dissatisfying mode of consumption and the rejection of hierarchical social relations in favor of a notion of autonomy based on the law of identity. In both cases, a notion of a self-identical subject determines the parameters of satisfaction, and this version of autonomous identity is symptomatic of slave morality in which difference is only suffered and never enjoyed. The postulation of self-identity as the ontological condition of satisfaction precludes the greater pleasures of affirming difference as difference and the derivative pleasures of hierarchical interchange. The dialectic is "slave" morality not in the sense of Hegel's "slave" who initiates the transition out of Lordship and Bondage into the Unhappy Consciousness, i.e., who carries the emancipatory principle of the *Phenomenology* in and through his "labor," but in the sense of the "slave" of Nietzsche's *Genealogy of Morals* who lacks the power of the nobility and, through a feat of envious transvaluation, comes to extoll his own limitations as evidence of moral superiority. The slave rationalizes incapacity as moral strength and, for both Nietzsche and Deleuze, Hegel's traveling subject is precisely such a slave. According to Nietzsche in "The Problem of Socrates", "It is the slave that triumphs in the dialectic. . . . The dialectic can only serve as a defensive weapon" (ff. 1:4). The will of Hegel's bondsman is a self-restricted will, even in the achievement of its ostensible emancipation. As long as emancipation is modeled on autonomy and self-realization, the emancipated bondsman will be restricted by the constraints of self-identity and will know neither pleasure nor creativity—essential features of the will-to-power. This emancipated bondsman will be shackled in a way that cannot be superseded within the terms of the *Phenomen-*

[210]

ology; he will always fear difference, and will never know how to act to affirm difference without having to assimilate that difference into himself. The Hegelian subject refuses the world outside itself, while its very "self" is enslaved to that world, constantly reacting against the externalities it encounters, never freely affirming that world as different, and deriving enjoyment from that affirmation; the Hegelian subject can only fear or appropriate the features of an external world, but because its fundamental project and deepest desire is to attain the self-identity of reflexive self-consciousness, it cannot enter into that world of alterity fearlessly, joyfully, creatively.

According to Deleuze, Nietzsche proposes fundamentally new meanings for the activities of affirmation and negation which invert and surpass the meaning and relation of these terms in Hegel's philosophy. Affirmation no longer carries the burden of effecting an ontological unity between that which affirms and that which is affirmed, for there is no being outside of the will-to-power: "Being and nothingness are merely the abstract expression of affirmation and negation as qualities *(qualia)* of the will-to-power" (p. 186). And yet the will-to-power is not an exclusively human capacity, but the internally differentiated dynamism of life. To affirm is not an anthropomorphizing projection, but a generative activity that, in and through its very activity, affirms the generativity of life itself. The subject does not need to struggle to become adequate to a countervailing world, but must *give itself up* to what is greater than itself—the will-to-power, creative life. As Deleuze emphasizes in his own exposition, "to affirm is not to take responsibility for, to take on the burden of what is, but to release, to set free, what lives" (p. 185).

Hegel's dialectic is considered anti-life inasmuch as it refuses the categories of affirmation and life for the categories of negativity or, according to Nietzsche, death. The philosophical expectations that the world can be analyzed in terms of truth and falsity, being and non-being, the real and the apparent are, according to Nietzsche, symptomatic of a pervasive hatred of life which rationalizes itself through the imposition of false conceptual constructs. These philosophical oppositions are meant to detain life, control and bury it, and safeguard the dialectical philosopher in a position of death-in-life. The postulation of identity, whether as the relation between subject and subject, between discrepant aspects of the world, or between the being of the world and its truth, is a strategy of

[211]

containment motivated by the slave's fear and hatred of the will-to-power as the principle of life. In Deleuze's words, "Nietzsche has no more belief in the self-sufficiency of the real than he has in that of the true: he thinks of them as the manifestations of a will, a will to depreciate life, to oppose life to life" (p. 184).

Clearly, we cannot explore in detail Nietzsche's various philosophical centerpieces—the will-to-power, the eternal return, the Dionysian, the musical Socrates—but our sketch of his position can reveal the challenge of a post-Hegelian formulation of the subject of desire. For Deleuze, Nietzsche provides a way to disjoin desire from negativity, and to account for the genealogy of the Hegelian position in terms of slave morality. The will-to-power provides an alternative model of desire which is based on the plenitude of life, its incessant fertility, rather than the negativity of self-consciousness. Nietzsche's critique of identity also has the consequence of decentering further the self-sufficient subject as the implicit agent and explicit aim of desire. As in Lacan, we see in Deleuze the genesis of this subject as a defense against a more primary, less philosophically tame, desire. In *Anti-Oedipus,* it is the coercive force of capitalism and the ideology of psychoanalysis that repress life-affirming desire, and in *Nietzsche and Philosophy,* it is the slave morality, but it is clear that capitalism and psychoanalysis *are* both slave moralities, and that life-affirming desire is, in both contexts, the Deleuzian telos of emancipation. This repressed desire is modeled on the will-to-power, but Nietzsche's notion is attributed by Deleuze to Spinoza's *conatus* which, placed within a modern political and cultural context, becomes for Deleuze the affective source of revolutionary change.

For Deleuze, the will-to-power is like Spinoza's primary desire to persist in one's being: both desires are empowered and enhanced through being affected by external phenomena. Desire is not that which aims for a thorough authorship of the world (Kojève, Sartre), but is that which is itself strengthened through its capacity *to respond* to what is inevitably external. Indeed, Deleuze understands Nietzsche's will-to-power as a developed *sensibility.* He quotes Nietzsche: "The will-to-power is not a being or becoming, but a *pathos*" (p. 62). Deleuze further argues that "it is difficult to deny a Spinozistic inspiration here. Spinoza, in an extremely profound theory, wanted a capacity for being affected to correspond to every quantity of force. The more ways a body could be affected the more force it had. This capacity measures the force of a body or expresses its power" (p. 62). In *Anti-Oedipus* Deleuze understands desire and the body to have been deprived of their capacity for response, and calls for a renewal of the body in terms of forces of "attraction and the production of intensities."[22] Spinoza thus offers Deleuze a way to understand the response to externality as an intensification of desire which resists the dialectical demand to appropriate this externality to a law of identity.

Interestingly enough, although Hegel criticized Spinoza for failing to understand the negativity that motors self-consciousness, Deleuze appears to applaud Spinoza for this very exclusion of the negative. Desire is thus understood by Deleuze as a productive response to life in which the force and intensity of desire multiplies and intensifies in the course of an exchange with alterity. Deleuze's "will" is not "willful," but responsive and malleable, assuming new and more complicated forms of organization through the exchange of force constitutive of desire. Because the field of force is abundant with energy and power, desire is less a struggle to monopolize power than an exchange that intensifies and proliferates energy and power into a state of excess. Beneath the contrived scarcity conditions which have produced desire as a modality of deprivation resides a ready abundance of life-affirming desire, and for Deleuze the political and personal task of a post-Hegelian erotics is to retrieve this Spinozistic persistence and to recast it in terms of the will-to-power. From this point of view, the Hegelian subject can be understood as a product of slave morality, a consequence of cultural malaise, the result as well as the agency of a life-negating desire.

Deleuze's theory prescribes a move from negative to productive desire which requires that we accept an emancipatory model of desire. In this sense he has politicized the Lacanian theory, arguing that productive desire, jouissance, is accessible to human experience, and that the prohibitive laws governing this desire can and must be broken. Marcuse's dialectical solution to politically repressed desire in *Eros and Civilization* is clearly unacceptable to a Deleuzian position inasmuch as Marcuse accepts the binary restrictions on desire and reconciles them in an Hegelian synthesis, i.e., the polarity of the sexes is overcome through a synthetic appropriation of bisexuality. Nietzsche's insistence on the nondialectical multiplicity of affects challenges the possibility of a self-identical subject and suggests that the will-to-power cannot be reduced to the internally

[213]

complicated structure of Hegelian desire. Although Nietzsche himself occasionally refers to a single dominating drive in terms of which various affects and forces are organized, Deleuze clearly prefers a reading of the will-to-power which resists such a unification of affects. For Deleuze, there is a significant difference between an internally multiplicitous desire in which the internality of various desires suggests a unifying structure of containment, and a fundamentally multiplicitous set of desires which can only be falsified by any effort to describe them as a unity.

Although a multiplicitous eros challenges the unitary directionality of desire, and even the dialectical "double object" of desire that we considered in the *Phenomenology*, it is less clear what kind of reality this ostensibly repressed desire(s) is supposed to have. If Deleuze accepts the Spinozistic elaboration of the will-to-power as a natural eros which has subsequently been denied by a restrictive culture, then he seems compelled to explain how we might gain insight into this natural multiplicity from within a cultural perspective. On the one hand, Deleuze criticizes the Lacanian reification of the juridical law as foundational to all culture and appears to offer, via Nietzsche, a strategy for the subversion and displacement of that juridical law. On the other hand, the strategy Deleuze promotes appeals to a different kind of reification, namely, the reification of multiplicitous affect as the invariant, although largely repressed, ontological structure of desire. If the inquiry into the structure of desire takes place within a culturally constructed perspective, then the analysis of desire is always implicated in the cultural situation it seeks to explain. The postulation of a natural multiplicity appears, then, as an insupportable metaphysical speculation on the part of Deleuze. Moreover, inasmuch as the critique of the cultural reification of desire as lack engages its own form of reification through an appeal to an ontologically invariant multiplicitous affectivity, it discards the benefits of the Lacanian position along with its disadvantages; in other words, the appeal to a precultural eros ignores the Lacanian insight that all desire is linguistically and culturally constructed. The Deleuzian critique of the prohibitive law, and the subsequent reification of desire as that which is always already repressed, requires a political strategy that explicitly takes account of the cultural construction of desire, that is, a political strategy that resists the appeal to a "natural" desire as a normative ideal.

Although Deleuze's critique of the Hegelian subject places him within

[214]

the postmodern effort to describe a decentered affectivity, his appeal to Nietzsche's theory of forces suggests that he understands this decentered experience as an ontological rather than a culturally conditioned historical experience. In effect, his appeal to a naturally multiplicitous affectivity is not unlike the Enlightenment appeal to natural desires that we find in Rousseau or Montesquieu. Ironically, Deleuze's ostensibly anti-capitalist position shares a number of philosophical assumptions with classical liberalism. Just as individuals are said to possess certain desires for pleasure (Bentham) or property (Locke) which are subsequently inhibited by the constraints of a social contract, so Deleuze's conception of an originally unrepressed libidinal diversity is subject to the prohibitive laws of culture. In both cases, desire is the locus of a precultural ideal, the essence of the individual, which is subsequently distorted or repressed through the imposition of anti-erotic political structures. Here Deleuze appears to undermine his original project to historicize desire, for his arcadian vision of precultural libidinal chaos poses as an ahistorical absolute.

Lacan argues, on the other hand, that the prohibitive law is precisely what engenders the culturally accessible experience of desire and precludes any appeal to a desire freed from all prohibition, and so questions whether desire can be conceptualized apart from the law. If Lacan is right in this respect, Deleuze's concern to displace the hegemony of the prohibitive law must be taken up by a position that subverts and proliferates this law from within the terms of culture itself. As we shall see, the theory of Michel Foucault appears to achieve precisely this: (1) the acknowledgment of the cultural construction of desire which does not entail an acceptance of the cultural reification of desire as lack and (2) a political strategy to displace the hegemony of the prohibitive law through the accentuation of that law's self-subverting and self-proliferating possibilities. Foucault thus offers a normative framework which entails a subversive struggle with existing prohibitions, a thoroughly cultural program which disavows any appeal to a desire that has a natural or metaphysical structure said to exist either prior or posterior to linguistic and cultural laws.

Despite his reification of the prohibitive law, Lacan nevertheless offers a critique of the kinds of experiences of desire that are possible within existing culture, and thereby begins the project elaborated by Foucault to wrest desire from the grips of the dialectical imagination. The limitation on the possibilities of that cultural experience may be unduly restrictive, but he does establish a limit to unrestrained metaphysical speculation on the structure and meaning of desire. This is not to claim that Lacan is free of metaphysical aspirations for desire, but that he realizes the necessary limit that culture establishes for such aspirations. This Kantian limitation on the experience of desire has a two-fold consequence; desire is always more than what we experience, although we cannot use language to describe this "more." Hence, desire is experienced as a kind of limit, the limits to language itself, the fate of a metaphysical aspiration which necessarily founders upon the limits set by linguistic prohibitions.

And yet, neither Deleuze nor Lacan are thoroughly freed of metaphysical aspirations for desire, and the metaphysical longings operative in their theories can be understood as so much residual Hegelianism. For both Deleuze and Lacan, there remains an elusive and tantalizing "beyond" to culturally instituted desire, the promise of a liberation, even if, in the case of Lacan, that promise can never be fulfilled. In each case, a version of absolute presence, albeit internally differentiated, is the final aim or *telos* of desire. For Lacan, this "Being" is barred from the human subject in much the same way as the synthesis of the real and rational remains a nostalgic ideal for Hyppolite. For Deleuze, the eradication of negativity from productive desire[23] culminates in an internally differentiated Eros in which the "differences" are understood as positive differentials of force rather than externally related moments of desire. In other words, for Deleuze, *the theory of forces replaces Hegel's doctrine of internal relations as the guarantor of the principle of plenitude.*

Although Deleuze and Lacan differ dramatically on the question of whether desire can be emancipated from the shackles of the prohibitive law, both theorists maintain that desire has an ontological status apart from this law; for Lacan, jouissance is the noumenal being of desire, that which structures the culturally concrete experience of desire but which is never fully known or experienced within the terms of culture. For Deleuze, the erotics of multiplicity is revealed as an always already existing possibility once life itself is freed from the constraints of slave morality. Whether as jouissance or life itself, this postulation of affirmation and plenitude is said to characterize desire internally as its essential structure and telos, although for Lacan this telos cannot be achieved. In this respect, it appears that both Lacan and Deleuze remain entranced by the metaphysical promise of desire as an immanent experience of the Absolute.

[216]

Whether satisfaction is conceived as a state prior to ontological difference (Lacan), or as the ultimate incorporation of differences as so many attributes of a life-affirming will-to-power (Deleuze), it remains a postulated presence and unity which denies the externality of difference. In this sense, then, neither position is freed of the Hegelian dream that the satisfaction of desire would establish the primacy of plenitude, the presumption of ontological integrity and immanent metaphysical place.

The interpretation of Lacan and Deleuze as subservient to the principle of identity and the pursuit of absolute presence casts serious doubt on the self-styled distinction between philosophers of identity and philosophers of difference. For both Lacan and Deleuze, ontological unity is primary and only becomes interrupted through the advent of cultural law which, consonant with most theories of the Fall, results in desire as an experience of relentless dissatisfaction. This unity or absolute presence then becomes the tacit but fundamental project of desire—the cause of love, according to Lacan—which is either imagined (Sartre, Lacan) or pursued through a revolutionary return to natural Eros (Deleuze). The Hegelian effort to transvaluate or supersede all negativity into an all-encompassing Being remains the constitutive desire of these ostensible post-Hegelian positions. The inexorable necessity of the *Phenomenology* seems no longer to serve as a persuasive narrative, and the psychoanalytic and Nietzschean routes engage fewer illusions about the autonomy of the subject and the dialectical structure of reason and experience. But the dream of reconstituting that lost unity of Being still structures these theories, whether through the notion of jouissance or the theory of forces, and no matter whether the dream can be realized.

Foucault: Dialectics Unmoored

There is no single locus of great refusal, no soul of revolt, source of all rebellions.—Foucault, *The History of Sexuality*

Foucault's first volume of *The History of Sexuality* questions whether the history of Western desire can be adequately explained within a dialectical framework which relies on binary oppositions. Freud's *Civilization and its Discontents* tended to explain desire as an instinct whose sublimation is the necessary consequence of a generally restrictive "civilization." Civilization is here understood to be a juridical and prohibitive set of institutions which both represses original instincts and is itself the sublimated form of those instincts. Marcuse's *Eros and Civilization* examines this notion of sublimation in light of a theory of Eros and suggests that sublimation constitutes the creative and erotic organization of all positive cultural formations. Eros is thus understood by Marcuse to be a nonrepressive and nonjuridical organizing principle of cultural production. In a sense, Foucault can be seen as emerging from this particular psychoanalytic and Hegelian heritage. Indeed, Freud identifies the juridical model of power, and Marcuse reveals the inadvertent generativity of that ostensibly repressive power through a speculative consideration of sublimation; for Foucault, however, this tension becomes reformulated as that between juridical and productive power, and the postulation of an "instinct" or an ahistorical form of Eros is denied. As a consequence, desire is not repressed by the juridical law, and neither is it a derivative or sublimated form of that originally repressed instinct. Desire is created by the repressive law itself, and has no other meaning than that which an historically specific form of juridical power inadvertently produces. The law that we expect to repress some set of desires which could be said to exist prior to the law succeeds, rather, in naming, delimiting and, thereby, giving social meaning and possibility to precisely those desires it intended to eradicate.

The "law," however, is encoded and produced through certain discursive practices, and so has its own historically specific linguistic modality. Medicine, psychiatry, and criminology become discursive domains in which desire is both regulated and produced, indeed, in which the regulation of desire is the mode of its cultural production. If the repressive law constitutes the desire it is meant to control, then it makes no sense to appeal to that constituted desire as the emancipatory opposite of repression. Indeed, for Foucault, desire is the inadvertent consequence of the law. And insofar as the law is reproduced through given discursive practices, these latter participate in the cultural production of desire. In a political elaboration of structuralist premises, Foucault argues that (a) language is always structured in a specific historical form and is, therefore, always a kind of *discourse,* and (b) that this discourse invariably recapitulates and produces given historical relations of power, and (c) these power-laden discourses produce desire through their regulatory practices.

[218]

Hence, for Foucault, there is no desire outside of discourse, and no discourse freed of power-relations. Foucault's notion of discourse includes functions that surpass those of conventional emancipatory models. Discourse is neither an epiphenomenal reflection of material relations, nor an instrument of domination, nor a conventional system of signs that embodies universalistic principles of communication. In his words, "discourse [is] a series of discontinuous segments whose tactical function is neither uniform nor stable . . . we must not imagine a world of discourse divided between accepted discourse and excluded discourse, or between the dominant discourse and the dominated one; but as a multiplicity of discursive elements that can come into play in various strategies" (*HS* 100). Emancipation cannot consist in ascending to a power-free discourse because, for Foucault, power and discourse have become coextensive. If there is to be an emancipatory potential in discourse, it must consist of the transformation rather than the transcendence of power. For Foucault, "discourse can be both an instrument and effect of power, but also a hindrance, a stumbling-block, a point of resistance and a starting point for an opposing strategy. Discourse transmits and produces power; it reinforces it, but also undermines and exposes it, renders it fragile and makes it possible to thwart it" (*HS* 101).

The binary configuration of power in terms of repression/emancipation reduces the multiplicity of power-relations into two univocal alternatives which mask the variegated texture of power. These constructs, even when intended as emancipatory, result in a restriction of the political imagination and, hence, the possibilities of political transformation inasmuch as "power is everywhere; not because it embraces everything, but because it comes from everywhere" (*HS* 93). The emancipatory model of power remains restricted to juridical forms which have become hegemonic, but are for that reason neither universal nor necessary. Like Deleuze, Foucault appeals to *productive* forms of power which have for the most part gone unnoticed in modern theories of political emancipation. Unlike Deleuze, however, he rejects any precultural notion of "true desire," and conceives of political transformation as a function of the *proliferation* of configurations of power and sexuality. The Nietzschean theory of forces which, for Deleuze, characterize the precultural ontology of desire becomes for Foucault a theory of discursive *power,* historically constituted and conditioned by the breakdown of monarchical forms of government and the ubiquity of modern war. Because discourse is fundamentally determined by the situation of modern power dynamics, and because desire is only articulated and implemented in terms of this discourse, desire and power are coextensive, and any theory that postulates desire as a "beyond" to power is, in modern terms, a cultural and political impossibility, or, worse, a reactionary deployment of power which conceals itself through an open denial of its own constitutive power-relations.

The hegemony of juridical power, regulatory and prohibitive laws, infiltrates civil society, cultural forms of life, and theories of psychic organization and development. Foucault identifies psychoanalysis as the cultural derivative of monarchical power-relations, that is, as the discursive sphere in which juridical law comes to govern affective life. Psychoanalytic discourse not only interprets the working of repression and desire, but creates or produces a new set of power-relations for desire. The understanding of desire within the framework of sexuality and repression necessitates *confession* as the emancipatory moment of desire. The "talking cure" does not relieve a patient of his desire, but becomes desire's new life: confession itself becomes eroticized. Because there is no desire relieved of power, confession becomes its own form of productive power, and desire becomes transmuted into confessional speech. Hence, the psychoanalytic treatment of desire results not in catharsis, but in the proliferation of desire as confessional speech; there is no "original" desire that one speaks "of," but the "speaking of" becomes desire's new historical form; desire is verbalized, and verbalization becomes the occasion for desire.

Foucault purports to be revealing an inadvertent consequence of psychoanalytic discourse, namely, that the juridical power of repression is transformed into the productive power of discourse, and that nowhere is an original or prelinguistic desire brought to light. Because psychoanalysis has established sexuality as the discursive domain of desire, Foucault concludes that sexuality and power, in its various forms, are coextensive. Overcoming repression does not entail the transcendence of power-relations; the discourse of emancipation proceeds to produce desire in its own terms. Foucault argues, "we must not think that by saying yes to sex, one says no to power" (*HS* 157).

Foucault sharpens Deleuze's political challenge to psychoanalysis by questioning the origins and hegemony of juridical law. He recognizes that

[220]

Lacanian psychoanalytic theory is an improvement upon theories that impute an ontological status to prelinguistic drives and instincts, but he underscores the failure of Lacan's structuralist interpretation to consider power outside of its juridical or prohibitive form: "What distinguishes the analysis made in terms of the repression of instincts from that made in terms of the law of desire is clearly the way in which they each conceive of the nature and dynamics of drives, not the way in which they conceive of power" (HS 82–83). Although Lacan has dismissed the notion of desire as "a rebellious energy that must be throttled . . . a primitive, natural, and living energy welling up from below," he has still retained a belief in a true desire prior to repression, a phenomenon that would, according to Foucault, announce an "outside" to discourse. According to Foucault, the repressive law is the discursive moment of desire's *production* rather than its *negation:*

One should not think that desire is repressed, for the simple reason that the law is what constitutes desire and the lack on which it is predicated. Where there is desire, the power-relation is already present: an illusion, then, to denounce this relation for a repression exerted after the event; but vanity as well, to go questing after a desire that is beyond the reach of power. (HS 81)

The juridical model of desire permits of only two kinds of tactics: the "promise of liberation" (Deleuze, Marcuse) or "the affirmation: you are always-already trapped" (Lacan). In either case, the binary restrictions on desire imposed by the juridical model of power remain intact. Hence, Foucault concludes that the genealogy of juridical power must be reconstructed and exposed, and that the possibilities of a response to that model which eludes its binary restrictions must be pursued. In effect, Foucault is arguing that both the psychoanalytic and liberationist views of desire are caught within a dialectical impasse conditioned by a false premise. Only by overcoming the juridical model of power will the modalities of desire become freed from the binary alternatives of repression and emancipation:

Whether desire is this or that, in any case one continues to conceive of it in relation to a power that is always juridical and discursive, a power that has its central point in the enunciation of the law. One remains attached to a certain image of power-law, of power-sovereignty, which was traced out by the theoreticians of right and the monarchic institution. It is this image that we must break free of, that is, of the theoretical privilege of law and sovereignty. (HS 89)

[221]

What Lacan understood as the culturally universal prohibition against incest, and what Deleuze referred to as the slave morality inculcated by capitalism and psychoanalysis, is reformulated by Foucault as the rule of monarchy which, it seems, has produced "subjects" whose desires are unavoidably linked with negativity. The presence of the negative is understood culturally as the effect of the juridical law, transcribed in psychoanalytic discourse as the repressive mechanism, and manifest in philosophical texts as the ontological negativity of human life—the "lack" that is the human subject. For Foucault, *the move from negativity to plenitude is understood, then, as a problem of shifting political paradigms.* This shift cannot be a dialectical inversion and, hence, an inadvertent affirmation of the self-identity of juridical power—that was the mistake of positions that impute an intrinsic emancipatory potential to desire. The problem for Foucault is to contrive a tactic of nondialectical subversion, a position beyond subjection and rebellion which alters fundamentally the form of the cultural nexus of power and desire. Foucault's notion of productive power clearly draws from the theory of forces promoted by Deleuze and Nietzsche. In *The History of Sexuality,* however, we can understand Foucault's appropriation of the theory of forces in the context of an Hegelian dialectic in ruins. Foucault radicalizes the critique of Hegelian autonomy as well as the progressive presumptions of Hegel's notion of historical change. The consequence is that the dialectic is unmoored from both the subject and its teleological conclusion. In what follows, I will show how this dialectic gone awry evolves into a principle of identity, and how Foucault prescribes the shift from a juridical to a productive model of desire in terms of such a change. Finally, I will consider whether Foucault's tactic of subversion is as nondialectical as he professes, and whether, in particular, Hegel's Life and Death Struggle returns in the work of Foucault as the contemporary situation of desire.

In my brief consideration of the unexpected consequences of the juridical model of power in psychoanalytic practice, we saw an instance of the shift from juridical to productive power. In that case, the postulation of repression necessitated the talking cure as a model of (limited) emancipation, but this very cure turned out to be an elaboration rather than a catharsis of desire. Instead of returning to the repressed desire, we encountered a desire produced through the law of repression which inadvertently gives rise to confessional speech as the new historical locus of sexuality and desire. The erotic possibilities of confession become, in Foucault's terms, exemplary of productive desire, itself produced by the juridical model, but essentially exceeding that model. For the juridical model to work, desire would be repressed, then recovered, and a return to an original meaning of desire would be facilitated. In Hegelian terms, the ostensible alienation of the subject from itself would be recovered through the work of psychoanalytic practice. Foucault's point is that psychoanalytic practice determines desire even as it interprets it, and because desire *is* its discursive function, and psychoanalysis its contemporary discursive context, psychoanalysis does not recover but, rather, *produces* desire.

The juridical model of power asserts an external relation between desire and power, such that power is exerted on desire, and desire is either silenced and censored in virtue of this power or resurfaces in a substitute form which appropriately cloaks its offensive aims. In either case, the juridical model maintains the assumption of an original and primary desire to which one *can* return, and *must* return if the estrangement characteristic of neurosis is to be overcome. In the case of Lacan, this return to original desire may not be possible, but its inaccessibility does not preclude the insistence on its ontological integrity. Foucault's theory of productive discourse suggests that the very notion of an original desire is manufactured by the juridical model in an attempt to consolidate and entrench its own power. Indeed, both the subject and its hidden desire are constructs deployed by a juridical discourse in the interests of its own self-amplification. But the juridical model always contains the possibility of subverting itself inasmuch as its confessional mechanisms of controlling desire become inadvertent loci for the production of desire, i.e., when the psychoanalytic confession is itself eroticized, the scene of guilt is confused with the scene of pleasure, and new possibilities of pleasure within discursive practices are created. Indeed, wherever there exists a discursive regulation of pleasure, there follows an eroticization of regulation, and a transformation of a scene of repression into an occasion for erotic play. As a result, the law is diverted from its repressive aim through its redeployment as a source of pleasure. In dialectical fashion, the ostensible opposition between desire and the law is subverted through an ironic reversal, and yet we will see that this reversal resists accommodation within a dialectical unity.

[223]

In the *Phenomenology* we considered the self-subverting dialectic of domination and oppression in the context of lordship and bondage. There the dialectical opposition between lord and bondsman becomes reconciled through the emergence of an enhanced notion of the subject. Foucault lacks any such subject, and so binary opposites fail to fall under any such law of immanence. Instead, binary oppositions, including those of juridical models of power, tend to create effects that are thoroughly unforeseen, to multiply and proliferate into new forms of power that cannot be adequately explained within the terms of binary opposition. For Hegel, the unanticipated consequences of binary opposition are eventually revealed as the unclaimed, unrecovered dimensions of the subject itself. *For Foucault, the inadvertent consequences of binary oppositions neither enlighten the subject involved nor restore the subject to an enhanced conception of its ontological place. Because the power-relations produced by discourse do not belong to a preestablished unified system of relations, they are indications of the incessant dispersal of the subject—the impossibility of a return to a dialectical unity.*

While the Hegelian subject resolves the binary oppositions it encounters through the recovery of an expanded conception of identity, Foucault's subject becomes schooled in its ever-expanding lack of agency and, concomitantly, in the ever-growing power of discourse. Indeed, discourse appears to covet the power of agency, "deploying," "producing," "intending," and "selecting" its means. In an interview, Foucault is asked what sense can be made of a strategy that is not initiated by a subject. He responds that one can understand a "coherent, rational strategy, but one for which it is no longer possible to identify a person who conceived it." And though there is no subject, he argues, there is "an effect of finalisation relative to an objective."[24] The subject is not wholly epiphenomenal, although it is determined almost entirely by prior strategies. These strategies are understood as permutations of power, and human subjects and their desires are understood as instruments of that power's self-implementation. Foucault understands the problems associated with such a personification of discourse and power, and qualifies his theory as follows: "one needs to be nominalistic, no doubt: power is not an institution, and not a structure; neither is it a certain strength we are endowed with; it is the name that one attributes to a complex strategical situation in a par-

[224]

ticular society" (*HS* 93). In another context, he writes: "power in the substantive sense, *le pouvoir*, doesn't exist . . . power means relations, a more-or-less organized, hierarchical coordinated cluster of relations."[25]

It would be as misguided to assign an original meaning to power as it would be to postulate an original meaning for desire. Foucault insists on the polyvalence of power; it is a dominant and more or less systematic movement which changes through the force of internal divisions and multiplications. It is not a self-identical substance that manifests itself in the tributaries of everyday life, but a relation that is continuously transformed in virtue of passing through the nodal points of everyday life. Lacking a discrete and unified origin, power is a kind of malleable purposiveness permanently uprooted in the world; the history of power is not a reconstruction of a unilinear or dialectical progression, but a series of innovations that elude the explanations of cosmogony, anthropogenesis, or teleology. Because power does not exist apart from the various relations by which it is transmitted and transformed, it is the very process of transmission and transformation, a history of these processes, with none of the narrative coherence and closure characteristic of the *Phenomenology*. Foucault thus remains a tenuous dialectician, but his is a dialectic without a subject and without teleology, a dialectic unanchored in which the constant inversion of opposites leads not to a reconciliation in unity, but to a proliferation of oppositions which come to undermine the hegemony of binary opposition itself.

Although Foucault occasionally refers to the shift from juridical to productive models of power as if it were an inevitability in a world no longer structured in Hegelian terms, he also makes clear that this shift is not a purely logical necessity, but, rather, a condition of historical circumstances. In a surprising turn of argumentation, Foucault attributes the emergence of productive power in modern times to the growing cultural and political influence of war:

It is a question of reorienting ourselves to a conception of power which replaces the privilege of prohibition with the viewpoint of tactical efficacy . . . the strategic model rather than the model based on law. And this not out of speculative choice or theoretical preference, but because in fact it is one of the essential traits of Western societies that the force relationships which for a long time had found expression in war, in every form of warfare, gradually became invested in the order of political power. (*HS* 102)

According to Foucault, war has become the contemporary experience of power, and civil society is structured as an occupied zone. In a peculiar kind of materialist vocabulary, Foucault appears to understand war as a determining base of experience which produces various forms of rationality and sexuality in its wake. Although Foucault prescribes a shift from juridical models of power to models predicated upon a war experience, he does not appear to be condoning war itself as a good way of life. He seems, rather, to be acknowledging power-relations as they are structured in contemporary terms, and to suggest that whatever modes of political and cultural transformation are available are, of necessity, available within the terms of war. Hence, if contemporary power-relations are, at least implicitly, war relations, we must look to "tactics," "strategies," "deployments" and "instrumentalities" to find our way out or, at least, through.

The question that concerns us is how desire is to be conceived as part of the experience of war. His answer appears to be that even sexuality has taken on the terms of "a struggle for life," and that the inadvertent consequence of warlike opposition is the intensification of life's value. The wholesale challenge to life that wars have threatened have inadvertently created a renewed desire for life, the intensification and multiplication of bodily pleasures, the promotion of sexual vitalism. Hence, the will-to-power, understood as the affirmation of life, becomes, for Foucault, the inadvertent consequence of the attempted negation of life, manifest culturally as the experience of sexuality as vital struggle, an experience determined by the pervasive presence of war relations throughout civil society. For Foucault, then, Nietzsche's life-affirming desire thus becomes a cultural possibility within the last century:

Since the last century, the great struggles that have challenged the general system of power were not guided by the belief in a return to former rights, or by the age-old dream of a cycle of time or a Golden Age. One no longer aspired toward the coming of the emperor of the poor, or the kingdom of the latter days, or even the restoration of our imagined ancestral rights; what was demanded and what served as an objective was life, understood as the basic needs, man's concrete essence, the realization of his potential, a plentitude of the possible. Whether or not it was Utopia that was wanted was of little importance; what we have seen has been a very real process of struggle; life as a political object was in a sense taken at face value and turned back against the system that was bent on controlling it. It was life rather than the law that became the issue of political struggles. (*HS* 144–45)

[226]

For Foucault, it is "life rather than the law," productive power rather than juridical power, that characterizes "political struggles," but because we know that sexuality and power are coextensive (*HS* 157), life characterizes the struggle of sexuality as well. Further, it is clear that for Foucault the major opponents in wars have become the forces of life and anti-life, and because war relations determine power-relations, and power-relations, sexual relations, it makes sense to conclude that, for Foucault, desire has become a Life and Death struggle.

We have seen Foucault return himself to an essentially Hegelian preoccupation with Life and Death, and a Nietzschean concern to see the forces of affirmation triumph over those of negation. Considered from this perspective, it becomes unclear whether Foucault, like Deleuze, is arguing for an ontology of desire that approximates the Nietzschean will-to-power, i.e., a Nietzschean rereading of Hegel's Life and Death struggle, or whether he is adequately depicting an historically conditioned, unprecedented form of desire. We may accept Foucault's assessment of modern warfare as essentially about survival, especially considering the effects of the nuclear threat, but the question remains whether his claim that vitalism is constitutive of all contemporary political struggles is an historically contingent claim or a claim of universal ontology, that is, a Nietzschean premise about the will-to-power which is in some sense *prior* to any of the historical observations that Foucault is making. Earlier in *The History of Sexuality,* Foucault calls for the overthrowing of juridical models of power because they are, in his words, "anti-energy" (*HS* 83). Although Foucault is generally critical of theories that attribute natural features to desire prior to acculturation and discourse, he seems in this instance to be doing precisely that. He argues against Freud that "sexuality must not be described as a stubborn drive, by nature alien and of necessity disobedient to a power which exhausts itself trying to subdue it" (*HS* 103). It seems, however, that the will-to-live, the will-to-power, is precisely such a "drive" in Foucault's own accepted discourse.

Moreover, in prescribing the overthrow of juridical models of power, Foucault faults such models for subduing the life-affirming energy characteristic of productive power. It seems, then, that juridical power acts "juridically" over productive power which, like Marcuse's Eros or Deleuze's internally differentiated will-to-power, is a long-repressed desire clamoring for emancipation. Either as pure energy, the will-to-power, or

[227]

e itself, productive desire seems less an historically *determined* than an historically *occasioned* desire which, in its origins, is an ontological invariant of human life. Foucault affirms as much when he defines the affirmation of "life" as "man's concrete essence, the realization of his potential, a plenitude of the possible" (*HS* 145).

Foucault attributes binary thinking to the domain of juridical power, but it seems that even his distinction between juridical and productive power is itself a juridical and binary distinction, the opposition between life and anti-life, affirmation and negation. Further, it seems that productive power relies on its opposite, juridical power, for its own existence; life gains its vitality, its essential productivity, in the course of struggle and resistance. Hence, affirmation seems conditioned by the threat of negation, just as the Hegelian subject who, risking his life, suffers the threat of death and resolves then to value and sustain life throughout the rest of his journey.

Foucault's understanding of desire as that which is awakened in the course of struggle and resistance assumes that domination always effects a generative consequence. On the one hand, it appears that Foucault minimizes the effects of domination, and sexual domination in particular, as an institution that might effectively preclude any response at all. After all, what is to distinguish generative domination and an effectively oppressive form of domination which immobilizes its object altogether? On the other hand, Foucault is perhaps suggesting only that there is a sense in which domination can be generative, not that all domination is, in fact, generative. I take it that in this second version of his theory, domination must be understood as a dynamic relation whose outcome is never fixed in the sense that effective domination immobilizes or destroys its object. Foucault seems to suggest that sexual domination, when it is not coerced, resembles an open game. Indeed, his political opposition to coercion is clear. In discussing the homosexual movement in an interview, he maintains that "there is the question of freedom of sexual choice that must be faced. I say freedom of sexual *choice* and not freedom of sexual acts because there are sexual acts like rape that should not be permitted whether they involve a man and a woman or two men."[26]

In discussing sadomasochism in the same interview, Foucault describes a scene of sexual conflict which is designed to sustain rather than resolve sexual tension. This is a version of desire that seeks its own reproduction and proliferation through the sustained struggle and conflict of the forces involved:

S&M is not a relationship between he (or she) who suffers and he (or she) who inflicts suffering, but between the master and the one on whom he exercises his mastery. What interests the practitioners of S&M is that the relationship is at the same time regulated and open. It resembles a chess game in the sense that one can win and the other lose. The master can lose in the S&M game if he finds he is unable to respond to the needs and trials of his victim. Conversely, the servant can lose if he fails to meet or can't stand meeting the challenge thrown at him by the master. This mixture of rules and openness has the effect of intensifying sexual relations by introducing a perpetual novelty, a perpetual tension and a perpetual uncertainty which the simple consummation of the act lacks. The idea is also to make use of every part of the body as a sexual instrument.[27]

In the above description, Foucault appears to defend the desirability of dissatisfaction, suggesting that the failure to achieve an erotic resolution of opposites is itself an eroticizing experience. Similar to the Deleuzian defense of an affirmative erotic multiplicity, Foucault's erotics of perpetual reversal is a generative activity which resists the possibility of closure. In this sense, dissatisfaction is no longer lamented, as it is in Sartre and Lacan, but celebrated as a sign of perpetual erotic possibility. The failure to achieve a final satisfaction for desire is, in Foucaultian terms, a significant achievement, the triumph of eros over an immobilizing law or, equivalently, the erotic mobilization of the law. Indeed, for Foucault, what from an Hegelian perspective would be understood as "futile" is now reappropriated as productive, generative, life-affirming. It is less the resolution of opposition than its erotic celebration that becomes the normative model for desire. Foucault further understands this generative opposition and subversive play as characteristic of sexuality in a post-dialectical age: "Perhaps the emergence of sexuality in our culture is an 'event' of multiple values: it is tied to the death of God and to the ontological void which his death fixed at the limit of our thought; it is also tied to the still silent and groping apparition of a form of thought in which the interrogation of the limit replaces the search for totality and the act of transgression replaces the movement of contradictions."[28]

[229]

Final Reflections on the "Overcoming" of Hegel

If Kojève halts the *Phenomenology's* progress at the struggle between lord and bondsman, and Hyppolite emphasizes the temporal flux of Life as the central moment of the text, and Sartre rewrites the dialectic of desire and recognition, it should not surprise us that Foucault, like Lacan, reformulates the Life and Death Struggle in contemporary terms. Both the French reception and the French criticism of Hegel appear, then, to take their bearings within the *Phenomenology's* Chapter 4. Indeed, it is striking to find how regularly even the most tenacious of post-Hegelians appear to remain faithful to the founding struggles of Hegel's desiring subject.

Foucault's break with the *Phenomenology* appears only partial. In the *Phenomenology*, the simple affirmation of life is inadequate because life must be repeatedly maintained. This necessitates the emergence of the bondsman who labors on life, and through that labor, learns the parameters of self-reflection, a capacity that eventually leads to his own revolt. Clearly, for Foucault, the discourse on life is not concerned with the development of the autonomous laborer, for that would posit a *telos* to life that is other than life, and that normative ideal, *qua* ideal, would prove to be anti-life. In a Nietzschean transvaluation of Hegel, Foucault appears to value the affirmation of life as the highest ideal, an ideal that works in the service of life and, therefore, cannot be part of any slave morality. Life, however, is not affirmed in a simple self-generated act; it requires resistance and struggle, and so requires a domain of Others, and a form of struggle. In conceding as much, Foucault seems to be acknowledging that the very promotion of life requires a way of life, and that this way of life is a certain kind of struggle. For Foucault, sexuality has become precisely such a way of life, a contemporary locus of struggle, because of the juridical management of reproduction in the interests of the politics of population control.[29] The colonization of reproductive technology, the medical isolation of homosexuality, the hysterization of women's bodies, the psychiatrization of perversions, have been medico-legal strategies for deploying sexuality in the interests of juridical discourses. The category of "sex" as a univocal signifier is precisely such a politically motivated construct, as is the category of "desire" which, according to Foucault, misses the point of sexuality as a complex discourse.

[230]

Sexuality is a domain of conflict for Foucault, one in which life-affirming desires are produced in the course of struggle and opposition. Eroticizing the master-slave relation, Foucault seems to envision the thorough eroticization of the body as a consequence of sadomasochistic jouissance, an eroticization of domination and submission which produces inadvertent intensities and pleasures, which proliferates kinds of pleasures and, hence, the entire field of sexual forces, working against the juridical reduction and localization of erotic pleasure. In such a struggle, domination does not result in oppression—that would be the consequence of a juridical power-relation. Rather, domination engenders creative and unexpected response. Productive power in the sexual domain thus becomes understood as a kind of erotic improvisation, the sexual version of Nietzsche's life-affirming creation of values.

Like Deleuze, Foucault appears to value life as a domain of pure possibility in which restriction and prohibition belong to the forces of anti-life. Struggle and resistance take the place of the law or, we might say, they *are* the law which has lost its rigidity and become malleable—the plasticity of the law. The law in its rigidity creates desire as a lack, but the law in its plasticity creates "the plenitude of the possible," desire as a creative act, a locus of innovation, the production of new cultural meanings. As in Hegel, desire reaches its limit nowhere, that is to say, it is an "absolute impulse" that only attains its satisfaction in the experience of the infinite back and forth of dialectical play. This notion of jouissance, what Sartre calls the imaginary and Lacan terms "Being," what Deleuze and Foucault understand as the affirmation of the will-to-power, seems to be what Hegel had in mind when he wrote not only that the infinite is self-consciousness, but that "self-consciousness is desire."

And yet it would clearly be wrong to conclude that these very efforts to overcome Hegel's *Phenomenology* can simply be reassimilated back into Hegel's framework. That is not the argument here. Hegel's subject can no longer be entertained, even in an imaginary domain, apart from the thesis of its very impossibility. With Foucault, it becomes more difficult to refer to "desire" without first asking after the specific historical discourse productive of the phenomenon. Both the "subject" and its "desire" have come to suffer the process of historicization, and the presumed universality of the Hegelian discourse becomes increasingly suspect. Indeed, it becomes crucial to ask just how this subject is constituted, under what conditions, and by what means. Moreover, are there concrete individuals whose desire approximates the desire of Hegel's subject? What gender are they, and to what extent is dialectical opposition considered to be characteristic of binary relations between the sexes?

Among French readers of Hegel, Julia Kristeva stands out as the one most concerned with a critique of Hegel from the point of view of an embodied, gendered individual. In her *Revolution in Poetic Language* (1974), she criticizes Hegel's subject as a "paranoid" psychological figure, one who denies the materiality of his body and the psychosomatic origins of affective life. "Desire" is the name given to the rationalist appropriation of drives, the logocentric resistance to the body that precedes conventional signification. Moreover, Kristeva aligns herself with the Feuerbachian critique of Hegel which, she maintains, "makes explicit the *real basis* of [Hegel's subject's] totalizing and unifying aspect. It reveals that certain social relations—the family, civil society, and the State—founded on this unitary subject and his desire, are the truth of Hegelian speculation in its *positivistic* aspect" (p. 136). Like Deleuze, Kristeva sees in the subject's initially hostile relation to the Other evidence of a slave morality of sorts, and argues that capitalism requires that each individual be pitted against every other in the competition for scarcely available goods. Distancing herself from a Marxist conclusion to the dilemma, she appears to agree with Foucault that the binary division of social agents into classes is an extension rather than a critique of the notion of the subject. In her view, capitalism induces a widespread schizoid disorder in which the disassociation from the body is central. The identification with a desiring subject whose main aim is the suppression of alterity is characteristic of a highly rationalistic and paranoid personality, one that is fostered and maintained by capitalist social relations. Hence, Kristeva concludes that "in the State and in religion, capitalism requires and consolidates the paranoid moment of the subject: a unity foreclosing the other and taking its place" (p. 139).

Kristeva's purpose is to explode this monadic structure of the subject through a return to the body as a heterogeneous assemblage of drives and needs. Although Lacan argued that there could be no return to this primary heterogeneity without the breaking of the incest taboo, Kristeva argues that such a return is possible through the medium of poetic language. The rhythms and sounds of poetic language, its plurivocity of meanings, recall and reformulate an infantile relation to the maternal body. This language has its own set of meanings, but these meanings are not included by Lacan's theory of signification or, for that matter, by most theories of linguistic meaning. They constitute the *semiotic* for Kristeva, a notion explained in *Desire in Language* (1977). Briefly summarized, the semiotic designates the somatic aspects of language, which includes the rhythms, pacing of breath, apparent non sequiturs, and polyvalences of speech. According to Kristeva, the semiotic designates the 'workings of drives' which are irreducibly heterogeneous. The emergence of the *symbolic* function of language, as in Lacan, requires the internalization of the incest taboo which, according to Kristeva, effects a transition from semiotic to symbolic speech. Although poetry is said to recapture the semiotic, it does so only within the terms of the symbolic; the unconstrained return to the semiotic would result in a leave-taking of cultural systems of communication and an entrance into psychosis.

Throughout her speculations in *Desire in Language,* Kristeva suggests that women sustain a different relation to the semiotic in virtue of the psychoanalytic necessity that some identification with the mother is necessary for female sexual development. Following Lacan, Kristeva argues that the symbolic constitutes the rule of the Phallus, and that the entire system of symbolic language is predicated not only upon the denial of dependency upon the maternal body but, as a consequence, implies the repudiation of femininity. The "subject" who emerges as a result of this internalized repression is necessarily dissociated from his own body as well, a subject whose unity is purchased at the expense of his own drives, and whose denial is renamed as *desire.*

Not far from this view is Simone de Beauvoir's claim in *The Second Sex* that it is mainly men who constitute the domain of subjects, and that women, in this regard, are the Other. Kristeva's contribution to this formulation is to suggest, not an equality among subjects, but the critical deconstruction of the subject to its psychosomatic origins. Although Kristeva adheres to a psychoanalytic account of primary drives which may well be questionable, she nevertheless presents a significant departure from the Hegelian program, a turn from a discourse on desires and subjects, to one which examines first the bodies from which, or against which, desires emerge.

In this sense, Kristeva's methodological procedure bears similarities to Foucault's, despite the latter's critique of psychoanalytic assumptions regarding drives and repression. For Foucault, the examination of bodies would require a reflection upon the history of bodies, the institutional conditions of their emergence in given forms and relations, the historical production of their signification. For Kristeva, this reflection would attend to the psychosomatic origins of identity, where one would presumably discover a primary heterogeneity of impulse and drive subsequently rendered uniform through the internalization of the incest taboo. In a sense, repression is, for Kristeva, an invariant historical scene, the mechanism through which nature is transformed into history, a universal truth or, at least, a highly generalized truth of Western culture. Although Foucault would doubtless take issue with the presumed primacy of the incest taboo, and would argue that regulative mechanisms are more varied and historicized than Kristeva admits, his position is similarly concerned with the construction of the subject via the denial of the body and the heterogeneity of its impulses.

Like Kristeva, Foucault suggests a departure from the Hegelian discourse on desire and a turn, instead, to a discourse on bodies. On a general level, this project would tenuously align him with some feminist inquiries that understand the historical situation of the body to be centrally concerned with gender, and which tend to claim that inquiries into the structure and aim of desire require a prior inquiry into the complex interrelations of desire and gender. If gender is, as Beauvoir claims, the body in situation, then the "history of bodies" that Foucault suggests ought theoretically to include a history of gender as well. In *The History of Sexuality*, however, and in his short introduction to the journals of Herculine Barbin,[30] Foucault takes issue with the category of sex as a peculiar product of the discourse on sexuality: "the notion of 'sex' made it possible to group together, in an artificial unity, anatomical elements, biological functions, conducts, sensations, and pleasures, and it enabled one to make use of this fictitious unity as a causal principle, an omnipresent meaning, a secret to be discovered everywhere: sex was thus able to function as a unique signifier and as a universal signified" (*HS* 154). That the body is figured as belonging to one of two sexes is evidence of a regulative discourse whose categories have become constitutive of experience itself, and which now appear, in their sedimented form, to be fully naturalized phenomena. As a result, Foucault is less interested in feminist inquiry that he is in a general displacement of the regulatory discourses on sexuality such as those that create the category of sex. Moreover, Foucault remarks that the opposition to juridical forms of sexuality ought not to operate within the terms of the discourse on desire: "the rallying point for the counterattack against the deployment of sexuality ought not to be sex-desire, but bodies and pleasure" (*HS* 157).

This critique of "the desiring subject,"[31] and the proposal to write a history of bodies[32] in its place constitutes a major conceptual reorientation which, if successful, would signal the definitive closure of Hegel's narrative of desire. In the introduction to the second volume of *The History of Sexuality*, Foucault describes the specific historical context in which the subject of desire has played its central role:

When I came to study the modes according to which individuals are given to recognize themselves as sexual subjects . . . at the time the notion of desire, or of the desiring subject, constituted if not a theory, then at least a generally accepted theoretical frame. This very acceptance was odd: it was this same theme, in fact, or variations thereof, that was found not only at the very center of the traditional theory, but also in the conceptions that sought to detach themselves from it.[33]

Foucault explains that this conception was inherited by the nineteenth and twentieth centuries "from a long Christian tradition" whose own references to "the flesh" as both limit and temptation produce human beings as fundamentally characterized by dissatisfied desire. Foucault cautions against simply accepting this conceptual framework in the historical investigation of sexuality, but proposes, rather, a genealogical investigation of how the desiring subject was historically produced. He explains, "this does not mean that I propose to write a history of the successive conceptions of desire, of concupisence, or of libido, but rather to analyze the practices by which individuals were led to focus their attention on themselves, to decipher, recognize, and acknowledge themselves as subjects of desire, bringing into play between themselves a certain relationship that allows them to discover, in desire, the truth of their being, be it natural or fallen."[34]

Foucault's method of genealogical inquiry consists of giving an account of how a given "truth" is produced from a set of power relations as a strategic moment in the self-amplification of power. The "truth" of the relation between desire and the subject, the "truth" that is ostensibly latent in every desire and which constitutes the secret, the essence, of the subject itself, is a fiction which a given discourse, indeed, an entire history of Western discourses, has required. If desire can be said to reveal the truth of the human subject, then self-investigation promises the truth of the subject. And with this posture so sanctified, both the "self" and its "truth" are admitted to be immanently locatable within the reflexive circle of thinking. What if Foucault were right, that the conceit of an immanently philosophical desire grounded the further conceits of the subject and its truth? Then Hegel's narrative would have entered fully the domain of the fantastic, and the phenomenology would require a genealogical account of the hidden historical conditions of its own structure.

But what justifies Foucault's turn to a history of bodies, and what are the implications of forfeiting the inquiry into desire for an inquiry that takes the body as its primary theme? Foucault would argue that juridical discourses have been mainly concerned with the regulation of bodies and that history has left its legacy, as it were, *on* the bodies of contemporaries. In Foucault's terms, "the body is the inscribed surface of events (traced by language and dissolved by ideas), the locus of a dissociated Self (adopting the illusion of a substantial unity), and a volume in perpetual disintegration." The task of genealogy, he maintains, is "to expose a body totally imprinted by history and the process of history's destruction of the body."[35]

The "dissociated Self" is understood to be a sublimated creation of the juridically repressed body, which suggests that the Subject itself is a fiction based upon the regulation of the body (here Foucault's theory clearly draws on Nietzsche's *Will to Power* in which the ego is understood to conceal the multiplicitous affectivity of the body and of instinctual life in general). Hence, for Foucault, the subject is dissociated *from* the body and the multivalent force relations of which it is constituted; this suggests that a history of the subject requires an account of the regulatory and repressive mechanisms, those strategies of subjection that gave rise to the "subject." Foucault's discussion of the body occasionally relies upon a naturalistic vocabulary (e.g., "the strength or weakness of an instinct") which is fairly questionable, and it also suggests, as I noted earlier, that the body is always the occasion for a play of dominations and regulations: "In a sense, only a single drama is ever staged in this 'non-place,' the endlessly repeated play of dominations. The domination of certain men over others leads to the differentiation of values; class domination generates the idea of liberty."[36]

The "destruction" of the body is, thus, the occasion for the manufacturing of values, the moment of the "disassociation" which gives rise to abstraction and to the subject itself as an abstraction. Inasmuch as this is a single scene repeated endlessly throughout the course of history, Foucault appears to subscribe to a single locus of historical change, a single tension between the body and strategies of domination which give rise to events and values alike. Here we can see that Foucault has elevated the scene of bodily conflict to an invariant feature of historical change, and it makes sense to ask whether war itself has not become romanticized and reified through this theoretical move.

There may be another sense in which the body can be understood as the "inscribed surface of events" that does not assume that the body is always subjected to domination, and that this "subjection" is the juridical generator of values. Rather than assume that all culture is predicated upon the denial of the body, and that inscription is both a moment of regulation and of signification, it seems that a more thoroughly historicized consideration of various bodies in concrete social contexts might illuminate "inscription" as a more internally complicated notion. How, for instance, are we to understand the body as the inscribed surface of the history of gender relations, race relations, and ethnicity? How does the aging body evince a history of aging, and how do various bodies signify social positions and even social histories? And to what extent can the body exhibit an innovative relation to the past which constitutes it? How do we conceive of the body as a concrete scene of cultural struggle?

Foucault appears to accept that the various regulatory mechanisms which govern the body are invariably negative and assist in the production of the dissociated self, the "subject" of desire. Why does Foucault appear to eschew the analysis of concrete bodies in complex historical situations in favor of a single history in which all culture requires the subjection of the body, a subjection which produces a "subject" in its wake?

Foucault's account in "Nietzsche, Genealogy, and History" is illuminated when we understand the tension between the dissociated Self and the "subjected body" as a reworking of the lordship-bondage dialectic. For Hegel, the bondsman is the body without consciousness, and the lord is the figure of pure abstraction which disavows its own corporeality. Foucault's genealogical account conflates these two figures into a relation of inversion which is not attributable to subjects of any kind. Indeed, for Foucault, this relation of inversion generates the fiction of the subject

[237]

itself. If we want to ask the question of who occupies these roles in a concrete social context, that is, for whom is dissociated cruelty a characteristic practice, and whose bodies are regularly subjected to this subjection, then it appears that Foucault's genealogical analysis must be supplemented by an account of the genesis and distribution of social roles. In fact, it is Hegel's account of lordship and bondage that accounts for this relationship in both reflexive and intersubjective terms, and so appears a more promising framework within which to answer such a question. Foucault may well give us an account of how the "subject" is generated, but he cannot tell us which subjects are generated in the way that he describes, and at whose expense.

Foucault's analysis of historical *Entstehung* appears essentially indebted to Hegel's lordship-bondage dialectic. But other problems remain: if there is a single drama to history, and if it consists in the conflictual scene in which the subjection or inscription of the body gives rise to significations, then either we must accept a personified notion of History as a signifier, or we must ask more specific questions about the production and distribution of power through the field of bodies and desires. If a history of bodies can be written that would not reduce all culture to this imposition of the law upon the body, then perhaps a truly specific account of bodies will be forthcoming, and desire will be understood in the context of the interrelationship between historically specific bodies.

Foucault's critique of the discourse on desire, on the figure of the "subject of desire," does well to remind us that desire is a name that not only accounts for an experience, but determines that experience as well, that the subject of desire may well be a fiction useful to a variety of regulative strategies, and that the "truth" of desire may well lie in a history of bodies as yet unwritten. Foucault challenges us to make fun of ourselves in our search for truth, in the relentless pursuit of the essence of our selves in the various flashes of impulse that lure us with their metaphysical promise. If the history of desire must be told in terms of a history of bodies, then it becomes necessary to understand how that history encodes itself in these most immediate phenomena; and if it is not a hermeneutics of the self that is required, then perhaps it is the narrative of a certain philosophically instructive comedy of errors. From Hegel through Foucault, it appears that desire makes us into strangely fictive beings. And the laugh of recognition appears to be the occasion of insight.

[238]

Notes

Introduction

1. See Unger, *Knowledge and Politics*, for a sustained criticism of desire as arbitrary.

2. Spinoza, *Ethics*, part 3, prop. 3.

3. Kant, *Critique of Practical Reason*, Preface, ff.#7; theorem 2, remark 1 (¶ 24).

4. See Diotima's final speeches in Plato's *Symposium*.

5. See Aristotle, *Nicomachean Ethics*, book 1, ch. 13, ¶1102b29–30, for an explanation of the unification of desires under a rational principle.

6. See note 3.

7. The term "repression" is used loosely in this context, although it will be considered in a more detailed fashion in chapter 4, opening section.

8. In fact, Nietzsche and Freud present different theories of psychic organization which do not rely on the principle of self-identity. We will see the extent to which post-Hegelian French thought relies on both of these theories in chapter 4.

9. Sartre refers to Hegel's "ontological optimism" in *BN*, 243.

10. The desire-to-be can be seen to be the first principle of Sartre's theory of the emotions inasmuch as all emotion problematizes this project to be. Negative emotions such as fear, distrust, sadness, and even jealousy, can be derived from the fear of not-being, and joy, pleasure, and enthusiasm can similarly be understood as temporary appearances of the project-to-be's success.

11. The final paragraph of the *Phenomenology* (¶ 808), closes on a note of significant nonclosure: the final word is "infinitude."

12. See Gadamer, "The Idea of Hegel's Logic" in his *Hegel's Dialectic*, for a discussion of the primacy of Becoming in Hegel's *Logic*.

13. Hegel, *Philosophy of History*, p. 102; see Shlomo Avineri, *Hegel's Theory of the Modern State*, (Cambridge: Cambridge University Press, 1972), pp. 234–38.

14. *Hegel's Lectures on the History of Philosophy*, E. S. Haldane and Frances H. Simson, trans. (New York: Humanities Press, 1974), 3:289.
15. Spinoza, *Ethics*, part 3, prop. 1.
16. Aristotle, *De Anima*, book 3, ch. 10., pp. 20–25.
17. Spinoza, *Ethics*, part 3, prop. 2, note.
18. For a more thorough discussion of Spinoza's solution to the mind/body problem, see Marx Wartofsky, "Action and Passion: Spinoza's Construction of a Scientific Psychology," in Marjorie Grene, ed., *Spinoza: A Collection of Critical Essays*, pp. 329–55 (Notre Dame: University of Notre Dame Press, 1973).
19. Hegel, *History of Philosophy*, 3:256.
20. *Ibid.*, p. 257.
21. *Ibid.*, p. 281.
22. Marx, *Hegel's Phenomenology of Spirit*, p. 44.
23. *Ibid.*, p. 48.
24. Hegel, *History of Philosophy*, 3:287.
25. For Fichte, perpetual longing is the human consequence of a dialectic without the ontological possibility of synthesis.
26. See my *"Geist ist Zeit:* French Interpretations of Hegel's Absolute", *Berkshire Review* (September 1985), for a more extended discussion of the Absolute as time.
27. See Jacques Derrida, "The Pit and the Pyramid: Introduction to Hegel's Semiology"; first presented as a paper at the Séminaire de Jean Hyppolite, at the Collège de France in 1968 and subsequently published in a collection in honor of Hyppolite, *Hegel et la pensée moderne, séminaire sur Hegel dirigé par Jean Hyppolite au Collège de France (1967–68)* (Paris: Presses Universitaires de France, 1970) and published in English in Derrida's *Margins of Philosophy*.

1. Desire, Rhetoric, and Recognition in Hegel's Phenomenology of Spirit

1. A "psychological novel." See M. H. Abrams, *Natural Supernaturalism,* "Hegel's 'Phenomenology of the Spirit': Metaphysical Structure and Narrative Plot," pp. 225–37.
2. Derrida argues in "The Pit and the Pyramid: An Introduction to Hegel's Semiology," that dialectical movement, in virtue of its circularity, circumscribes a stationary place which precludes the possibility of movement. This leads Derrida to argue that for Hegel, the process of signification is a kind of death-in-life, a posture of stasis which implicitly refutes its own claim to being a kind of movement. Derrida's assumption, however, is that Hegel's system, understood in terms of his semiology, is completed and self-sufficient, when it is precisely that assumption that first requires clarification.
3. Diderot's *Jacques le fataliste* renders a master-slave dialectic which clearly influenced Hegel's own discussion of the dynamic. Diderot implicates his reader directly, exaggerating the polemical purpose of the text, and indirectly setting up the relation between text and reader as its own dialectic of power. Hegel's narrative

[240]

1. Hegel: Desire, Rhetoric, Recognition

strategy is less self-consciously polemical, avoiding the direct assertion of pro-
nouns. In part, this narrative strategy appears to conform to his design to show
the dramatic emergence of the subject, i.e., the impossibility of simple reference
to an "I" or a "you" precisely because we cannot yet be sure what these desig-
nations mean.

4. Kierkegaard, *Repetition*, p. 200 (freely interpreted).
5. Nietzsche, *The Will to Power*, ¶ 535.
6. Nietzsche's critique of morality and philosophical abstraction generally
reveals one kind of lie that aids in the living of a "slave's existence," but in "Truth
and Lie in an Extra-Moral Sense," he argues that the "truth" counterposed to
this lie is itself a kind of necessary falsehood. In *Beyond Good and Evil*, it becomes
clear that concepts are such necessary falsehoods, that they invariably reduce the
multiple significations from which they are generated, i.e., that they are "dead"
rather than living, metaphorical, fluid. The stages of the *Phenomenology* can be
read as frozen moments in a necessarily fluid movement; hence, they are necessarily
false, but nevertheless informative, if deconstructed into the suppressed multiplicity at their origin.

7. Rosen, *Hegel: An Introduction to the Science of Wisdom*, p. 159.
8. Taylor, *Hegel*, p. 146.
9. See Gadamer, *Hegel's Dialectic: Five Hermeneutical Studies*, p. 62,
ff.7.
10. *Goethe's Faust*, part 1, p. 146.
11. Spinoza, *Ethics*, part 4, Preface, p. 88.
12. See Findlay, *Hegel: A Reexamination*, p. 96.
13. Rosen, *Hegel: Introduction to the Science of Wisdom*, p. 41.
14. For a discussion of this notion of self-alienation in terms of the religious
concept of ecstasy, see Rotenstreich, "On the Ecstatic Sources of the Concept of
Alienation," *Review of Metaphysics*, 1963.
15. The "experience" of the *Phenomenology* ought not be understood as
ordinary experience, but, rather, as the gradual and insistent cultivation of philosophical truths embedded in ordinary experience. Werner Marx accounts for
the distinction between natural and phenomenal consciousness in *Hegel's Phenomenology of Spirit: A Commentary on the Preface and Introduction*, pp. 12–
16. Although Hegel occasionally claims to begin his phenomenological narrative
with ordinary experience [¶ 8: "It has taken such a long time . . . (to) make
attention to the here and now as such, attention to what has been called 'experience,' an interesting and valid enterprise")] he also claims that philosophy must
now lift Spirit beyond the realm of pure sense. The philosophical cultivation of
sensuousness into an all-embracing truth begins not with "ordinary experience"
or daily life, but with the philosophical assumptions of ordinary experience.
Hence, the "experience" of the *Phenomenology* is never devoid of philosophical
appropriation; although the referent is implicitly the ordinary experience of human beings, this referent is never disclosed as outside of the philosophical language
that interprets it.

16. In German: "Es ist für das Selbstbewusstsein ein anderes Selbstbewu-sstsein; es ist ausser sich gekommen. Dies hat die gedoppelte Bedeutung: erstlich, es hat sich selbst verloren, denn es findet sich als anderes Wesen; zweitens, es hat damit das Andere aufgehoben, denn es sieht auch nicht das Andere als Wesen, sondern, sich selbst im Anderen." Hegel, *Phänomenologie des Geistes*, p. 146.

17. For a subject whose ideal is that of self-sufficiency, self-estrangement might well be understood as a threat to that project and that identity. Anger thus makes sense as a counterpart to ecstasy for such a subject.

18. The struggle for recognition was reconceived a number of times throughout Hegel's early writings, but the *Phenomenology* establishes the struggle as consequent upon the experience of desire for and by another. Although Kojève and Leo Strauss have interpreted this struggle as emerging from a conflict of desires over goods, the scarcity of which sets individual wills against each other, this interpretation has been deftly refuted by the scholarship of Ludwig Siep in "Der Kampf um Anerkennung;" "Zur Dialektik der Anerkennung bei Hegel"; and "Zum Freiheitsbegriff der praktischen Philosophie Hegels in Jena," pp. 217–28. In his "Der Kampf um Anerkennung" Siep traces the evolving conception of the struggle for recognition throughout the Jena writings, and discovers that Hegel's conception of the struggle between self-consciousness differs significantly from Hobbes' notion of the conflict of interests that forms the basis of contractarian legal theory. While Hobbes understood the conflict of desires to give rise to an artificial state apparatus which would limit the (naturally) limitless freedom of egoistic individuals, Hegel developed the view that the struggle for recognition gave rise to a concept of the individual essentially defined in terms of a larger cultural order, which, rather than limiting the individual's freedom, provided for its concrete determination and expression. In the *System der Sittlichkeit* (1802–3), Hegel viewed the struggle for recognition, not as a pursuit of property or personal honor but of the integrity of the family. The struggle was enacted within the family as a struggle between members who must reconcile their individual wills with the exigencies of collective family life, and as a struggle between distinct families for recognition. The act of recognition ensures that the individual is no longer a discrete entity, but is, rather, *"ein Glied eines Ganzen" (System der Sittlichkeit,* p. 50). That recognition aids in the construction of a collective identity is reinforced by Henry Harris' analysis of the *System der Sittlichkeit* in "The Concept of Recognition in Hegel's Jena Manuscripts" Hegel-Studien, Beiheft 20.

In the *Realphilosophie II* (1805–6), Hegel reconceives the struggle for recognition as a pursuit of property and honor, but even here it is not the individual who seeks recognition of his own interests, but, rather, a set of individuals who seek to find recognition for their common identity. Hegel here develops his notion of absolute freedom which calls for the surpassing of individual wills: "die einzelnen haben sich durch Negation ihrer, durch Entäusserung und Bildung zum Allgemeinen zu machen" *(Realphilosophie II,* ¶ 245). The *Realphilosophie II* envisions the struggle for recognition as *following* the breakdown of a contractual agree-

[242]

ment; hence, the struggle does not, as it does for Hobbes, signify the need for a contract, but, rather, for an ethical community based on nonartificial, i.e., natural, ties.

In every case in the Jena writings, Hegel conceives of the struggle for recognition as one that is resolved through a discovery of a prior unifying ground which remains concealed throughout the struggle itself. Both of the above cited texts resolve the struggle through positing love or family as its necessary solution. This struggle for à community based on *agape* is prefigured in Hegel's early essay on love *(Die Liebe),* written between 1797 and 1798. By the time of the *Phenomenology* (1806) Hegel views the struggle for recognition as motivated by the demands of reciprocal desire, but the life and death struggle emerges as an intermediary stage of this development. *Siep points out\that the struggle for recognition is often misconceived as a struggle that begins with the life and death struggle, but he argues that the life and death struggle is itself precipitated by the prior struggle for recognition implicit in desire:* "Die Bewegung des Anerkennens beginnt nämlich nach Hegel damit, dass es 'ausser sich' ist, sich als 'Fürsichseiendes aufhebt' und sich nur im Anderen anschaut. . . . Diese Struktur entspricht nicht dem Kampf, sondern der Liebe. . . . Nicht der Anfang der Bewegung des Anerkennens, sondern erst der Schritt des Selbstbewusstseins, 'sein Andersein auf(zu)-heben,' ist im Kampf auf Leben und Tod verkörpert" (Siep, "Der Kampf um Anerkennung," p.194).

The struggle for recognition arises, then, not from a primary competitive attitude toward the other, but from the experience of desire for and by another. Specific desires for property, goods or positions of social dominance must be, according to Hegel's framework, seen as derivative expressions of the desire for a community based on love. Desire is, thus, not originally an effort of acquisition or domination, but emerges in such forms only when a community based on the principles of reciprocal recognition has not yet been developed.

19. See Gadamer, "Hegel's Dialectic of Self-Consciousness," p. 66: "self-consciousness . . . is unable to achieve true being-for-self without overcoming its attachment to life, i.e. without annihilating itself as mere 'life.' "

20. Kierkegaard, *Sickness Unto Death,* p. 18.

21. It is not merely the failure of desire that precipitates the experience of death in life, for desire is *itself* an expression of the negative. The failure to achieve substantial being, which is, strictly speaking, not the failure of desire, but the failure of satisfaction, must be viewed in Hegelian terms as philosophically important. Prefiguring Kierkegaard's frustration with those "too tenacious of life to die a little," Hegel claims in his preface that "the life of the spirit is not the life which shrinks from death and keeps itself untouched by devastation, but rather the life which endures it and maintains itself in it" (¶ 32). Walter Kaufmann's translation of the rest of the paragraph elucidates the project to which devastation, the failure of desire, the experience of death in life, gives rise: "Spirit gains its truth only by finding itself in absolute dismemberment. This power it is—not as

the positive that looks away from the negative—as when we say of something, this is nothing or false, and then, finished with it, turn away from it to something else: the spirit is this power only by looking the negative in the face and abiding with it. This abiding is the magic force which converts the negative into being," Kaufmann, *Hegel: Texts and Commentary*, p. 50.

2. Historical Desires: The French Reception of Hegel

1. See Koyré, "Rapports sur l'état des études hégéliennes en France."
2. Hegel's early theological writings were edited and made available in 1907 by Henri Niel in German, as the *Theologische Jugendschriften*. Wahl cites this edition, as well as the histories of Hegel's development by Rosenkranz (1844), Haym (1857), and Dilthey (1905) as central to his own investigation of the tragic element in Hegel's early religious writings through the *Phenomenology of Spirit*. He quotes very few French texts in his work with the exception of Léon Brunschvicg's *Le Progrès de la conscience dans la philosophie occidentale* (Paris: 1927). Before the publication of Kojève's lectures (1933–39) and Hyppolite's *Genèse et structure de la "Phénoménologie de l'esprit de Hegel"* both in 1947, only Henri Niel's *De la médiation dans la philosophie de Hegel* stands out as a major, full-length study in French. The publication of the *Phenomenology* in French by Hyppolite from 1939 through 1941 prompted a good number of critical articles in various French philosophical and intellectual journals.

Hyppolite gives an account of Hegel's emergence into French intellectual life during and after the war years in pp. 230–41 in his *Figures de la pensée philosophique*. He credits the interest in Bergson in the 1920s with introducing certain themes, i.e., life and history, into French intellectual life which ultimately made a serious consideration of Hegel possible. Mikel Dufrenne in "L'actualité de Hegel" also likens Hegel's dialectical notion of becoming with the notion of *durée* in Bergson. Only Mark Poster among the major intellectual historians of the period sees in the turn to Hegel a reaction against Bergson.

3. Merleau-Ponty, *Sense and Non-Sense*, pp. 109–10.
4. Simone de Beauvoir, *Force of Circumstance*, p. 34.
5. Alexandre Koyré, *Études d'histoire de la pensée philosophique*, (Paris: Armand Colin, 1961), p. 34.
6. See Descombes, *Modern French Philosophy*, p. 14.
7. Dufrenne, "L'actualité de Hegel," p. 296.
8. See Dufrenne, pp. 301–3; and Henri Niel, "L'interprétation de Hegel," p. 428.
9. For a consideration of Kojève's view of nature, see Dufrenne's "L'actualité de Hegel." Kojève's view is problematic not only in the context of Hegel's apparently more complex view, but also in terms of contemporary scientific accounts of nature. Kojève is clearly writing in the context of a philosophical tradition that maintains a view of natural existence as static and nondialectical; he does not

consider the possibility that nature is itself an evolving system, nor does he consider the kinds of "reasons" that account for evolutionary schemes in nature. In his single-minded account of nature as brute and unintelligible, he seems to discount the possibility of a dynamic conception of nature.

10. For a discussion of Kojève's atheistic interpretation of Hegel, and a defense of Hegel's theism, see Niel, "L'interprétation de Hegel." In his *Introduction to the Reading of Hegel,* Kojève calls for an overcoming of Christian society, and appears to subscribe to the conventional Marxist view of religion as a mystification. See also Kojève's "Hegel, Marx et le christianisme," p. 340. Hyppolite in "Note sur la préface de la *Phénoménologie de l'esprit* et le thème: l'Absolu est sujet" in *Figures, 1* rejects this interpretation of Hegel as an atheist—as do Niel and Wahl—claiming instead that the very meaning of God is transformed within the Hegelian system such that it is not vulnerable to the criticisms of the conventional Marxist view.

11. Hegel, *Jenaer Realphilosophie,* p. 4.

12. Hyppolite claims. "There is little doubt that in general Kierkegaard is right against Hegel, and it is not our purpose here to enter a defense of the Hegelian system against Kierkegaard's attack. What interests us is to reveal in Hegel, as we find him in his early works and in the *Phenomenology,* a philosopher much closer to Kierkegaard than might seem credible. This concrete and existential character of Hegel's early works has been admirably demonstrated by Jean Wahl in his work on *The Unhappy Consciousness in Hegel"* (CE 22–23).

13. Hyppolite, "The Human Situation in the Hegelian Phenomenology," in his *Studies on Marx and Hegel,* p. 169. See also CE 26–27.

14. See also GS 163.

15. Goethe, *Faust,* p. 146.

16. See Klaus Hartmann, *Sartre's Ontology: A Study of Being and Nothingness in the Light of Hegel's Logic* (Evanston: Northwestern University Press, 1966).

3. Sartre: Imaginary Pursuit of Being

1. See Sartre, *Imagination: A Psychological Critique,* ch. 9, "The Phenomenology of Husserl" for Sartre's early understanding of the *Ideas* as laying the framework for a non-solipsistic psychology.

2. Husserl's theory of intentionality may be seen as exemplifying the principle of ontological harmony that we considered in the context of Hegel. Aron Gurwitsch's many comparisons between Husserl and Leibniz give credence to the claim that Husserl's doctrine of intentionality is an effort to reinterpret the doctrine of internal relations in terms of a modern epistemology.

3. See Gurwitsch, "On the Intentionality of Consciousness."

4. David Hume, *A Treatise on Human Nature,* T. H. Green and T. H. Grose, eds. (London, 1890), 1: 505–06.

5. *Ibid.,* p. 491.

6. Sartre refers throughout *The Transcendence of the Ego* to the *Phenomenology of Internal Time Consciousness* as portraying a non-egological theory of intentionality which he himself accepts; see *TE* 39, 42, n.21.

7. *PI* 10: "the image . . . is complete at the very moment of its appearance."

8. "This act . . . can posit the object as nonexistent, or as absent, or as existing elsewhere; it can also "neutralize" itself, that is, not posit its object as existing."

9. Sartre uses the expression "degradation" to refer to the state of consciousness in emotion throughout *E*; in *PI* he implies that consciousness, as imaginary, is involved in a purposeful project of self-obfuscation, a belief in plenitude which turns out to be an "essential poverty" (p. 11).

10. "I" 4: "there is nothing in (consciousness) but a movement of fleeing itself" and (p. 5), "everything is finally outside."

11. Robert Solomon, "Sartre on Emotions," in Schilpp, *The Philosophy of Jean-Paul Sartre*, p. 284.

12. *BN* 384: "The first apprehension of the Other's sexuality in so far as it is lived and suffered can be only *desire;* it is by desiring the Other (or by discovering myself as incapable of desiring him) or by apprehending his desire for me that I discover his being-sexed. Desire reveals to me simultaneously *my* being-sexed and *his* being-sexed, *my* body as sex and *his* body." Also, see page 382: "My original attempt to get hold of the Other's free subjectivity through his objectivity-for-me is *sexual desire.*" The understanding of desire in exclusively sexual terms can be found in Marcuse's "Existentialism," p. 326 and Natanson's *A Critique of Jean-Paul Sartre's Ontology*, p. 44.

13. This broader conception of desire is discussed at length in the section "Existential Psychoanalysis" where desire is identified with the for-itself conceived as a lack: "Freedom is precisely the being which makes itself a lack of being. But since desire . . . is identical with lack of being, freedom can arise only as being which makes itself a desire of being" (BN 567).

14. Spinoza, *Ethics,* part 3, prop. 6.

15. The cited excerpts are my translations from the French transcript of this session published as "Conscience de soi et connaissance de soi," *Bulletin de la Societé Française de Philosophie* (1948) 13: 49–91.

16. See Hartmann, *Sartre's Ontology,* p. 21, n. 59.

17. Although Sartre appears to be aligned with the Nietzschean criticism of egological views of consciousness (see *TE*), we can nevertheless consider what a Nietzschean criticism of Sartre's postulation of a unified subject might be like. Nietzsche's *Will to Power* supports a view of the fundamental multiplicity of desires, and the unified self as a deceptive construct. In section 518 of that text, Nietzsche argues against the idea of the self as a unity: "If our 'ego' is for us the sole being, after the model of which we fashion and understand all being; very well! Then there would be very much room to doubt whether what we have here is not a perspective illusion—an apparent unity that encloses everything like a horizon. The evidence of the body reveals a tremendous multiplicity. . . . " (p.

281). To this purpose one ought also to consult sections 489, 492, and 259. According to Nietzsche, the principle of identity that structures egological theories serves a normative purpose; the positing of a singular or unified identity masks a wish to overcome the multiplicity of the body, the contradictoriness of desires, "the systematic reduction of all bodily feelings to moral values" (section 227). For Nietzsche, ontology cloaks morality, and morality is motivated by a desire to overcome the body altogether. One might extrapolate from this position a criticism of Sartre's view that desire is internally unified and that it seeks a transcendence of facticity. These positions could then be seen not as a consequence of an ontological situation, but as a transcription of a religious wish into the rationalizing language of ontology. In section 333, Nietzsche explains, "it is only this desire 'thus it ought to be' that has called forth that other desire to know what 'is.' For the knowledge of what is, is a consequence of that question: 'How? is it possible? why precisely so?' Wonder at the disagreement between our desires and the course of the world. But perhaps the case is different: perhaps that 'thus it ought to be' is our desire to overcome the world." See chapter 4 of this text for further discussion.

18. Jean-Paul Sartre, "Self-Portrait at Seventy," in his *Life/Situations*, p. 11.

19. Sartre describes both sadism (*BN* 378) and masochism (*BN* 405) as "failures" of desire. The true aim of desire he defines as "reciprocal incarnation" (*BN* 398), but then goes on to claim that this is a *necessary* failure (*BN* 396). Sadism and masochism appear to be the most pronounced ways in which reciprocity breaks down into non-reciprocal exchange.

20. See Hegel, "The Revealed Religion," pp. 453–78 in the *Phenomenology*.

21. For an interesting article tracing Sartre's cartesianism and its eventual dissolution, see Busch, "Beyond the Cogito."

22. See Marcuse, "Existentialism," p. 330.

23. Monika Langer, "Sartre and Merleau-Ponty: A Reappraisal," in Schilpp *The Philosophy of Jean-Paul Sartre*, pp. 300–25.

24. Sartre clearly does not consider the "look" as a figurative expression insofar as it can be a "rustling of branches" or "the slight opening of a shutter" (*BN* 257–58). Objects can manifest a look, and a look can persist in the mode of memory or anticipation: cf. *The Words*: "Even in solitude I was putting on an act. Karlemamie and Anne Marie had turned those pages long before I was born; it was their knowledge that lay open before my eyes. In the evening they would question me: 'what did you read? What have you understood?' I knew it, I was pregnant, I would give birth to a child's comment. To escape from the grown-ups into reading was the best way of communing with them. Though they were absent, their future gaze entered me through the back of my head, emerged from their pupils, and propelled along the floor the sentences which had been read a hundred times and which I was reading for the first time. I who was seen saw myself" (p. 70).

25. Merleau-Ponty's *Phenomenology of Perception* sought to refute the notion,

subscribed to by Sartre in *PI*, that perception confronts a factic world which is brutely given at an insurpassable distance from consciousness. Perception is not a mode of knowing the world which requires distance between the perceiving agent and the world it knows: for Merleau-Ponty, perception is already flesh, a sensuous act which apprehends an object in virtue of a common sensuousness. See also "The Intertwining" in his *The Visible and the Invisible.*

26. *BN* 308: "The point of view of pure knowledge is contradictory; there is only the point of view of *engaged* knowledge."

27. Sartre refers to emotion as "an intuition of the absolute" (*E* 81), a phrase that is echoed in Hyppolite's "CE" 26, when he claims that "desire is an absolute impulse."

28. See *BN* 615: "Generally speaking, there is no irreducible taste or inclination. They all represent a certain appropriative choice of being. It is up to existential psychoanalysis to compare and classify them. Ontology abandons us here."

29. Sartre, "Itinerary of a Thought," pp. 50–51: "The reason why I produced *Les Mots* is the reason why I have studied Genet or Flaubert: how does a man become someone who writes, who wants to speak of the imaginary? This is what I sought to answer in my own case, as I sought it in that of others."

30. Barnes, *Sartre and Flaubert*, p. 2.

31. Sartre uses this term in *FI* ix. He also entitled a lecture on Kierkegaard "The Singular Universal," delivered at an international colloquium entitled "Kierkegaard Living" in Paris in April 1964. A translation by Peter Goldberger can be found in Josiah Thompson, *Kierkegaard: A Collection of Critical Essays* Garden City, N.Y.: Anchor Books, 1972.

I will be using only volume 1 of *The Family Idiot* in my discussion; the succeeding volumes, available in French in the Gallimard editions, are not considered here mainly because the first volume elaborates the theory of desire more explicitly than the later volumes. The English version of volume 1 also attends to the problem of childhood experience and its relation to the literary imagination. The later volumes cover the material and cultural traditions from which Flaubert labored, and thus do not attend the problem of how the dialectic of desire and recognition constitute personal identity. Certainly, these themes are taken up in a limited way in the succeeding volumes, but Sartre's efforts seem more concerned with a reconciliation of psychoanalysis and Marxism than with a concretization of his own earlier theory.

32. Sartre, "Itinerary of a Thought," p. 52.

33. *Ibid.*

34. See Sartre, *What Is Literature?*, pp. 35–37.

35. Douglas Collins argues that in *SG* "the most powerful outside influence is Hegel," that "the master-slave relationship . . . reappears in *Saint Genet* as the framework for moral questions" and that "in *Saint Genet* all issues are approached dialectically." Sartre clearly departs from Hegel's program in Collins' view: "Hegel's individual consciousness, without being annulled, becomes at one with itself

and others, whereas Sartre's unhappy consciousness must resort to a more earthly cure . . . the projection of the self upon the other." *Sartre as Biographer,* pp. 84–85.

36. Without recognition, Sartre argues, a child lacks a sense of personal rights. Flaubert does not dare to desire in his early years, for desire itself presupposes belief in the right and capacity to be fulfilled: "In order to desire one has to have been desired; because he had not internalized—as a primary and subjective affirmation of the self—this original affirmation of objective, maternal love, Gustave never affirmed his desires or imagined they might be satisfied. Having never been valorized, he did not recognize their value. As a creature of chance, he has no right to live, and consequently his desires have no right to be gratified; they burn themselves out, vague transient fancies that haunt his passivity and disappear, usually before he even thinks to satisfy them . . . he is consumed by the negative of desire, by envy" (*FI* 409).

37. See Freud's explanation of ego formation in *Beyond the Pleasure Principle,* in which the experience of loss precipitates the formation of an ego 'shell' for protection. See also Freud's discussion of ego formation in "Mourning and Melancholia" for which the notion of internalization is central. In that essay, Freud claimed that the loss of a loved one becomes internalized as part of the ego itself, at least in the case of melancholia. Mourning is distinguished from melancholia insofar as it does not essay to "preserve" the other through incorporating the other into the ego; the mourner recognizes the other as both *other* and *lost.* Later in *The Ego and the Id* Freud argued that the work of melancholia, the incorporation of lost loved ones into the ego itself, provides a model for understanding all ego formation. In this developed theory, Freud seems to be arguing in consonance with Sartre that the 'self' is wrought through the internalizations of early losses.

38. Interview with Sartre, "On the Idiot of the Family," in Sartre's *Life/Situations,* p. 112.

39. *Ibid.,* p. 113.

40. *Ibid.,* p. 110.

4. *The Life and Death Struggles of Desire: Hegel and Contemporary French Theory*

1. This consideration of the contemporary reception of Hegel's conception of desire in France is necessarily restricted in scope. The chapter considers a selective number of works by Lacan, Deleuze, and Foucault, and also contains shorter discussions of Derrida and Kristeva. Clearly, there are a number of French intellectuals whose work is not only significant in itself, but significantly influenced by a critical reading of Hegel, and this inquiry cannot hope to do justice to this array of intellectual enterprises. Among the most clearly influential students in Kojève's seminar who are not considered here are Georges Bataille, author of

Érotisme and, earlier, *L'Histoire de l'érotisme,* and a critical discussion of Hegel via Nietzsche in his *Sur Nietzsche, volonté de chance;* Maurice Merleau-Ponty, author of several comparative discussions on Hegel and existentialism, and one who thought that the dialectical method offered the possibility of a concrete revision of Husserl's doctrine of intentionality; Raymond Aron, Pierre Klossowski, Eric Weil, and Alexandre Koyré, among others. Hyppolite's seminar spawned a number of other prominent thinkers: Paul de Man, Jacques Derrida, and Michel Foucault. Colleagues who benefited from long-standing intellectual dialogues with Hyppolite were Claude Lévi-Strauss and Georges Poulet. Yet other thinkers became influential as critics of Hegel: Tran Duc Thau, whose *Phénoménologie et matérialisme dialectique* sought to resolve both Hegelian and Husserlian idealism into Marxism, and Louis Althusser, whose critique of the subject sought to put an end to Hegelianism through structuralist and Marxist means. Jean-François Lyotard waged a similar critique of Husserl in his *La Phénoménologie* and called for a Marxist-Freudian conception of pleasure and desire in his *Economie libidinale.* As followers of a theological appropriation of Hegel exemplified by Henri Niel, Jean Wahl, and Hyppolite, other philosophers like Emmanuel Levinas and Paul Ricoeur drew upon Hegelian themes in the formulation of their highly eclectic theories. Simone de Beauvoir's *Second Sex* employs a dialectical framework as well for understanding the nonreciprocal relations between the sexes, and her novel, *L'Invitée (She Came to Stay),* opens with the Hegelian epigraph: "Each consciousness seeks the death of the Other."

2. Foucault's essay was published in *Hommage à Jean Hyppolite* (Paris, PUF, 1971), translated as *Language, Counter-Memory, and Practice,* Donald F. Bouchard and Sherry Simon, trs. Donald F. Bouchard, ed. (Ithaca: Cornell University Press, 1977).

3. Derrida's essay was originally presented in Hyppolite's seminar in 1968 and later published in Jacques d'Hondt, *Hegel et la pensée moderne* (Paris: PUF, 1970) and translated in *Margins of Philosophy.* See also "An Hegelianism Without Reserve," in *Writing and Difference.*

4. Michel Foucault, "Nietzsche, Genealogy, and History," in his *Language, Counter-Memory, Practice,* p. 142. Subsequent page references in the text refer to this essay.

5. Jacques Derrida, *Glas: Que reste-t-il du savoir absolu?,* p. 169.

6. The German, *Verneinung,* is translated into French as *la dénégation.* Lacan's comments can be found in "Introduction au commentaire de Jean Hyppolite." The notion of denial is of special interest to Lacan and Hyppolite because it is understood to be an intellectual denial of repression and, thus, constitutes a double negation. Lacan remarks that "the ego that we speak of is absolutely impossible to distinguish from the imaginary captations of which it is thoroughly constituted . . . we are obliged to understand the ego from beginning to end in the movement of progressive alienation where self-consciousness situates itself in the *Phenomenology* of Hegel" (p. 374, my translation).

[250]

4. Hegel and Contemporary French Theory

7. Hyppolite in Lacan, *Écrits* (PUF), p. 883.

8. See Freud, "Instincts and their Vicissitudes," *General Psychological Theory*, Philip Rieff, ed. (New York: Macmillan, 1976), pp. 87–89.

9. Lacan, "Of Structure as an Inmixing . . . ," p. 193. Subsequent page references in the text refer to this essay.

10. See J. Melvin Woody and Edward Casey, "Hegel, Heidegger, Lacan: The Dialectic of Desire," in Smith and Kerrigan, *Interpreting Lacan* . They argue that the supersession of desire in the *Phenomenology* is equivalent to its transcendence, and consider that Hegel was wrong to dismiss desire as an elementary form of self-consciousness. A quite different interpretation which argues that desire is not eliminated but, rather, rendered foundational to the progress of the *Phenomenology* is to be found in Stanley Rosen's *Hegel: An Introduction to the Science of Wisdom*, p. 41.

11. See Gadamer, "The Dialectic of Self-Consciousness," *Hegel's Dialectic* p. 62 ff.

12. In the French edition of *Écrits* (PUF), Hyppolite contributes a lecture on the Hegelian possibilities of *Verneinung* cited above, suggesting that the defense against eros which every psychological defense tacitly effects is subject to a second-order negation in the work of psychoanalytic practice, and that successful transference is the resultant eros of this double negation. In effect, Hyppolite sees a confirmation of dialectical logic in the practice of psychoanalysis. The double negation effective in transference is the unity *(Vereinigung:* literally, binding) achieved through the labor of the negative (repression and, then, substitution).

13. See *Feminine Sexuality: Jacques Lacan and the École Freudienne*.

14. *Ibid.*, p. 109.

15. *Ibid.*, p. 151.

16. *Ibid.*, p. 170.

17. Deleuze and Guattari, *Anti-Oedipus*, p. 28.

18. *Ibid.*, p. 29.

19. Nietzsche, *Genealogy of Morals*, p. 36.

20. *Ibid.*, p. 38.

21. Deleuze, *Nietzsche and Philosophy*, p. 9. Subsequent page references in the text refer to *Nietzsche and Philosophy*.

22. Deleuze and Guattari, *Anti-Oedipus*, p. 339.

23. Deleuze argues that the will-to-power or productive desire entails the thorough eradication of negativity, although the negative may be deployed by productive desire in the service of its own self-enhancement. Whether this second sense of negativity is different from Hegelian negativity is not immediately clear because Deleuze does not specify its sense.

28. Foucault, "Preface to Transgression," in his *Language, Counter-Memory, Practice*, p. 50.

29. *Ibid.*, p. 147.

30. See Foucault, *Herculine Barbin*.

31. Foucault, *The Use of Pleasure*, p. 5.
32. HS 152; Foucault, *Discipline and Punishment*, p. 25.
33. Foucault, *The Use of Pleasure*, p. 5.
34. *Ibid.*, p. 5.
35. Foucault, "Nietzsche, Genealogy, and History," p. 148.
36. *Ibid.*, p. 150.
24. Foucault, *Power/Knowledge*, p. 198.
25. *Ibid.*,.
26. Interview with Foucault, *Salmagundi (Winter 1982–83)*, p. 12.
27. *Ibid.*, p. 20.

Bibliography

The following bibliography is restricted to those works I have used in the preparation of this inquiry and is in no sense comprehensive. It is mainly devoted to works that explicitly treat Hegel's *Phenomenology of Spirit,* the works of Alexandre Kojève and Jean Hyppolite, and selected works of Jean-Paul Sartre, Jacques Lacan, Gilles Deleuze, and Michel Foucault. For more comprehensive bibliographies of Hegel, Sartre, and Kojève see:

Contat, Michel and Michel Rybalka. *Les Écrits de Sartre.* Paris: Gallimard, 1970.
Lapointe, François. *Jean-Paul Sartre and His Critics: An International Bibliography, 1938–1980.* Bowling Green, Ohio: Philosophy Documentation Center, 1981.
Roth, Michael S. "A Bibliography of Alexandre Kojève." Forthcoming in *Revue de Métaphysique et de Morale.*
Steinhauer, S. J. Kurt *Hegel: An International Bibliography.* München: Verlag Dokumentation, 1978.

Works by Gilles Deleuze

Différence et répétition. Paris: Presses Universitaires de France, 1972. *L'Anti-Oedipe* (with Felix Guattari). Paris: Éditions de Minuit, 1972. *Anti-Oedipus: Capitalism and Schizophrenia.* Robert Hurley, Mark Seem, and Helen R. Lane, trs. New York: Viking Press, 1977.
L'Idée d'expression dans la philosophie de Spinoza. Paris: Éditions de Minuit, 1968.
Nietzsche et la philosophie. Paris: Presses universitaires de France, 1973. *Nietzsche and Philosophy.* Hugh Tomlinson, tr. New York: Columbia University Press, 1983.

[253]

Bibliography

Présentation de Sacher-Masoch, le froid et le cruel. Paris: Éditions de Minuit, 1967. *Masochism: An Interpretation of Coldness and Cruelty.* New York: Braziller, 1971.

Works by Michel Foucault

Herculine Barbin dite Alexina B., presenté par Michel Foucault. Paris: Gallimard, 1978. *Herculine Barbin, Being the Recently Discovered Memoirs of a Nineteenth Century French Hermaphrodite.* Richard McDougall, tr. New York: Pantheon, 1980.
Histoire de la sexualité. 1:*La Volonté de savoir.* Paris: Gallimard, 1976. *The History of Sexuality.* Vol. 1: *An Introduction.* New York: Vintage, 1980. *Histoire de la sexualité.* 2: *L'Usage des plaisirs.* Paris: Gallimard, 1984. *The History of Sexuality.* Vol 2: *The Use of Pleasure.* Robert Hurley, tr. New York: Pantheon, 1985. *Histoire de la sexualité.* 3: *Le Souci de soi.* Paris: Gallimard, 1984. Vol. I cited in text and notes as *"HS."*
Language, Counter-Memory, Practice: Selected Essays and Interviews. Donald F. Bouchard, ed. Donald F. Bouchard and Sherry Simon, trs. Ithaca: Cornell University Press, 1977.
Les Mots et les choses. Paris: Gallimard, 1966: *The Order of Things: An Archaelogy of the Human Sciences.* New York: Vintage, 1973.
Power/Knowledge: Selected Interviews and Other Writings, 1972–77. Colin Gordon, ed. and tr. New York: Pantheon, 1980.

Works on Michel Foucault

Baudrillard, Jean. *Oublier Foucault.* Paris: Éditions Galilée, 1977.
Dreyfus, Hubert L. and Paul Rabinow. *Michel Foucault: Beyond Structuralism and Hermeneutics.* Chicago: Chicago University Press, 1983.
Guédez, Annie. *Foucault.* Paris: Éditions universitaires, 1972.
Lemert, Charles C. and Garth Gillan. *Michel Foucault: Social Theory as Transgression.* New York: Columbia University Press, 1982.
Megill, Allan. *Prophets of Extremity: Nietzsche, Heidegger, Foucault, Derrida.* Berkeley: University of California Press, 1985.
Minson, Jeffrey. *Genealogies of Morals: Nietzsche, Foucault, Donzelot, and the Eccentricity of Ethics.* London: Macmillan, 1985.
Rajchman, John. *Michel Foucault: The Freedom of Philosophy.* New York: Columbia University Press, 1985.
Sheridan, Alan. *Michel Foucault: The Will to Truth.* London and New York: Tavistock, 1980.

[254]

Bibliography

Works by G. W. F. Hegel

Note: I have made use of Hegel's *Sämtliche Werke*, both the Lasson and Hoffmeister edition (1928) and the Glöckner edition (Jubilaumsausgabe, 1927).

Enzyklopädie der philosophischen Wissenschaften, Erster Teil, Die Wissenschaft der Logik. Frankfurt: Suhrkamp Verlag, 1970. *Hegel's Logic.* Oxford: Clarendon Press, 1975.
Geschichte der Philosophie. G. Lasson, ed. Leipzig, 1940. *Hegel's Lectures on the History of Philosophy.* E. S. Haldane F. H. Simson, trs. New York: Humanities Press, 1968.
Grundlinien der Philosophie des Rechts. Frankfurt, Suhrkamp, 1983. *Philosophy of Right.* T. M. Knox, tr. Oxford: Clarendon Press, 1942.
Jenaer Realphilosophie 1: Die Vorlesungen von 1803/4. J. Hoffmeister, ed. Leipzig, 1932; *Jenaer Realphilosophie 2: Die Vorlesungen von 1805/6.* J. Hoffmeister, ed. Leipzig, 1932. Both republished under the title *Jenaer Realphilosophie.* Hamburg: Felix Meiner Verlag, 1967.
Phänomenologie des Geistes. Frankfurt: Suhrkamp Verlag, 1970. *Hegel's Phenomenology of Spirit.* A. V. Miller, tr.; J. N. Findlay, ed. Oxford: Clarendon Press, 1977.
Politische Schriften, Nachwort von Jürgen Habermas. Frankfurt: Suhrkamp Verlag, 1966. *Political Writings.* T. N. Knox, tr. Oxford: Clarendon Press, 1964.
Schriften zur Politik und Rechtsphilosophie. G. Lasson, ed. Leipzig, 1913.
System der Sittlichkeit. Hamburg: Felix Meiner Verlag, 1970.
Theologische Jugendschriften. H. Nohl, ed. Tubingen, 1907. *Early Theological Writings.* T. M. Knox, tr. Philadelphia: University of Pennsylvania Press, 1971.
Vorlesungen über die Philosophie der Weltgeschichte. G. Lasson, ed. Hamburg: Felix Meiner Verlag, 1968; *Hegel's Philosophy of History.* J. Sibtree, tr. New York: Dover, 1962.
Wissenschaft der Logik. G. Lasson, ed. Hamburg: Felix Meiner Verlag, 1966–67. *Hegel's Science of Logic.* A. V. Miller, tr. Oxford: Clarendon Press, 1969.

Works on G. W. F. Hegel: French Reception, Commentary and Articles

Adorno, Theodor. *Zur Metakritik der Erkenntnistheorie: Drei Studien zu Hegel.* Frankfurt: Suhrkamp Verlag, 1963.
Bieml, Walter. "Das Wesen der Dialektik bei Hegel und Sartre." *Tijdschrift voor Philosophie* (1958), vol. 20.
Bloch, Ernst. *Subjekt-Objekt: Erlauterungen zu Hegel.* Berlin: Aufbau, 1951.
Boey, Conrad. *L'Aliénation dans "La Phénoménologie de l'esprit."* Paris: Desclec de Brouwer, 1973.

Bibliography

Borel, Alain. *Hegel et le problème de la finitude.* Paris: La Pensée Universelle, 1972.

Brockard, Hans. *Subjekt: Versuch zur Ontologie bei Hegel.* München: Pustet, 1970.

Brunschvicg, Léon. *Le Progrès de la conscience dans la philosophie occidentale.* 2ᵉ éd. Paris: Presses Universitaires de France, 1953. 2 vols.

Cooper, Barry. *The End of History: An Essay on Modern Hegelianism.* Toronto: University of Toronto Press, 1984.

Darbon, Michel. "Hégélianisme, marxisme, existentialisme." *Les études philosophiques* (1949), 4:346–70.

Dove, Kenley Royce. "Toward an Interpretation of Hegel's *Phänomenologie des Geistes.*" New Haven, c. 1966. Microfilm.

Dufrenne, Mikel. "L'actualité de Hegel." *Esprit* (September 1948), no. 16.

Findlay, John N. *Hegel, A Reexamination.* New York: Macmillan, 1958.

Fink, Eugen. *Interpretationen der "Phänomenologie des Geistes."* Frankfurt: Klostermann, 1977.

Fulda, Hans. *Materiellen zu Hegels "Phänomenologie des Geistes."* Frankfurt: Suhrkamp Verlag, 1973.

Gadamer, Hans-Georg. *Hegel's Dialectic: Five Hermeneutical Studies.* P. Christopher Smith, tr. New Haven: Yale University Press, 1976.

Garaudy, Roger. *Dieu et mort: Étude sur Hegel.* Paris: Bordas, 1966.

Garaudy, Roger. *La Pensée de Hegel.* Paris: Bordas, 1966.

Gauvin, Joseph, ed. *Hegel-Studien Beiheft 14, Wörtindex zur Phänomenologie des Geistes.* Bonn: Bouvier, 1977.

Goldfarb, Denis J. "Kojève's Reading of Hegel." *International Philosophical Quarterly* (1982), 22:275–94.

Gorland Ingraud. *Die konkrete Freiheit des Individuums bei Hegel und Sartre.* Frankfurt: Klostermann, 1978.

Guinday, Guillaume. *Le Drame de la pensée dialectique: Hegel, Marx, Sartre.* Paris: Vrin, 1976.

Habermas, Jürgen. "Arbeit und Interaktion." In *Technik und Wissenschaft als Ideologie.* Frankfurt: Suhrkamp Verlag, 1969.

Harris, Henry. "The Concept of Recognition in Hegel's Jena Manuscripts." In *Hegel-Studien Beiheft 20: Hegel in Jena.* Bonn: Bouvier, 1980.

Hartmann, Klaus. *Grundzüge der Ontologie Sartres in ihrem Verhaltnis zu Hegels Logik: eine Untersuchung zu "L'Être et le néant."* Berlin: de Gruyter, 1963; *Sartre's Ontology.* Evanston: Northwestern University Press, 1966.

Heidegger, Martin. *Hegel's Concept of Experience.* New York: Harper and Row, 1970.

Hondt, Jacques D', éd. *Hegel et la pensée moderne, séminaire sur Hegel dirigé par Jean Hyppolite au Collège de France (1967–68).* Paris: Presses Universitaires de France, 1970.

Ilting, K. H. "Anerkennung. Zur Rechtfertigung praktischer Sätze." In *Probleme der Ethik—zur Diskussion gestellt.* G. G. Grau, ed. Freiburg: K. Alber, 1972.

Bibliography

Kaufmann, Walter, ed. *Hegel: Texts and Commentary.* Garden City, N.Y.: Anchor, 1966.

Kimmerle, Heinz. *Das Problem der Abgeschlossenheit des Denkens.* Bonn: Bouvier Verlag, 1970.

Koyré, Alexandre. *Études d'histoire de la pensée philosophique.* Paris: Armand Colin, 1961.

Koyré, Alexandre. "Rapports sur l'état des études hégéliennes en France." *Revue d'histoire de la philosophie* (April–June 1931), vol. 5, no. 2.

Lichtheim, George. *Marxism in Modern France.* New York: Columbia University Press, 1966.

Lyotard, Jean-François. *La Phénoménologie.* Séries *Que sais-je?* Paris, 1954.

MacIntyre, Alasdair, ed. *Hegel: A Collection of Critical Essays.* New York: Notre Dame, 1972.

Marx, Werner. *Hegel's Phenomenology of Spirit: Its Point and Purpose. A Commentary on the Preface and Introduction.* Peter Heath, tr. New York: Harper and Row, 1975.

Niel, Henri. *De la médiation dans la philosophie de Hegel.* Paris: Aubier, 1945.

Niel, Henri. "L'interprétation de Hegel." *Critique* (1947), No. 3.

Patri, Aimé. "Dialectique du Maître et de l'Esclave." *Le contrat social* (1961), 5:231–35.

Pelczynski, Z. A. *Hegel's Political Philosophy: Problems and Perspectives.* Cambridge: Cambridge University Press, 1971.

Pitkethley, Lawrence. "Hegel in Modern France (1900–1950)." PH.D. dissertation, University of London, 1978.

Pöggeler, Otto. "Hegel und die Griechische Tragödie," In *Hegel-Studien Beiheft* 1. Bonn: Bouvier, 1961.

Poster, Mark. *Existential Marxism in Postwar France.* Princeton: Princeton University Press, 1975.

Riedel, Manfred. *Theorie und Praxis im Denken Hegels.* Stuttgart: Kohlhammer, 1965.

Rosen, Stanley. *G. W. F. Hegel: An Introduction to the Science of Wisdom.* New Haven: Yale University Press, 1974.

Rotenstreich, Nathan. "On the Ecstatic Sources of the Concept of Alienation." *Review of Metaphysics* (March 1963), vol. 16.

Rotenstreich, Nathan. *From Substance to Subject: Studies in Hegel.* The Hague: Martinus Nijhoff, 1979.

Roth, Michael S. "A Note on Kojève's Phenomenology of Right." *Political Theory.* (1983), 2:447–50.

Schmidt, Friedrich W. *Zum Begriff der Negativität bei Schelling und Hegel.* Stuttgart: Metler Verlag, 1971.

Siep, Ludwig. "Zur Dialektik der Anerkennung bei Hegel." In *Hegel-Jahrbuch 1975.* Köln: Pahl-Rugenstein Verlag.

Siep, Ludwig. "Zum Freiheitsbegriff der praktischen Philosophie Hegels in Jena." *Hegel-Studien Beiheft 20.* Bonn: Bouvier, 1980.

Siep, Ludwig. "Der Kampf um Anerkennung. Zur Auseinandersetzung Hegels mit Hobbes in den Jenaer Schriften." *Hegel-Studien, Band 9.* Bonn: Bouvier, 1974.
Smith, Colon. *Contemporary French Philosophy.* New York: Cambridge, 1979.
Solomon, Robert. *In the Spirit of Hegel: A Study of G. W. F. Hegel's "Phenomenology of Spirit."* New York: Oxford University Press, 1983.
Taylor, Charles. *Hegel.* Cambridge: Cambridge University Press, 1975.
Taylor, Charles. *Hegel and Modern Society.* Cambridge: Cambridge University Press, 1978.
Wahl, Jean. *Le Malheur de la conscience dans la philosophie de Hegel.* Paris: Presses Universitaires de France, 1951.
Weiss, P. "Existenz und Hegel." *Philosophy and Phenomenological Research* (1948), 8:206–16.

Works by Jean Hyppolite

"The Concept of Existence in the Hegelian Phenomenology." In *Studies on Hegel and Marx.* John O'Neill, tr. New York: Basic Books, 1969. Cited in text and Notes as "CE."
Études sur Marx et Hegel. Paris: Rivière, 1955. *Studies on Marx and Hegel.* John O'Neill, tr. New York: Basic Books, 1969.
Figures de la pensée philosophique, I and *II.* Paris: Presses Universitaires de France, 1971. Cited in text and Notes as *"F."*
Genèse et structure de la Phénoménologie de l'esprit de Hegel. Paris: Presses Universitaires de France, 1948. *Genesis and Structure of Hegel's "Phenomenology of Spirit."* Samuel Cherniak and John Heckman, trs. Evanston: Northwestern University Press, 1974. Cited in text and Notes as "GS."
Logique et existence: Essai sur la logique de Hegel. Paris: Presses Universitaires de France, 1953.

Works by Alexandre Kojève

Études d'histoire de la pensée philosophique. Paris: Presses Universitaires de France, 1971.
"Hegel, Marx et le christianisme." *Critique,* Décembre 19, 1946.
Introduction à la lecture de Hegel. Paris: Presses Universitaires de France, 1941. *Introduction to the Reading of Hegel.* James H. Nichols, tr., Allan Bloom, ed. Ithaca: Cornell University Press, 1980. Cited in text and Notes as *"IH."*
Tyrannie et Sagesse. Paris: Gallimard, 1954. "Tyranny and Wisdom." Michael Gold, tr. In Leo Strauss, ed., *On Tyranny.* Ithaca: Cornell University Press, 1963.

[258]

Bibliography

Works by Jacques Lacan

Écrits. Paris: Éditions du Seuil, 1970–72. Écrits: A Selection. Alan Sheridan, tr. New York: Norton, 1977.

Feminine Sexuality: Jacques Lacan and the École Freudienne. Juliet Mitchell and Jacqueline Rose, eds.; Jacqueline Rose, tr. New York: Norton, 1985.

The Language of the Self. Anthony Wilden, tr. Baltimore: Johns Hopkins University Press, 1968. Originally published as "Fonction et champ de la parole et du langage en psychanalyse" in La Psychanalyse, vol. 1, Paris, 1956, and in the author's original (1966) version of Écrits.

"Of Structure as an Inmixing of an Otherness Prerequisite to Any Subject Whatever." In Richard Macksey and Eugenio Donato, eds., The Structuralist Controversy: The Languages of Criticism and the Sciences of Man. Baltimore: Johns Hopkins University Press, 1975.

Les Quatre concepts fondamentaux de la psychanalyse. Originally published as vol. 2 of the author's Le Séminaire de Jacques Lacan. Translated by Alan Sheridan as The Four Fundamental Concepts of Psychoanalysis. London: Hogarth Press, 1977. Cited in text and Notes as "FFCP."

Le Séminaire de Jacques Lacan. Vols. 1, 2, 11, 20. Jacques-Alain Miller, éd. Paris: Éditions du Seuil, 1973.

Works on Jacques Lacan

Clément, Catherine. Vies et légendes de Jacques Lacan. Paris: Grasset, 1981. The Lives and Legends of Jacques Lacan, Arthur Goldhammer, tr. New York: Columbia University Press, 1983.

Gallop, Jane. Reading Lacan. Ithaca: Cornell University Press, 1985.

Mannoni, Maud. La Théorie comme fiction: Freud, Groddeck, Winnicott, Lacan. Paris: Éditions du Seuil, 1979.

Smith, Joseph H. and William Kerrigan, eds. Interpreting Lacan. New Haven: Yale University Press, 1983.

Turkle, Sherry. Psychoanalytic Politics: Freud's French Revolution. New York: Basic Books, 1978.

Works by Jean-Paul Sartre

Baudelaire. Paris: Gallimard, 1947. Baudelaire. Martin Turnell, tr. New York: New Directions, 1967.

Cahiers pour une morale. Paris: Gallimard, 1983.

Critique de la raison dialectique. Vol. 1: Théorie des ensembles pratiques. Paris: Gallimard, 1960. Critique of Dialectical Reason. Alan Sheridan Smith, tr. Atlantic Highlands, N.J.: Humanities Press, 1976.

[259]

Esquisse d'une théorie des émotions. Paris: Hermann, 1939. *The Emotions: Outline of a Theory.* Bernard Frechtman, tr. New York: Philosophical Library, 1949. Cited in text and Notes as *"E."*

L'Être et le néant: Essai d'ontologie phénoménologique. Paris: Gallimard, 1943. *Being and Nothingness: An Essay in Phenomenological Ontology.* Hazel E. Barnes, tr. New York: Philosophical Library, 1956. Cited in text and Notes as *BN.*

L'Idiot de la famille: Gustave Flaubert de 1821 à 1857. 3 vols. Paris: Gallimard, 1971. *The Family Idiot,* vol. 1 Carol Cosman, tr. Chicago: University of Chicago Press, 1981. Cited in text and Notes as *"FI."*

L'Imaginaire: Psychologie phénoménologique de l'imagination. Paris: Gallimard, 1971. *The Psychology of Imagination.* New York: Philosophical Library, 1948. Cited in text and Notes as *"PI."*

L'Imagination. Paris: Presses Universitaires de France, 1963. *Imagination: A Psychological Critique.* Forest Williams, tr. Ann Arbor: University of Michigan Press, 1963.

"Intentionality: A Fundamental Idea in Husserl's Phenomenology," Joseph Fell, tr. *Journal of the British Society for Phenomenology* (May 1970), 1(2):4–5. Cited in text and Notes as "I."

"Itinerary of a Thought." *New Left Review* (November-December 1969).

Les Mots. Paris: Gallimard, 1964. *The Words.* Bernard Frechtman, tr. New York: Vintage, 1981.

Saint Genet, comédien et martyr. Paris: Gallimard, 1952, *Saint Genet: Actor and Martyr.* Bernard Frechtman, tr. New York: Braziller, 1963. Cited in text and Notes as *"SG."*

Sartre par lui-même, texte du film réalisé par Alexandre Astruc et Michel Contat. Paris: Gallimard, 1977. *Sartre by Himself.* Richard Weaver, tr. New York: Urizen, 1978.

Situations 2. Paris: Gallimard, 1948: *What Is Literature?* Bernard Frechtman, tr. New York: Philosophical Library, 1949 (partial translation).

Situations 3. Paris: Gallimard, 1949. *Literary and Philosophical Essays.* Annette Michelson and Wade Baskin, trs. New York: Criterion, 1955.

Situations 10. Paris: Gallimard, 1976. *Life/Situations: Essays Written and Spoken.* Paul Auster and Lydia Davis, trs. New York: Pantheon, 1977.

La Transcendance de l'ego: Esquisse d'une description phénoménologique. Paris: Librairie Philosophique J. Vrin, 1965. *The Transcendence of the Ego.* Forrest Williams and Robert Kirkpatrick, trs. New York: Noonday Press, 1957. Cited in text and Notes as *"TE."*

Works on Jean-Paul Sartre: Commentary and Articles

Barnes, Hazel E. *Sartre and Flaubert.* Chicago: University of Chicago Press, 1981.

Beauvoir, Simone de. "Merleau-Ponty et le Pseudo-Sartrisme." *Les Temps Modernes* (1955), vol. 10, no. 2.

Bibliography

Busch, Thomas. "Beyond the Cogito: The Question of Continuity in Sartre's Thought." *The Modern Schoolman* (March 1983), vol. 60.

Caws, Peter. *Sartre: Arguments of the Philosophers.* London: Routledge, Kegan Paul, 1979.

Collins, Douglas. *Sartre as Biographer.* Cambridge: Harvard University Press, 1980.

Corvez, Maurice. *L'Être et la conscience morale.* Paris: Nauwelaerts, 1968.

Danto, Arthur. *Jean-Paul Sartre.* New York: Viking Press, 1975.

Dempsey, Peter J. *The Psychology of Sartre.* Cork: Cork University Press, 1965.

Desan, Wilfrid. *The Tragic Finale.* New York: Harper and Row, 1960.

Fell, Joseph P. *Emotion in the Thought of Sartre.* New York: Columbia University Press, 1965.

Fell, Joseph P. *Heidegger and Sartre: An Essay on Being and Place.* New York: Columbia University Press, 1979.

Grene, Marjorie. *Sartre.* New York: Harper and Row, 1973.

Jeanson, Francis. *Le Problème moral et la pensée de Sartre.* Paris: Éditions du Seuil, 1965. *Sartre and the Problem of Morality.* Robert Stone, tr. Bloomington: Indiana University Press, 1980.

Maier, Willi. *Das Problem der Leiblichkeit bei Jean-Paul Sartre und Maurice Merleau-Ponty.* Tübingen: Niemayer, 1964.

Marcuse, Herbert. "Existentialism: Remarks on Jean-Paul Sartre's *L'Être et le néant.*" *Philosophy and Phenomenological Research,* vol. 8, no. 3.

Martin-Deslias, Noël. *Jean-Paul Sartre, ou la conscience ambiguë.* Paris: Éditions Nagel, 1972.

Merleau-Ponty, Maurice. *The Phenomenology of Perception.* Colin Smith, tr. London: Routledge, Kegan Paul, 1962.

Merleau-Ponty, Maurice. *Sense and Non-Sense.* Hubert and Patricia Dreyfus, trs. Evanston: Northwestern University Press, 1964.

Merleau-Ponty, Maurice. *The Visible and the Invisible.* Alphonso Lingis, tr. Evanston: Northwestern University Press, 1967.

Natanson, Maurice. *A Critique of Jean-Paul Sartre's Ontology.* The Hague: Martinus Nijhoff, 1973 (reprint).

Natanson, Maurice. "Phenomenology and Existentialism: Husserl and Sartre on Intentionality." In Joseph Kockelmans, eds., *Phenomenology: The Philosophy of Edmund Husserl and its Interpretation.* Garden City, N.Y.: Doubleday, 1967.

Natanson, Maurice. "The Sleep of Bad Faith." *New Literary History* (Autumn 1980), 12:97–106.

Niel, André. *Jean-Paul Sartre, héros et victime de la conscience malheureuse: Essai sur le drame de la pensée occidentale.* Paris: Éditions Courrier du Livre, 1966.

Schilpp, Paul A. *The Philosophy of Jean-Paul Sartre.* Library of Living Philosophers Series, vol. 16. Open Court, 1981.

Stern, Alfred. *Sartre: His Philosophy and Existential Psychoanalysis.* New York: Delacorte Press, 1967.

Theunissen, Michael. *Der Andere: Studien zur Sozialontologie der Gegenwart.* Berlin: de Gruyter, 1965.

Thody, Philip. *Jean-Paul Sartre: A Literary and Political Study.* London: Hamilton, 1960.

Verstraeten, Pierre. *Violence et éthique: Esquisse d'une critique de la morale dialectique à partir du théâtre politique de Sartre.* Paris: Gallimard, 1972.

Warnock, Mary, ed. *Sartre: A Collection of Critical Essays.* Garden City, N.Y.: Anchor, 1971.

Related Works

Abrams, M. H. *Natural Supernaturalism: Tradition and Revolution in Romantic Literature.* New York: Norton, 1971.

Archard, David. *Marxism and Existentialism.* Ulster: Blackstaff Press, 1980.

Aristotle. *Nicomachean Ethics.* Martin Ostwald, tr. Indianapolis: Bobbs-Merrill, 1962.

Aristotle. "De Anima." In *Introduction to Aristotle.* Richard McKeon, ed. New York: Modern Library, 1947.

Aron, Raymond. *Marxism and the Existentialists.* New York: Harper and Row, 1965.

Bataille, Georges. *L'Érotisme.* Paris: Éditions de Minuit, 1965.

Bataille, Georges. *Sur Nietzsche.* Paris: Éditions de Minuit, 1945.

Beauvoir, Simone de. *Force of Circumstance.* Richard Howard, tr. New York: Putnam, 1965.

Brooks, Peter and Joseph Halpern, eds. *Genet: A Collection of Critical Essays.* Englewood Cliffs, N.J.: Prentice-Hall, 1979.

Culler, Jonathan. *Flaubert: The Uses of Uncertainty.* Ithaca: Cornell University Press, 1974.

Derrida, Jacques. *Glas: Quereste-t-il du savoir absolu?* Paris: Denoël Gauthier, 1982.

Derrida, Jacques. *L'Écriture et la différence.* Paris: Éditions du Seuil, 1967. *Writing and Difference.* Alan Bass, tr. Chicago: Chicago University Press, 1978.

Derrida, Jacques. *Marges de la Philosophie.* Paris: Éditions du Seuil, 1972. *Margins of Philosophy.* Alan Bass, tr. Chicago: University of Chicago Press, 1982.

Descombes, Vincent. *Modern French Philosophy.* Cambridge: Cambridge University Press, 1980.

Diderot, Denis. *Jacques the Fatalist and His Master.* J. Robert Loy, tr. New York: Norton, 1959.

Flaubert, Gustave. *Madame Bovary.* Edouard Maynial, éd. Paris: Garnier, 1961. *Madame Bovary.* Lowell Bair, tr. New York: Bantam, 1981.

Flaubert, Gustave. *Trois Contes.* Paris: Garnier, 1965.

Freud, Sigmund. *Civilization and Its Discontents.* James Strachey, tr. London: Hogarth Press, 1950.

Bibliography

Freud, Sigmund. *General Psychological Theory.* Philip Rieff, ed. New York: Macmillan, 1976.

Freud, Sigmund. *New Introductory Lectures.* James Strachey, tr. London: Hogarth Press, 1948.

Genet, Jean. *Les Bonnes.* Paris: L'Arbalète, 1976.

Genet, Jean. *Haute Surveillance.* Paris: Gallimard, 1965.

Genet, Jean. *Journal du Voleur.* Paris: Gallimard, 1949. *The Thief's Journal.* Bernard Frechtman, tr. New York: Bantam, 1965.

Genet, Jean. *Les Nègres.* Paris: Barbezat, 1959.

Genet, Jean. *Notre-dame-des-fleurs.* Paris: Gallimard, 1975. *Our Lady of the Flowers.* Bernard Frechtman, tr. New York: Grove Press, 1963.

Goethe's Faust. Philip Wayne, tr. London: Penguin, 1972.

Gurwitsch, Aron. "On the Intentionality of Consciousness." In Joseph Kockelmans, ed., *Phenomenology: The Philosophy of Edmund Husserl and Its Interpretation.* Garden City, N.Y.: Doubleday, 1967.

Heller, Agnes. *A Theory of Feelings.* Assen: Van Gorcum, 1979.

Hobbes, Thomas. *Leviathan.* W. G. Pogson Smith, ed. Oxford: Clarendon Press, 1929.

Husserl, Edmund. *The Crisis of European Sciences and Transcendental Phenomenology: An Introduction to Phenomenological Philosophy.* David Carr, tr. Evanston: Northwestern University Press, 1970.

Husserl, Edmund. *Experience and Judgment: Investigations in a Genealogy of Logic.* Ludwig Landgrebe, ed. James S. Churchill and Karl Ameriks, trs. Evanston: Northwestern University Press, 1973.

Husserl, Edmund. *The Phenomenology of Internal Time Consciousness.* Martin Heidegger, ed.; James S. Churchill, tr. Bloomington: Indiana University Press, 1964.

Kant, Immanuel. *Critique of Practical Reason.* Lewis White Beck, tr. Indianapolis: Bobbs-Merrill, 1977.

Kierkegaard, Soren. *Philosophical Fragments.* Howard Hong, tr. Princeton: Princeton University Press, 1962.

Kierkegaard, Soren. *Repetition: An Essay in Experimental Psychology.* Howard and Edna Hong, trs. Princeton: Princeton University Press, 1983.

Kristeva, Julia. *La Révolution du language poétique.* Paris: Éditions du Seuil, Jardin, and Louis Roudiez, trs. New York: Columbia University Press, 1980.

Kristeva, Julia. *La révolution du language poétique.* Paris: Editions du Seuil, 1974. *Revolution in Poetic Language.* Margaret Walker, tr. New York: Columbia University Press, 1984.

Kristeva, Julia. *Polylogue.* Paris: Éditions du Seuil, 1977; and Σημειωτιχη: *Recherches pour une sémanalyse.* Both partially translated in *Desire in Language: A Semiotic Approach to Literature and Art.* Leon S. Roudiez, ed.; Thomas Gora, Alice Jardine, and Leon S. Roudiez, trs. New York: Columbia University Press, 1980.

Lyotard, Jean-François. *Économie libidinale*. Paris: Éditions de Minuit, 1974.

Lyotard, Jean-François. *La Phénoménologie*. Paris: Presses Universitaires de France, 1954.

Merleau-Ponty, Maurice. *Le Visible et l'invisible*. Claude Lefort, éd. Paris: Gallimard, 1964. *The Visible and the Invisible*. Alphonso Lingis, tr. Evanston: Northwestern University Press, 1968.

Nietzsche, Friedrich. *The Will to Power*. Walter Kaufmann and R. J. Hollingdale, trs. New York: Vintage Books, 1968.

Nietzsche, Friedrich. *On the Genealogy of Morals*. Walter Kaufmann, tr. New York: Vintage Books, 1967.

Owen, Wendy. "A Riddle in Nine Syllables: Female Creativity in the Poetry of Sylvia Plath." Ph. D. dissertation, Yale University, 1985.

Rella, Franco. *Il mito dell' altro: Lacan, Deleuze, Foucault*. Milano: Feltrinelli, 1978.

Rilke, Rainer Maria. *Duino Elegies*. J. B. Leishman, tr. New York: Norton, 1963.

Rorty, Amelia Oksenberg, ed. *Explaining Emotions*. Berkeley and Los Angeles: University of California Press, 1980.

Solomon, Robert. *The Passions*. (Garden City, N.Y.: Anchor Books), 1976.

Spinoza, Benedict de. *On the Improvement of the Understanding, The Ethics, Correspondence*. R. H. M. Elwes, tr. New York: Dover, 1955.

Steegmuller, Francis, ed. *The Letters of Gustave Flaubert, 1830–1857*. Cambridge, Mass.: Belknap Press, 1979.

Stevens, Wallace. *The Palm at the End of the Mind*. New York: Vintage, 1971.

Strasser, Stephen. *Phenomenology of Feeling: An Essay on the Phenomenology of the Heart*. Pittsburgh: Duquesne University Press, 1977.

Strauss, Leo. *The Political Philosophy of Hobbes: Its Basis and Genesis*. Oxford: Clarendon Press, 1936.

Unger, Roberto. *Knowledge and Politics*. New York: Free Press, 1975.

Index

Abrahms, M. H., 240*n*1
Absolute, the, 21–23, 25, 27, 196, 203
Althusser, Louis, 249–50*n*1
Anger, 48, 49
Aristotle: on desire and moral philosophy, 4; desire in *de Anima*, 11
Aron, Raymond, 249–50*n*1
Aufhebung, 41, 183, 187

Barbin, Herculine, 234
Barnes, Hazel, 156
Bataille, Georges, 249–50*n*1
Baudelaire, Charles, Sartre on, 157
Beauvoir, Simone de, 61–62, 172, 233, 249–50*n*1

Casey, Edward, 251*n*10
Choice: and bad faith, 130–31; original and fundamental, in Sartre, 123–27; prereflective, 121–38
Collins, Douglas, 248–49*n*35
Concept *(Begriff)*, in Hegel, 26, 72, 75, 84–88, 178

Deleuze, Gilles, 6, 14, 204, 205–17, 251*n*23; and forces, 216; and Foucault, 215–17, 219–22; and Lacan, 213–15; and Nietzsche, 206–17; and Spinoza, 212–13
De Man, Paul, 249–50*n*1

Derrida, Jacques, 14, 177–79, 183–84, 249–50*n*1; on fictive status of the "subject," 179; and irony, 178–79; on mastery, 178–80; relation to Hegel, 184, 240*n*2
Descartes, René, 11–12; Cartesian thought, 11, 15, 149, 176, 189, 196, 247*n*21
Desire: animal, 66–67; as arbitrary, 1–2; and belief, 152–53; and "consciousness," 25–42; and death, 54–55, 89–92, 243–44*n*21; and deception, 22–23, 73, 88–89, 117, 126–27; and domination, 52–56, 77, 138–41, 144–47, 228–29, 231; and Explanation, 28–31; and externalization, 25–28, 65, 155, 164, 171–73, 185–86; and Force, 26–28; and freedom, 55–56, 91; as generating history, 44–45; and the imaginary, 95–96, 101–21, 187, 250*n*6; and language, 17–23, 68, 90–92, 156–74, 177–84, 186–204, 217–23, 238; and Life, 55, 83–85, 92; and need, 56; and the negative, 9, 10, 41, 63–64, 81, 90, 96, 113, 169–72, 200–1, 206, 239*n*10, 243*n*21, 251*n*23; in *Phenomenology*, 4, 7, 9, 17–60, 242*n*18; as practical, 3; as rational, 2–3; and satisfaction, 35, 88, 94–95, 167–69, 219; and "self-consciousness" in *Phenomenology*, 32–42; and self loss, 47–50; and time, 71–74; and work (or labor), 57, 65–71, 75–

[265]

Index

anthropology, 64, 75, 82; and posthistorical time, 64–65; on reciprocal recognition, 68, 76–77; and Sartre, 71, 75, 92–99, 121, 151; seminar participants, 249–50*n*1
Koyré, Alexandre, 61–62, 249–50*n*1
Kristeva, Julia, 232–34

Lacan, Jacques, 6, 114, 175, 185, 186–204; on "desire as a "lack," 191, 192–93; and "difference," 188–89; and Freud, 191, 198–99, 201; and Hegel, 189, 195, 199–200; and Hyppolite, 187–88, 192, 197–98, 250*n*6; on jouissance, 194, 203; and Kojève, 192, 197–98; *see also under* Deleuze, Gilles; Foucault, Michel; Sartre, Jean-Paul
Langer, Monika, 140
Levinas, Emmanuel, 249–50*n*1
Lévi-Strauss, Claude, 201, 249–50*n*1
Life, concept of, 36–37, 38, 39, 40, 82, 85
Life and death struggle, 51–53, 227
"Look," the, *see under* Sartre, Jean-Paul
Lordship and bondage: Deleuze on, 207–10; Foucault on, 177–80; Kojève on, 77; Lacan on, 200–1; and post-Hegelianism, 237; *see under* Hegel. G. W. F.
Lyotard, Jean-François, 249–50*n*1

Magic, 115, 118–19, 147, 150–52
Marcuse, Herbert, 140, 213–18, 227
Marx, Karl, 59, 64; and Foucault, 232; and Kristeva, 232; and Sartre, 157
Marx, Werner, 12, 241*n*15
Merleau-Ponty, Maurice, 61, 147–48, 247–48*n*25, 249–50*n*1

Negation, 9, 41, 63–64, 81, 90, 96, 113, 178, 250*n*6
Niel, Henri, 244*n*2, 245*n*10, 249–50*n*1
Nietzsche, Friedrich, 14, 17, 23, 177, 179–81; Deleuze and, 206–17; Foucault and, 179–86, 219, 222, 226–27, 231, 236; Sartre and, 241*n*6, 246–47*n*17; 251*n*23

Other, the, 10, 13, 20; and desire, 1, 25, 41; and Genet, 159; and Hegel, 46–53, 57–59; and Hyppolite, 85–86; and Kojève,

67, 68, 74, 75, 77; and Kristeva, 232; and Lacan, 191–97, 200, 201; and Sartre, 95, 121, 137, 138, 140–46, 150–52, 154–55, 161, 172–73; and self, 25, 31, 40

Plato, on eros, 4, 9
Pleasure, 145–46, 152, 209
Poster, Mark, 244–2
Post-Hegelianism: critique of Hegel's system as "totalizing," 6, 14; Deleuze and, 212–17; history of, 175–78, 216–17; Hyppolite and, 79–80; Kojève and, 68–70, 230; and rereading "Lordship and Bondage," 230–31; Sartre and, 92–99
Poulet, Georges, 249–50*n*1
Prereflective consciousness, 128–29, 132–35, 141–42
Presence: Derrida on, 178, 185, 197; Foucault on, 222; metaphysics of, 14, 176, 216; Sartre on, 116–18, 148, 150, 153–54

Recognition: in *The Family Idiot*, 162, 164–72, 249*n*36; Kojève on, 68, 76–77; in *Saint Genet*, 159–63; struggle for, 50–59, 242–43*n*18
Repression, 4, 239*n*7
Ricoeur, Paul, 249–50*n*1
Rilke, Rainer Marie, 156
Rosen, Stanley, 24–25, 45
Rotenstreich, Nathan, 241*n*14

Sadism, *see* Foucault, Michel; Sartre, Jean-Paul
Sartre, Jean-Paul: *Baudelaire*, 157; and the body, 137–54, 162; on desire as a "vain passion," 14, 36; on emotion, 118–21, 239*n*10, 248*n*27; *The Family Idiot*, 248*n*31; on Flaubert, 122–23, 130, 156–76, 248*n*29, 249*n*36; and Freud, 127–28, 161, 171, 249*n*37; and Hegel, 8, 92–101, 120, 129, 131, 133–35, 136, 141, 145, 147, 151, 154, 155, 160, 164, 170; and Hyppolite, 132–36, 151; on the imagination, 102–21, 246*n*9; and Kojève, 71, 75, 92–99, 121, 151; on the "look," 140–43, 159, 163, 166, 247*n*24; and Nietzsche, 246–47*n*17; as post-Hegelian,

[267]